COLONEL STA

THE MEMOIRS OF
W. A. TILNEY
1868–1947

A Soldier's Life in England, India,
The Boer War and Ireland

———

EDITED BY HIS GRANDDAUGHTER
NINI MURRAY-PHILIPSON

[handwritten inscription:] To F. from H. Aug 2007 to pass on to I.C.

MICHAEL RUSSELL

© Nini Murray-Philipson 2001

First published in Great Britain 2001
by Michael Russell (Publishing) Ltd
Wilby Hall, Wilby, Norwich NR16 2JP

Reprinted 2002

Typeset in Sabon by Waveney Typesetters
Wymondham, Norfolk
Printed and bound in Great Britain
by Biddles Ltd, Guildford and King's Lynn

Contents

Preface

These memoirs carry an interest that goes beyond the individual. William Arthur Tilney is typical of his background – one could say archetypal. In that alone, this document he left behind is a treasure for the sheer immediacy and genuineness of it. Here is a figure of vividly authentic flesh and blood who could have stepped straight from the pen of John Buchan. No side, no affectation, no playing a part. W. A. Tilney wholly hangs together as a man of his class and his time. We know what he felt and why he felt it. All that in itself makes this valuable to any student of the time or to his own immediate family.

Yet W. A. Tilney was also an original in much of what he was engaged in as a professional soldier. In each of the theatres of war or military activity in which he participated – South Africa, India, France, Ireland, or back here at home – W. A. Tilney set new balls rolling, invariably as a consequence of thinking for himself, standing up for his bright ideas, and sticking to his principles. Hence there are footnotes to history here of some consequence – not least in the use of balloon reconnaissance he initiated in South Africa, and in his authorship of *Marching or Flying by Night without a Compass with Time Table of Directional Stars*, which went through several printings and was for years an item of compulsory study at Staff College.

A deep-rooted Christianity shines through Tilney's approach to life – a faith of such simplicity and innocence that even his prejudices seem almost forgivable in our own obsessively tolerant age. His father died when W. A. Tilney was fifteen; his mother died the following year. His father, realising that he had but a short time to live, called for his sons from Eton. He told them to make God your best and truest friend. When W. A. Tilney had a particularly dangerous mission or when he was seriously ill – as with malaria or trench fever – it was on God that he relied utterly. He had no time for the High Church Anglican priest who depended on ritual and dressing up, but great admiration for Gell, the boxer turned priest who used beer for the communion cup when the wine ran out. Certainly, he had no time for the Roman Catholic Church. Today this may seem quite inadmissible, but in his day such a prejudice was more the rule than the exception in people of his provenance. It was during his time in Ireland that his encounters with the Roman Catholic Church cut him to the quick. In the period 1916–22 the Catholic priests he castigated were rather ignorant Irish patriots who saw the British as an occupying alien force. English Catholics were seen as owing an allegiance to the Pope in Rome – and how could that be squared with being 100 per cent English? W. A. Tilney was outraged that the Pope refused to condemn the murder of homecoming Irish ex-servicemen.

The Jews also came in for sharp criticism. They too were seen at the time as being unpatriotic. They had the name for going wherever there was money to be made. W. A. Tilney knew that British Jews went to Johannesburg to make money in the mines but they did not want to jeopardise their fortunes when it came to taking sides in the Boer War. This equivocation he contrasts with his cousin George Tilney whose property was confiscated by Kruger.

One of the most moving episodes in the memoirs is the execution of Isaac, his native servant. There is not a trace of racial superiority in his telling of this event. One feels this was every bit as big a loss to him as the death of his great friend Ava Dufferin during the siege of Lady-smith.

Having fought in the Boer War and the First World War and seen death at horribly close quarters, he was far more shocked by the inhuman treatment meted out by the Irish to their countrymen who had fought for Britain during that war. The death of a soldier doing his duty was quite different from the murder of the disabled and shell-shocked. Meanwhile, wherever he was, W. A. Tilney was immersing himself into all the sport and dashing society that was in reach. It was as if his sport, and soldiering, and life were all of the same continuum, each nourishing the other. He adored his hunting, his fishing, his shooting – whether in England or Ireland or India. Physically he must have been tough – but he drove himself hard. Whoever heard of swimming in the sea in February as a cure for trench fever! At Sutton Bonington today you can see trophies from the polo field ... and across the room a display of his many presents from Queen Mary.

W. A. Tilney never questions the existence of God. He does not wrestle with philosophy or moral theory – whether, for example, war as such was right or wrong. His memoirs are 'men's talk'. It would seem that he put his wife, Hylda, on a pedestal, yet of what sort of a relationship they had the memoirs breathe – characteristically – not a word.

Here is a life story told as it was lived with pluck, high courage, high humour and truth to himself. His experiences were a raconteur's dream; and he himself was the natural raconteur.

Part I

I was born on 18 June 1868, my parents being Colonel R. J. Tilney, CB, of Parkside, Liverpool, and Grove Hill, West Kirby, Cheshire, and my mother Eliza Rhodes of Nennerton, Henley-on-Thames, and sister of 'Squire Rhodes', who Cecil Rhodes of Rhodesia used to tell me was a cousin of his. My grandfather in April 1836 was one of the founders of the Liverpool Stock Exchange. It was then called the Liverpool Shareholders' Association.

My earliest recollection is being taken up to London to see Lady Victoria Tilney Long Wellesley, who lived near the present Park Lane. She ordered me to sit alongside her on a settee and I well remember what little room there was for my small body, for she was wearing a semi-crinoline.

My father was shortly afterwards bidden to Windsor Castle where he was created a CB, for having been one of the pioneers of the Volunteer Movement. He was intensely keen on this new movement and then had command of the 5th Liverpool Rifle Volunteers. In later years I was told that he maintained the Regiment chiefly at his own expense.

When about eight years old I was sent to Fendalls, Windlesham House, Bagshot, Surrey, where my brother R. H. Tilney (known as 'Monkey') had been for a year before me. It was supposed to be a very up-to-date school and run on modern lines.

Jerram, the writer of the boys' Latin Grammar in partnership with Fendall, was a horrible old man. The bullying among the boys was of the worst description, but my father had brought up my brothers and me on hard tack and insisted from childhood that we should be taught boxing. My brother Monkey and I had to box daily from childhood until we went to Eton. We found being able to look after ourselves to be of the greatest value throughout our lives.

When I joined Fendalls, the last arrivals were put into a corner of the gymnasium and catapulted by the senior boys, to see if the new boys could stand pain. A boy named Hardy, a regular bully, hit me on the hand with the first 'volley' and as my father had instilled into us that a Tilney should not be afraid of anyone in the world, I promptly went for

Hardy and knocked him down. He happened to knock his head against the 'round-about' pole and was taken to hospital. This stopped the bullying for me. Hardy was seriously injured. For some reason best known to Fendall and Jerram, I got a good caning for defending myself.

We had some cousins, the O'Haras and Houstons, at Fendalls, and they were indeed thoroughly Irish. One day Houston, who in after life commanded the 11th Hussars, drank a bottle of ink for a bet and seemed no worse.

When thirteen years of age I was sent to R. A. H. 'Mike' Mitchell's House at Eton where my brother had been for a year. As a lower boy I was continually in trouble, chiefly through laziness in my studies and my pugnacity.

When Monkey and I arrived at Eton one of the amusements of the big boys was to get up pugilistic encounters. 'Let us see the Monkeys fight' was a common byword and amusement at Mike's. Dear old Mike knew everything, but 'turned his blind eye'. Sometimes in the evening, after prayers, he would come to our room – Monkey and I had a joint one – and say in the kindest way: 'Why, Major [or Minor], what have you been doing to get two black eyes?'

Some of the promoters of these combats became great men in after years. At Mike's dinner Harry Forster (Lord Forster), Freeman Thomas (Lord Willingdon), General Davies and even Lord Plumer referred to these episodes, although the latter had left Eton before it became the vogue to have prize fights.

When the Guards came back from the Egyptian campaign, there was a grand parade in the Quadrangle of Windsor Castle, at which the Eton Volunteers were present. Some of us Lower Boys bet Bob Beresford that when 'Present Arms' took place, he would not let off a round of blank. I was about three files from Bob Beresford when Queen Victoria came down the steps to the Quadrangle and the 'Present' took place and off went Bob's rifle. There was tremendous excitement, for everyone thought that the Queen had been shot at, but the parade was carried through. At the end of the parade our arms were examined and the culprit having been detected, he was well 'swished' immediately he got back.

Our holidays were very happy for we generally went to the Gotts at Armley (my grandmother) or to Copgrove and Norton Conyers. Here we learnt the first rudiments of sport.

We had hunted in Cheshire since childhood and were thoroughly spoilt by our father, who provided us with excellent ponies. Armley

House at that time was quite in the country, with a good trout stream, and we used to spend many hours tickling trout and playing in the water.

When I was about fifteen, my father was frequently going to London to consult Dr Jenner. One's boy's mind did not realise that there was anything seriously wrong, until he wrote to Monkey at Eton that Dr Jenner had told him some bad news. Even then we hardly realised that he was to be shortly taken away, until Mike sent for us (I thought I was to be swiped) and said that we had to go at once to our father.

When we arrived he was in bed and said with a smile, 'My boys I am shortly going to be taken away from you. God will take care of you, treat Him as your best and truest friend and never disgrace the name you bear, for no Tilney, as far as we know, has done so for a thousand years!'

He was proud of being a member of the Tilney family because he had studied its records very carefully at the College of Heralds and said that for centuries they had been straight, honourable and God-fearing gentlemen. When we were children my father used to take us to Norfolk, Suffolk and elsewhere to see the family tombs and places that had been in the possession of the Tilney family. We returned to Eton, and not long afterwards Mike told us that our father was dead. The funeral was at Liverpool and many people speak about it to this day, for it was attended by thousands of all classes. He was buried just outside the present Cathedral. He was a wonderful father and a most kind, affectionate man, but had the utmost distrust of Roman Catholics and used to tell us the story of Elizabeth Tilney and Lady Jane Grey.[1]

---

1 The Tilney family were large landowners in East Anglia in the fifteenth and sixteenth centuries. They had various royal connections. Elizabeth (*née* Tilney) and her husband the 2nd Duke of Norfolk were the grandparents of Henry VIII's second wife Anne Boleyn and his fifth wife Catherine Howard. A different Elizabeth Tilney (a cousin of Elizabeth Norfolk) was lady-in-waiting to Lady Jane Grey, great-niece of Henry VIII. She attended Jane at her wedding to Lord Guildford Dudley, heir to the Duke of Northumberland. On Edward VI's death in 1553 Northumberland proclaimed sixteen-year-old Jane queen, but influential opinion was rallying in support of Mary. With Elizabeth Tilney in attendance, Jane, queen for nine days, was beheaded at the Tower of London and her body interred in the Chapel of St Peter-ad-Vincula, between the decapitated corpses of her great-uncle's wives, Anne Boleyn and Catherine Howard. Another related Tilney – Edmund – was appointed by Anne Boleyn's and Henry VIII's daughter, Elizabeth, to be Master of Revels in 1579. Edmund Tilney held this key ministerial office on the queen's behalf until her death in 1603, and on King James's behalf until 1610 when Edmund died. It thus fell to him to license for public presentation (and publication) all or most of Shakespeare's plays, or alternatively to censor them – in particular, or course, for any whiff of sedition.

Although he hated his politics he was a great friend of Mr Gladstone, and as boys we were much with the Gladstone family.

We went back to Eton next half and then our mother died. So at the age of sixteen, I found myself an orphan.

After my father's death, we lived at Ponfield, Herts, and at Colne Park, Essex, with my mother's sister, Mrs Peel. After this Monkey and I were left in the care of trustees, with my father's brother, George – who lived at Watts House, Bishops Lydeard, Somerset, and was Secretary to the Devon and Somerset Stag Hounds – as our guardian. I don't envy the task he had in looking after us. My younger brother, Jimmy, four years my junior, was sent to Wellington College and did not give much trouble.

CHALLENGED TO A DUEL

When I left Eton I was sent to Frank Townsend's at Clifton, whilst my brother R. H. Tilney went to Brasenose College, Oxford. Frank Townsend was then in the Gloucestershire Eleven and here I met the brothers Grace. It was from W. G. Grace that I learned how to play cricket. I also frequently saw C. T. Studd whom W. G. described as the best all round cricketer he had ever seen. C. T. subsequently became the famous missionary. He used to tell us boys that the chief aim in life was to make Jesus your best personal friend and then you would have peace here on earth, with the certainty of eternal life in the world to come. On summer evenings, two or three of us used to go to the nets, really to 'fag' for the Graces. Townsend let us off evening study on these occasions. Indeed, to get off our work was the attraction, so there was quite a competition to attend these nets. We liked W.G. much better than his brothers and whenever he was batting, he put 10/- on the wicket. I'm sure now that he sometimes allowed us to bowl him out, to make us keener to come up to the nets and fag the balls for them.

Townsend's was a rowdy Army crammer's establishment. Among the young fellows were some excellent athletes, including E. C. Bredin, England's champion hundred yard sprinter and quarter-miler, and Harris. When Bredin got stale we applied our energies to bicycle racing.

The bicycles of those days were of the big wheel type[2] with solid rubber tyres. We used to compete at most of the West Country Meetings and had great successes. At the Clifton Zoo on one occasion, the

2 Presumably the penny-farthing.

first race Bredin rode in, we made a lot of money. It was arranged that Harris and I should make the pace for Bredin, whom we backed for all we were worth. He, being a novice, started at long odds. The coup came off, although I took a bad toss and broke my jaw.

We resolved to try on the same game at Bath during the Horse Show week and bought the best and biggest bike obtainable for Bredin. It looked a certainty and we put our shirts on Bredin for a win. We told W. G. Grace to do the same, as he used to give us a sovereign or two to put on for him. On our arrival at the track at Bath, we saw a new sort of bicycle described as 'a multiplier'. We took little notice of this curiosity and laughed when it appeared on the track ridden by a man named Clark. I made the pace a hot one, in a five mile race, but could not shake off this little bicycle and looked round for Bredin after about four miles, and found he was half a lap behind Clark. The latter on the multiplier bicycle won easily, and we were all broke.

I managed to pay the bookies, but had nothing left, so had to appeal to my guardian and trustees for money. They decided to send me to France during the summer holidays to learn French at Châlons-sur-Marne.

Pasteur Andraunt had six pupils, all cramming for the Army, and also a very pretty wife. The poor little man could keep no sort of discipline and allowed us to do anything we liked.

Cecil Noel of Catmos, Oakham, and I had a dog cart in which we drove a tandem, much to the surprise and annoyance of the Frenchmen, for we used to gallop down the boulevards making terrific blasts on a coaching horn. This was eventually stopped by the authorities – after we had been fined several times. One day we were driving the tandem gently along the boulevard, when we espied Mme Andraunt walking arm in arm with a French officer, a big swell wearing red breeches and decorated with the Légion d'Honneur. They were coming towards us and Cecil Noel said, 'I'll bet you a fiver you don't hit Mme's lover with a plum', at the same time handing me a bag of large blue plums.

I took the bet and hit the man full in the face. He proved to be Major Rabot of the French Cavalry. Two days afterwards three French officers appeared at Andraunt's establishment and presented me with a challenge which I had to accept. I didn't know anything about swords or firearms, nor did we understand who had the choice of weapons, so a friend of mine named Lukis (who became a general in the British Army afterwards) was deputed to find this out. The answer was swords! So I at once repaired to the Maître d'Escrime and never worked so hard at anything in my life.

Almost three days before the duel was to have taken place I was arrested and taken to the railway station with a ticket for London. Andraunt was in tears, his Mme almost in hysterics. There was such confusion that Andraunt forgot to give me my money for food on the journey. I had about ten francs in my pocket and landed at Charing Cross penniless, about dusk at the end of August.

I carried my small luggage to the Golden Cross Hotel (it was a Saturday), took a room and wrote to George Tilney, my guardian. On the Sunday the proprietor demanded payment, so on Monday morning I pawned my heavy baggage at a shop near Vaughan's, the gun-maker, in the Strand.

I came back to the hotel very dejected and paid my bill, for the proprietor would allow me no food except on payment. I was sitting at breakfast when an old man with a long white beard came to my table and asked what was the matter. He was a kindly old soul, so I made a clean breast of my difficulties, telling him that I was an orphan and, having been expelled from France, was afraid of stirring up my cousins and aunts in London, but that I had written to my guardian.

The old gentleman, named Graham, was a perfect Dickens character and after a lot of advice and admonition gave me a fiver on the strict understanding that it would be returned when I had gained touch with my guardian.

In the middle of the week, my trustees and guardian arrived at the Grand Hotel and I had a most unpleasant interview. Thank goodness Henry Rhodes and Charlie Mason took a sporting view of my escapade and the latter took over the guardianship. Charlie had been helped when young by my father, and never could anyone have had a better friend than Charlie Mason was to my two brothers and myself, for he and Ina parented us all – till his death in 1914. I owe these two dear people my heartfelt gratitude for all they did for us.

We spent the Easter and summer holidays at our maternal grandmother's, the Rhodeses, at Hennerton, Henley-on-Thames. Our three uncles, Henry, William and Herbert, being keen sportsmen, we were well broken in to all sorts of sport. The Wargrave Backwater belonged to the Hennerton Estate and being strictly private was a splendid stream for trout and all sorts of coarse fish, so during the holidays we lived on and in the river most days. In those days the water was crystal clear with a gravel bottom, and there was a beautiful bathing pool at the boat house. Every morning 'the Squire' took us all down to bathe before breakfast and those who could not swim were thrown in and if in difficulties hauled out by one of the uncles. Herbert Rhodes was stroke of the Cambridge boat for three years, when Cambridge won the Oxford-Cambridge Boat Race each time.

Lords Desborough and Grenfell were close friends of our three uncles and as hard as they were, always full of fun, and tremendous sportsmen.

I was sent back to Townsend's at Clifton, where I lived at the house of Townsend's mother.

E. C. Bredin was then champion runner of England in two events, and as the bottom was knocked out of our bicycle and foot racing – for at the latter his form was perfectly known – we employed our spare time at and in the prize-ring, and also did a lot of rat-pit and badger-baiting competitions, which were legal, or I should say not illegal, at that time (1887).

THE CHARM OF THE 'ELEPHANT MAN'

About this time I became acquainted with one of the most extraordinary aberrations the world knew, namely the 'Elephant Man'. Having no definite home, I had to spend a good deal of my holidays knocking about London, and having made a resolve to see everything, I joined the Portland Prison Mission and used to go into the worst parts of London, visiting. I visited the Chinese and the abortion quarters in the East End, where I heard of this terrible-looking human being. Soon after, a letter appeared in *The Times* saying he was being cared for in the London Hospital, as his appearance in the streets terrified women and children.

As a Tilney ancestress had practically started the London Hospital – and endowed it – I wrote to ask leave to see this man. His appearance has frequently been described in the papers and it was indeed revolting, but he had a charming personality. I got to know him quite well. One day I commiserated with him on his lonely life, for at that time he only went out when it was dark. His reply made a very deep impression on me. He said that he had hired himself out for a year or so before to an Austrian showman, and had been 'shown' over many parts of the Continent, receiving a percentage of the profits. The showman, however, at the end of his contract, bolted, leaving him penniless. He was befriended by a man in Austria who, he said, told him about Christ. He said, 'Although I have such a terrible appearance in the body, my spirit lives with Jesus and I am one of the happiest people on earth.' He said this when the Senior House Surgeon was with us in the hospital.

His room was near the Cancer Ward. Sometimes most nauseous effluvia came through the door. When we got outside I told the House Surgeon how horrible it must be and he got the quarters changed. I told Princess Mary at White Lodge about him and she and Queen Alexandra were kind to him.

Through the Portland Mission I got to know Lees, who had been unsuccessfully hanged three times and was then in Portland Prison on a sentence of penal servitude for life. He had a cell next to the Hoxton murderer, a horrible-looking man. One day, when I was with the Governor on his round of visits, he remarked of Lees, 'I feel certain that man is innocent, for he is a charming fellow and very religious.' Some years afterwards, I got a letter from the Sub-Governor to say that the real murderer had made a full confession of the crime (which took place in Devonshire) on his deathbed and that Lees had been released.

When I was commanding the 17th in India, I came across a missionary who knew Lees well and said he was one of the greatest powers for good in the East End of London. As far as I remember, Lees's story was that the rope broke twice and the third time the trap door would not open. He said that before the Governor and me – and that God had wrought a true miracle in his life and that he would eventually be set free.

When I heard the news of his release, I thought that this indeed was as good a miracle as any in the Bible.

INTO THE CAVALRY

Having passed into Sandhurst, it was arranged for me to go into the 60th Rifles. However, a cousin of ours commanded the 7th Hussars, and he persuaded me to transfer to the Cavalry. I made an exchange with Lascelles, brother to Lord Harewood, and got £1,500, since it was much easier to pass the examination for Cavalry than for Infantry. Cox and Co. used to arrange these exchanges. It is curious how small events may completely change the whole course of one's life.

I would have passed into Sandhurst my first go and was staggered by the receipt of a W.O. letter briefly stating that having been proved 'cribbing' during the examination, my name had been erased from the list of successful candidates. It transpired afterwards that a boy named Tighe, who sat next to me, had cribbed my version of the Trinomial Theorem figure by figure, and when I attended the W.O., accompanied by my guardian, I was shown Tighe's paper and my own. Luckily for me the Military Secretary had been a friend of my father so they allowed me to attend the next exam on my repeating before them the Trinomial Theorem, which I had learnt by heart. I lost a term at Sandhurst, but I passed all right the next time.

My brother Monkey and I had hunted from Shenington Rectory near Banbury (the Rev. Blythman's) with the Warwickshire and also from Upton (W. H. Jenkin's place) quite close. A fellow Etonian, 'Cheesey' Soames, and I used to ride gallops for 'Jinks' at Upton and as he had some of the best steeplechasers in the world we thought a lot of ourselves.

Jinks was a really fine boxer – I think he had been amateur middle-weight champion – and we used to attend pugilistic encounters all over the country. He asked me to come with him to Liverpool for the Grand National and other races. He had three horses in the Grand National and when Cheesey and I rode those horses in their gallops and then went as his guests for the big race, we considered ourselves second to none in the racing world.

The sequel to this sporting tour was that I lost about £800 in ten days, which cured me from betting for the remainder of my life, for I said to myself 'If Jinks and his fellow trainers can be so wrong as to the chance of their horses have of winning [for he had advised me throughout], what chance have I, or any ordinary individual?' Jinks was brother-in-law to Lord Jersey who at that time had a lot of horses in training.

When we returned to Warwickshire, we heard that a fellow named Thomas, who had been at Eton with us and also at Blythman's, had met a Jesuit priest who asked him to have some tea at his house outside Wroxton Abbey. This priest had apparently mesmerised Thomas, for when we got to Blythman's, 'old B.', as we called Blythman, was much perturbed and told us that Thomas owned Birrons in Kent and would come into a considerable amount of money when he came of age, and that this priest had Thomas completely under his influence.

The result was tragic, for Thomas could never shake off the Jesuit, who led him into every form of debauchery. When Thomas finally died, he left everything to the Roman Catholics. He had been a friend of mine at Mike's house at Eton, and his downfall brought home to me my father's warning 'Never trust the Roman Catholics!' This was fully confirmed in my subsequent experiences.

I had been a sore trial to my new guardian, Charlie Mason, and the trustees, for I had to appeal for money to pay off my racing debts. The trustees decided that instead of hunting in Warwickshire I should go abroad. Charlie Mason's mother, my Aunt Susan, had a beautiful villa in Algiers and they planned that I should stay some time there but they allowed me funds to go on a shooting trip first.

ADVENTURES IN NORTH AFRICA

I chose Morocco, which at that time was a wild and almost savage country. My aunt knew Playfair, the ambassador at Algiers, very well, and he was kind enough to arrange passports. So with a gun and rifle I set off.

I was full of the spirit of adventure at that time, for since I had been left an orphan I had spent part of my holidays with the Webbs at Newstead Abbey, Notts. Old Webb had travelled with Speke and Stanley in Africa and was a very keen big game hunter. For the Newstead covert shooting, old Webb used to have any of his explorer friends who happened to be in England. The yarns they told filled me with enthusiasm and I almost chucked all idea of the Army in order to follow an explorer's life.

I met Stanley[3] at Newstead before he set out on his trip in search of Emin Pasha[4] in darkest Africa. I did not like him at all, for one Sunday at lunch he laughed at me about going to church. The Webb family told me that he was an agnostic and did not believe in religion and he, certainly from his conversation, bore out this opinion.

They (the old explorers) were extraordinary men and drank quantities of Dom, a potent Dutch liqueur, and talked about their experiences in Africa the whole time after dinner, till late into the night.

I was staying at Newstead after Stanley returned from his trip in Africa. I think it was in 1891. I shall never forget what a changed man he was. The first night there was a big party in his honour and Stanley stood up when he had escorted Miss Webb into dinner and said to old Webb, 'We have not yet said Grace.' He proceeded to do so in a very

---

3 Stanley is chiefly remembered for his expedition into central Africa to find David Livingstone. Stanley reached Livingstone in November 1871 and greeted him with the now famous words, 'Dr Livingstone, I presume?'
4 Emin Pasha, Governor of Equatoria province of Egypt, had been cut off by the Mahdist revolt of 1882. Sir William McKinnon, Chairman of the Imperial British East African Co., launched a rescue fund and invited Stanley to lead the expedition of 1887–89.

fervent manner. The next day Stanley came to church and walked back with me through the park, when he told me how he had been converted to be a follower of Christ. The story appears in his book *In Darkest Africa*. He was particularly friendly to me and this increased my longing to become an explorer.

On my first shooting trip, after setting off for Morocco, I heard that it was impossible to get far along the road to Fez. So I went on a cargo boat to Melilla, a filthy smelling port, where there seemed to be nothing but mongrel Frenchmen, Spaniards and low-caste Arabs. At Melilla our ambassador at Algiers had sent two guides – they were Arab shepherds – and I proceeded with gun and rifle into the hills through Beni Snassem, Themsen and Sidi Bel Abbas to Oran.

I shot a lot of game, generally slept in the open as I had no tent, and the only alternative, which was always available, was with a mongrel French girl. Denying myself the latter luxury is what got me through, for the Moors in the mountains were ready to do me in on the slightest pretext, and as I was at the time practically unarmed and unguarded, they did not interfere with me. The head guide had been given credit at the bank at Oran for about £100, if he delivered me safely there after the shooting tour.

At Oran I was alarmed and horrified to hear that a disease called 'black pox' was ravaging the place. By this time I could make myself fairly well understood by the Chief Guide, and after searching for a bed, heard that a white man was in the hotel nearest to the sea. It was a miserable place kept by a Frenchman. At lunch I met the white man who had been sent there as correspondent to the *Graphic*. I will not give his name, for a more miserable coward I have seldom come across. He died during the siege of Ladysmith.

He was paralytic with funk lest he should contract this black pox, and since he slept every night with the Frenchman's eldest daughter with all the windows closed, I thought he was for it. I had heard my old explorer friends say so often that in these circumstances the best place to sleep is the roof and never to 'go large' with the women. After we had waited five days a Messagerie Maritime cargo boat turned up. It was a coaster going to Tunis, so I decided to go as far as Bougie, Algeria, where I was told there was plenty of sport in the mountains. The only other occupants of the steamer were an American and his two daughters. The daughters had a marionette show which they worked at the various places we stopped at, whilst the father was buying all the old brass and bronze cannons, guns, *et cetera*, procurable along the coast.

The correspondent of the *Graphic* got off at Algiers, the chief reason being that the Captain had explained that the boat could not go any faster because the boilers were unsafe. At Algiers I saw Playfair, the ambassador, and thanked him for all he had done for me. He begged me not to proceed in this boat, but to wait for another; however, I had all my kit aboard, so we continued along the coast.

The afternoon before we got to Bougie, the Captain objected to my landing, as the channel was dangerous and his engines in bad repair. The American came to my rescue as the girls had arranged to give a marionette show in Bougie and there was a lot of copper and brass to be bought. So we landed.

The day after, whilst I was in the Chabet Pass, a hurricane came on and the boat that had brought me ashore was lost with all hands and passengers at the mouth of the Bougie Channel!

The fate of my American friends depressed me, so I harked back to Algiers where I stayed in my Aunt Susan's lovely villa and spent my time riding all day and got to know many of the Zouave and Foreign Legion officers. They had paper chases twice a week and we used to go into the hills, boar shooting. The officers' morals were awful and some of the Punitive Corps (as the unit was known) were real criminals who were condemned to serve their sentence in the Foreign Legion.

I learnt a good lesson in life here which was 'avoid a row at all costs when in a foreign country' and later in life I found this to apply equally at home. After the bi-weekly paper chases, there was a dance and I happened to 'get thick' with a girl 'walking out' with a lieutenant of the Chasseurs d'Afrique. The results were unpleasant, for one evening, after my dancing with her, Lacontier, the lieutenant, smashed me in the face before everyone as I was leaving the ballroom. I just laughed and thought no more of it. But the next day he and two officers came to my aunt's villa, just before lunch, with a challenge. Two or three days earlier I had got my orders to join Sandhurst in a month's time, so as there were only two female cousins staying with my aunt I thought it best to consult the ambassador Playfair, one of my aunt's greatest friends. When I took the paper to him, he roared with laughter, for apparently it was this good man who had got me out of the scrape at Châlons, Charlie Mason (my guardian) having asked his advice and help. He wrote me out a letter in answer to the challenge – in, of course, perfect French – to say that as I was appointed a Cadet, it was against regulations for an officer of the British Army to fight a duel, but that if

Lacontier wished, I would fight with anything he chose in the Salles d'Armes for 500 francs a side. The next day, just as I was going out riding with Norah Mason, I was surprised to see the same three officers appear at my aunt's. They called me '*lâche*', and other abuse which I could not understand was volleyed at me, so I just rode away laughing and that evening got a long rigmarole letter to say Lacontier would fight me the next afternoon in the Salle d'Armes with rapiers. I remember my joy that he had not chosen 'Le Savotte' at which I had heard he was an expert. He was a lanky athletic man who could have beaten me easily at this game, of which I had only learnt the rudiments at Le Havre. I was, however, after the training I received at Châlons, a proficient swordsman for my age. I have never worked harder at anything than I did with the Maître d'Escrime at Châlons when called out by Rabot.

So we proceeded the next afternoon to the Salle d'Armes, which was full of French and Arab officers. I lodged my stake, £25 in golden sovereigns, with the umpire, a French cavalry colonel. After what seemed an interminable jaw and ceremony, we began to fight. As soon as we crossed swords, I saw that he had been badly taught and that I could disarm him at any time. He held the rapier single stick fashion, and my Châlons instructor had shown me time after time how to disarm an opponent who did this. Boxing had made me very quick on my feet and I managed to avoid his first attack with some difficulty, as he was very agile and longer in the arm, but he gave me an opening and down went his rapier to the ground. There was great commotion, followed by much excited talk and then, with extravagant ceremony, I was presented with the stakes. In extremely bad French I refused to take anything, but went over to Lacontier and gave him the lot, after shaking him warmly by the hand, and then retired. Playfair came up to dinner and told my aunt that I had better be off, as the officers had misunderstood my bad French and action in handing back the stakes to Lacontier, which they took to be a further insult. This incident cost me £25, but it gave the English community something to talk about and incidentally brought me subsequently to the notice of the Duke of Cambridge, Commander in Chief of the British Army.

I went from Algiers to Constantine and Hammam Mesquotine. At the latter place I explored the Cave of Djebel Twya which had never been bottomed before. When I got to the bottom it was one vast series of halls, covered with Roman and Carthaginian hieroglyphics. So absorbed was I that I dropped the reel of cotton which would show me the way back and out. The guides had refused to come further than the subterranean river and mighty waterfall so I had gone on alone as I was determined to get to the bottom. When I had explored these vast halls, I looked for the cotton thread. I had given the guide my watch and had lost track of the time. At last I felt myself weakening and sat down in a sort of gallery.

I only had half a torch left, so I gave up all for lost. I shall never forget the cold sweat that came over me and as I write now I can hear and picture the mighty roar of the underground waterfall and river. I knelt and made a desperate prayer to God, that He would save me, and I was strengthened to get up and ascend a steep passage, praying all the time that God would lead me into safety. Again my strength gave way and I sat down to meet my end.

I was almost comatose and had given up all hope of rescue, when I heard voices and looking up saw a glint of daylight far above me. I shouted back as best I could and was told in Arab-French that the rescue party would lower a rope through the aperture I had seen and haul me up. When I had been dragged up, the Arab guide who was still there told me that the rescue party had been sent from Hammam Mescoutine that morning by a family named Dorrien Smith. I had been in the Cave of Djebal Twya for thirty-six hours.

When I arrived at Hammam Mesquotine, I found the English family Dorrien Smith who, having heard of my mad adventure, sent a party to rescue me.

I made off shortly afterwards for a trip into the Sahara Desert to Biskra, which at that time bordered the desert on the main caravan route. I was told there were a quantity of antelope a day's march from Biskra, and thought I would put in a week there before returning to Marseilles, via Tunis. The hotel at Biskra in 1887 was a mere caravanserai and the village chiefly Arab, with a brigade of Chasseurs d'Afrique and a Punitive Battalion. All the 'amusements' took place in the Arab quarter, so after early dinner I went to a dancing hall and the first man I met was Lacontier, who greeted me most warmly. When I told him the object of my visit to Biskra, he said he would show me all the shooting to be had.

The next day I hired four camels and we proceeded to an oasis fifty or sixty miles from Biskra where quails abounded. Lacontier was overjoyed with this quail shooting and bombarded them the whole of the first two days, much to my amusement. He was a desperately bad shot at any time, but as he only had a carbine, four or five quail *per diem* pleased him immensely. I soon got tired of this form of sport and also, I regret to say, of his company, for his one idea in life was 'women' and he did not apparently interest himself in anything else. The successful seduction of any woman seemed to be his goal in life. He had been transported from France for rape to a place where this (for the French) was no crime, so instead of being punished, he was in his paradise.

After three days I could not stand his company any longer. He was a vicious bully of the worst type. There is little wonder that the French were loathed by the Arabs. This devil sent his orderly every night with an order to the sheikh to send him a maiden. All the French officers of the Foreign Legion I met were of the same pattern, except a man named Huguet, who afterwards became a man of importance.

I journeyed by easy stages to Batna, saw the great ruins and Roman towns of Tangroat, Timbad, and a wonderful place about forty miles from Carthage, and reached Tunis about three weeks before I had to join Sandhurst. The Duc de Luynes and family had come there with an English doctor, Stephenson, who was one of the most curious men I have ever met. As far as I could gather he was supposed to be in charge of a boy who was mentally defective, but the doctor spent his days collecting bones at Carthage. One day he asked me to accompany him and never shall I forget my amazement when he started to dig up a grave near the elephant stables and became like a maniac. To his disgust a Frenchman or Arab had been deposited there and the grave contained nothing of interest. He then rushed off elsewhere. At that time Carthage was unprotected from such vandals and the natives sold rare Carthaginian coins and jewellery for mere songs. I bought a gold piece for two francs, which I sold on my way through Paris for one pound. This Dr Stephenson always wore a frock tail coat, into the huge pockets of which he stuffed bones, coins and anything valuable he could excavate from the graves. Later he took me round the jail and lunatic asylum in Tunis. At this time Tunis was a Suzerainty, uncontrolled by the French. The hospital was chiefly run by the French, but the asylum by the Arabs. The poor creatures were caged and those who were also criminals were chained by the waist to a sort of dog kennel. Some of these were almost naked and very emaciated. The prison was worse than any account of the Bastille.

The de Luynes family were very nice to me. When I was bidding them farewell, I unfortunately remarked I was going to Malta, en route for England. Stephenson at once asked to accompany me, as I spoke French and he did not. As I could not shake him off, he journeyed with me to Malta, where we stayed three days and he took me to see the embalmed monks. He spent hours examining those dried-up corpses and when he joined me outside, I saw a dried-up arm protruding from his tail coat pocket! At Carthage, I had thought he was merely robbing the graves of all their valuables, coins, and so on, but this incident at Malta fairly beat me, for when he came to the hotel, he packed the monk's arm most carefully in a huge trunk, which contained nothing else but human bones. I found a man who was going direct to Liverpool by sea at Malta, so packed off Stephenson with him and proceeded via Marseilles to Paris.

I had by this time resolved to see and judge everything possible, as I had heard so many tales from the famous explorers I had met at Newstead. So during my week in Paris, I went to most of the poorest parts of the town, including some of the lowest haunts, and was horrified to see the degradation to which human beings can sink. I had previously been to the Chinese and thieves' quarters in London, and also the abortion homes in the East End of London, but these were nothing to what I saw in Paris.

My first term at Sandhurst was an eventful one, for I made some great friends – Frank Teck and Algy Fitzroy who, as I write this, has become Speaker of the House of Commons. As I had an allowance of £1,000 a year, I had tremendous fun hunting with the Staff College Drag, Garths, and the surrounding packs. I had played a lot of rugger at Townsend's, and before I left Sandhurst got my colours for rugger and soccer.

It happened in this way. Towards the end of my time at Sandhurst I played rugger regularly for the College, but when the RMC were playing against the London Hospitals, six of us contracted what they called 'sweater rash' from the blue of our sweaters. As we were covered with sores we couldn't play any more rugger. The RMC soccer goal-keeper happened to get sick and I was asked to take his place, so got my colours at that game as well. I was told that no one had got their colours in both games in the same half before.

A ROYAL CHRISTMAS

At the end of my first term at Sandhurst, I was asked to spend Christmas at White Lodge in Windsor Park and remember the funk I was in at the prospect of going there on such a family occasion. But on my arrival I was soon put at my ease, their home life being perfect, and Princess Mary and the whole Teck family showing me great kindness. Altogether I spent six Christmases with them at White Lodge.

Sidney Greville, George Arthur and I used to go there two days before Christmas. At first Frank, Algy and Princess May (later Queen Mary)[5] were the only others, besides the Duke and Princess Mary. Adolphus (Dolly) was there the first Christmas with me before he joined the 17th. It was all fixed up for me to go to the 7th Hussars and this first Christmas at White Lodge changed the whole course of my life.

We spent Christmas in a thoroughly old English manner, going to Holy Communion early at the little church at Combe. As the young people had to walk there (about two miles) each way, it might have been excusable to miss midday service, but Princess Mary always expected us to go. In the afternoon of my first Christmas there, I was summoned back when out walking with the others, and told by the footman that the Duke of Cambridge, the C-in-C. of the Army, was having tea with Princess Mary and wanted to see me. I have seldom been more frightened and agitated. All my misdeeds rose up in my mind and I was only saved from making a complete fool of myself by my father's dying words: 'Never be afraid of anyone or anything, put your trust in God and He will look after you.' So in I went and after much bowing, the dear old man ordered me to sit by him. He told me that he had had the greatest respect for my father, and said he had heard of my wish to go into the 7th Hussars and that it would be all right. He then, to my horror, asked me if I was the cadet who had fought the French officer for £25 at Algiers.

I replied very timidly: 'I am sorry to say that I did get into some trouble there.' They all burst into fits of laughter and he clapped me on the back saying, 'You must come into my regiment.' He was the Colonel in Chief of the 17th Lancers. When Lord Wolseley, who was with the Duke, began to question me about my duel I began to feel more at home and told them how I had been obliged to become a swordsman at Châlons. They were much amused and were asking me all sorts of awkward questions when Princess May and her brothers walked in. This finished the conversation, but the old Duke often chaffed me about my wild life afterwards.

---

5 Princess Mary, granddaughter of George III was married to the Duke of Teck. Their daughter, called Princess May to distinguish herself from her mother, was engaged to Albert Edward, eldest son of Edward VII, who died in January 1892. In July 1893 she married George, Duke of York. On the death of Edward VII, she was crowned with him (as Queen Mary and George V) in Westminster Abbey in 1911.

Princess May gave me a Christmas present of a silver match box that Christmas (1887), and she never omitted to honour me with a Christmas present ever since, even during the South African War and in the Great War (by which time she was Queen). She sent a special messenger with it to me in the trenches at Festubert (a khaki Shetland sweater).

Life at White Lodge was a perfect pattern of what a Christian home could be, although there was plenty of chaff and laughter. Princess Mary was almost like a second mother to me; she used to lecture me, but always with a twinkle in her eye. She had an important influence on my life and I can easily recall her precepts.

Prince Dolly (afterwards the Marquess of Cambridge) had been invalided home from India after typhoid. He was usually there when I used to come over from Sandhurst for weekends at White Lodge. One Sunday afternoon Princess May, Prince Dolly and I were walking down the avenue in front of White Lodge when a messenger came to say that Queen Victoria wished to see Princess May and Prince Dolly. So back we went. Naturally I went to my bedroom to keep out of the way, but soon I was sent for by Princess Mary, although never anticipating that I would see Queen Victoria.

When I came in, I saw the Queen in an armchair with Prince Eddie seated on her left, the Duke of Teck standing behind them, and Princess May sitting on a footstool in front of the Queen. Princess Mary came to the door and walked me up to the Queen. Doing my best obeisance I caught the eye of Princess May, who was smiling, and to my horror the Queen ordered me to sit down on a footstool quite close. I had been instructed that you should never turn your back on royalty and as Princess Mary was sitting between myself and the Queen, there was no alternative, but to sit sideways. The Queen said she knew and had heard a great deal about my father, and spoke at length about the Volunteer Movement. She said she was very pleased to hear that I was going into the Duke of Cambridge's Regiment and hoped I liked Sandhurst. She expressed her sympathy at my being left an orphan when so young. On her making a bow, I understood that I had to leave. After making my best bow, I backed towards the door, but when passing Princess May's footstool, down I came on my behind, for she had put out her foot to trip me. There were roars of laughter and I fled from the room, which was the drawing room overlooking Richmond Park.

When I got back to my bedroom, it was about 4 p.m. I went alone for a walk and met Prince Eddie walking with Princess May. They told me to come in to tea, for the Queen had not yet gone. Everyone was in the highest spirits, and from the drift of the conversation, I guessed that Prince Eddie had proposed to Princess May and had been accepted.[6]

Princess Mary put me at my ease, by telling me that the Queen thought I would be a nice companion for Prince Dolly, and that I was to accompany him on his country house visits.

I shall never forget that night, for Princess May, who was a very pretty girl, looked radiantly beautiful. I sat between Princess May and Prince Dolly and they ragged me properly as to my deportment before the Queen and after dinner they showed me the correct bow from the hips. Prince Dolly was on sick leave for most of the winter and we had a happy time, for I attended him on most occasions for shooting, visits, balls, *et cetera*. We went for a week to Warwick Castle, when some of the most beautiful women in England were among the party – Lady Warwick, Millicent, Duchess of Sutherland, the Duchess of Leinster, Lady Westmorland, Lady Ormonde and Lady Lanesborough. There were six guns and we hunted on the days we did not shoot. Lady Ormonde afterwards became a mother-friend to me and this friendship lasted to her death in 1927. She virtually brought me out into London society.

Our next visit was to Eaton (the Duke of Westminster) for a fortnight's hunting and shooting. The Duke provided his guests with beautiful horses, but they were never fit, always too fat, so one never saw the end of a run properly.

MISS BAKER-WHITE'S NOT-SO-WHITE ALLIANCE

In April 1889 I was gazetted to the 17th Lancers and ordered to the Cavalry depot at Canterbury. Captain Steele, Bertram Portal, Tim Maryon-Wilson and Lionel Fortescue were the 17th Lancers officers. Poor Steele, who had had a bad fall playing polo in India, was soon sent to a 'home' where he died. The points which struck me most when joining the 17th were the number of different coats an officer had to buy and wear. One seemed to require a different kit for every class of parade. There was no appearance of military enthusiasm among the officers; their zeal was centred on dress – tunic, mess jacket, stable jacket, fur patrol, ordinary patrol, two serges, two cloaks, all bought at extravagant prices. The Adjutant of the Cavalry Depot was Captain

6 It is generally agreed that the proposal in fact took place at Luton Hoo in November 1891.

Ridley, 7th Hussars, who made me captain of the cricket eleven, and as I was fairly efficient in my duties, life at the depot centred chiefly on cricket and polo. Colonel Russell of the 12th Lancers was CO but we rarely saw him. Colonel Stuart was second in command and he let it be known that he was the direct descendant of Charles I. As neither CO took much interest in military affairs, the whole show was run by Ridley. My cricket, thanks to W.G.'s training, was successful and we had a good season.

There were some people called Baker-White who had a large house outside Canterbury and used to entertain the subalterns royally. They had an heiress daughter, who was captured by a very good-looking sub-altern named Thompson. Ridley took upon himself to tell the father of the girl that he knew for certain that Thompson's father was a half-caste Indian babu (native merchant). The father of the girl tried to make his daughter break off the engagement and the next thing we heard was that the War Office had accused Captain Ridley of making untrue state-ments about an officer. I must say at the time no one believed that Ridley's statement was accurate. The couple married.

In August I went out in the troopship *Malabar* to India. Mr and Mrs Thompson were fellow passengers. The ship was overcrowded to a dis-graceful degree, owing to the Pandjeh affair with Russia.[7] Four officers and fourteen men died from heat apoplexy in the Red Sea, as there were no punkahs and we ran short of fresh water. In those days the orderly officer of the night watch had to go through the whole ship's sleeping quarters, including the women's quarters. An officer named Keyworth, who was at Sandhurst with me, was orderly one very hot night in the Red Sea. In the terrible heat the women lay quite naked in their quarters and Keyworth, having drunk too much, 'lay up' in the ladies' empty berth. The orderly officer was found at dawn with nothing on and

---

7 Alarm bells rang in Calcutta and Whitehall when news came that the Russians were working flat out to extend their railway to Afghanistan. The Amir of Afghanistan had agreed to subject the conduct of his foreign affairs to the control of the government of India. It was accepted that British and Russian officers should together demarcate the northern boundary of Afghanistan. In 1885, before the Russians sent a boundary repre-sentative and while the Amir was conferring with Lord Dufferin, they attacked and drove an Afghan force from Pandjeh (a small oasis town on the Russian Afghanistan border). News of the event arrived in London a week later and provoked fury and dismay in the press and in Parliament. The outbreak of war was expected daily, but the Amir kept his head: he did not want his country turned into a battlefield. For the next few years rever-berations from the Pandjeh affair rumbled on. Troops were sent out from England to bol-ster those already in India – hence the overcrowding on the *Malabar*.

sound asleep. He was to be tried by general court martial but Captain Fanshawe (afterwards Admiral Fanshawe) of the *Malabar* changed the order to a trial by their brother subalterns of which there were 300 or so on board.

The court martial was most solemnly conducted and he was sentenced to twelve strokes with the cat. I was told off as one of the three executioners and we had to give four strikes apiece, which we did, till the blood poured down the poor fellow's back. Captain Fanshawe issued a written explanation as to why he had ordered this, instead of allowing him to be tried by general court martial of which the result would have been to lose his commission for a certainty, whereas he wanted to give that fellow a chance of making good. This he did and as I write he is a man of consequence in the world.

On our arrival at Bombay, I was contemplating the scenery when I heard a woman scream and saw Mrs Thompson hugging Captain Fanshawe, crying 'Save me, save me!' It was soon apparent what was the cause of Mrs Thompson's hysterics for in a launch at the gangway steps was a fat black babu with a still fatter wife. Thompson's father and mother! They were very rich Bombay people and had sent their children to be educated in England as infants, and to grow up and pass themselves off as white people. The ship's doctor said that babies of black parents, if sent straight to cold climates, grew up olive in complexion and if their parents were of the Aryan race they were difficult to detect from English, except that the whites of their finger nails were grey in colour, and their hands, instead of being warm-blooded, were snakish to feel and touch. For telling the truth and warning Miss Baker-White's father, Ridley virtually lost his commission as he was never subsequently employed or promoted.

The 17th were quartered at Lucknow and on landing at Bombay I received instructions from the Regiment to fit myself out with ponies from the Arab stables at Bombay, so spent a week at Watson's Hotel. One day at lunch time some Indian jugglers appeared and having done some wonderful tricks, asked the people on the verandah if they would like to see a mango grow out of the pavement. We went outside and surely a mango did grow up out of the middle of the footpath outside Watson's Hotel. The jugglers then asked if we would like to see a special performance of a boy climbing a rope in the air. All I can say is that the juggler threw a coil of rope skywards and a small boy climbed up it until within about six feet from the ground, the juggler made passes and the boy fell to the ground. No one present – and there were certainly twenty-five or more – could affix any explanation as to how the trick was done, but it was the most wonderful I have ever seen.

Having bought three ponies at the Arab stable, and two from de Lisle of the DLI (he stuck me badly with a runaway pony and one that shied off the ball), I proceeded to join the Regiment, where I had a good welcome and was soon tried for the polo team as Toby Rawlinson, brother to Harry Rawlinson (subsequently Lord Rawlinson), was invalided home. Renton was captain of the polo team and the others were Ted Miller and George Miller. I was to play No. 1, but, unfortunately, I got typhoid before the Inter-Regiment Tournament.

I had been in India six months and most of my time had been spent in the riding school and at polo, so when I was invalided home, at the end of 1890, I knew little of regiment drill or soldiering generally.

BOXING AND BEARS

As I was at a loose end of four or five months, I spent some of this time at Foxford on the Moy in Mayo with my brother, Monkey. Lord Lucan had been kind enough to give us all his fishing and shooting, so we had a most enjoyable time on Loch Cullen and Loch Conn. We made great friends with the inhabitants and started a very successful football club. We noticed that a number of the players had curly red heads and we remarked on this to the Resident Magistrate who replied: 'Ah, Father Sullivan [the local priest] is a great sire!'

Monkey always wore our father's gold watch chain with our mother's diamond ring attached to it at the opposite end to the watch. One day when salmon fishing on the Moy, the ring was detached through the butt of the rod catching the chain and the ring was lost in the river. Monkey was very much distressed at the loss and offered a reward for £25 for its recovery. We returned to Foxford the following year in August, and this time were accompanied by Erle Drax from Dorsetshire with whom we shared expenses. One day we were all fishing the Moy, we happened to be lunching near where Monkey had lost the ring the year before, and suddenly Drax said 'What is that in the water?' There was the ring on the top of a flat rock.

Some of the boys in Foxford told us that Father Sullivan was a member of the Clan a Liel, and had been organising poaching parties to net and burn (spearing salmon with torches) over part of the river, which we had leased for the season with another month to run. Monkey and I, therefore, went one night to see if this was correct and about 2 a.m. came upon the party. We were good with our fists and as we took the party unawares made short work of them, but were astonished to see both our ghillies, the blacksmith, baker, and 'the boots' of the hotel among the party of seven. All these were members of the football club we had started and financed, and had looked upon as our friends. We got to bed about 4 a.m. and after a very sound sleep in a double-bedded room, rose for breakfast. When we got downstairs, we found Erle Drax and the resident magistrate, MacDermott, in the coffee room, but not a particle of any sort of food or drink. Father Sullivan had ordered us to be boycotted and no appeals to the landlord or Biddy the maid were of any avail. MacDermott suggested we should all go to his house. We had a most excellent breakfast with him and then went to shoot duck on Loch Cullen. When we returned about tea time, Mac-Dermott met us some distance from his house and told us that we had been 'proclaimed' and that he could not answer for our safety. Old Drax was all for staying out our time, but that evening 'the boys' attacked and murdered the proprietor of the town store. MacDermott came to our rooms at dawn to say we would be shot for certain unless we left at once. He had ordered his side car to take us to Ballina. So escorted by two policemen, we bolted – Old Drax in the worst of tempers, for he had paid his half share of the fishing and we had only had a fortnight out of six weeks.

On the return home of the Regiment we were quartered at Shorncliffe. Colonel Benson was still Colonel and we subalterns had a rough time, for some of us knew nothing about our profession. Coventry, who had risen from the ranks, was Adjutant, and typical of that period of 'smart soldier'. His 'zenith of life' was exactitude of drill movement, perfect military turn-out, and as a 17th Lancer, to consider himself superior to any other being in the world. We were quartered in huts without any heating and it was an unusually cold winter. We found all water in our rooms to have turned into a block of ice every morning. We only had two parades a week, the other times being occupied by the subalterns in Riding School and foot drill. At each event during the day we had to put on a new sort of kit: in the morning a serge, then a fur patrol with astrakhan borders, a stable jacket for the stables, a serge and overalls for foot drill in the afternoon and mess kit in the evening. Tim Maryon-Wilson hunted the Drag and I acted as First Whip. When he got smashed up and subsequently died, I had the pleasure of hunting the hounds, which was a deterrent to my military career as I had begun to work for entry into Staff College and had my energies diverted.

Gerald Portal had been entrusted with a mission to Zanzibar and his brother Raymond was then serving in the Infantry at Shorncliffe. I was most anxious to join this pioneering expedition to East Africa. I approached the authorities, but got a very cold reception and was told, if I wanted to go buccaneering, I ought not to have joined the 17th Lancers!

Ava (Lord Dufferin's son who was subsequently killed at Ladysmith) became a great friend of mine, as we were both very keen on boxing and sport and we used to go to London as often as possible to support various fights.

Whilst at Shorncliffe, I was appointed ADC to General le Quesne and in that capacity met Hylda Paget, who had come down with her mother to Folkestone. In these days of soldiering, everything was show. The best officers were judged to be the smartest in every detail of appearance. We had to get our first chargers from Brown, a dealer in Buckingham Palace Road, London, at fabulous prices. A splendid first charger was necessary if you were to be in favour with the authorities. So after visiting Messrs Brown I bought a beautiful dark chestnut, with black mane and tail. General du Quesne had a full dress parade shortly afterwards and as I wanted to look very fine, I brought out Brown's chestnut. All went well until the march past, when the splendid-looking animal took the bit in his teeth and mounted the General's charger – it was a mare and this devil Brown had stuck me with 'a rig'. After this misdemeanour I was sent back to Regimental duty.

Had it not been for this period of ADC-ship, I probably would not have got to know Hylda,[8] who subsequently became my wife. I was tried for the polo team the first year the Regiment came home, but did not play at Hurlingham. I was fifth man. I accompanied Prince Dolly on a round of shooting visits in the autumn of 1891 and whilst we were at Berkeley Castle he told me that Prince Eddie was seriously ill – he died 14 January 1892. All hearts bled for Princess May, for she was about twenty-four, most fascinating, beautiful and charming, with a ready wit. During Prince Eddie's lifetime, Prince George had been a frequent visitor to White Lodge and with his breezy sailor manners, he made himself extremely popular with everyone. So later on there were great rejoicings at the announcement of his engagement to Princess May in the Spring of 1893. They were married on 6 July of that year.

8 Hylda Sophia Paget, only daughter of Sir Ernest and Lady Paget of The Hall, Sutton Bonington, Leicestershire.

The Regiment brought a tame bear, Lizzie, from India, which was looked after by a private named Gipsy Clark. He was a real gipsy and one of his boasts was that he had never washed his body. One winter's night, when I happened to be orderly officer, I was awakened by a man who said that Lizzie had gone to Folkestone and that some of the inhabitants were terrified. Having found Clark we proceeded towards Folkestone and seeing a crowd at the Shorncliffe end of the Leas, we went there to find Lizzie sitting on the roof of an outhouse eating a bun. It was about 5.30 a.m. and bitterly cold. The crowd consisted mainly of lodging house inmates in their night attire with overcoats. Lizzie had got into someone's kitchen, upset a milk bowl, roused the inmates and they in their turn had roused other people. They looked upon Lizzie as a wild animal, whereas she was as tame as a dog, and when she saw Clark came down from the roof and followed him to Shorncliffe.

Soon after this the great landslide took place near Folkestone, in which many people lost their lives. I was out about 6.30 a.m. with the hounds, accompanied by the kennel huntsman, Brown, and hearing that many people had been buried alive, we made for the spot, the cliffs to the east of Shorncliffe and north of Folkestone. We managed to rescue a woman, man and one boy, but others were dead under the debris and earth. It was a horrible sight. We excavated three children, whose father and mother had been killed, but they were saved through their being in cots with high sides.

DRAG HUNTING . . . AND FISTICUFFS

At this time, the winter of 1891, Lawrence (afterwards Sir Herbert Lawrence) told me of a good horse owned by a dealer, Green, at Canterbury. I was hunting the Drag and had a great need for a good one. He and I went to Canterbury, where we saw a beautiful black horse, price £120, which he guaranteed as a good hunter. He also had a grey which jumped a five-barred gate in the dealer's yard, but Green said little about it and would not give me a guarantee. We bought back both, myself the black and Lawrence the grey.

We took them both out the next week with the Drag on the hills above Shorncliffe, to a meet called 'the Black Horse Line' and off the hounds went, with Lawrence at their tails. My black put both feet in the ground and wouldn't move, nor could I get it near a fence. Towards nightfall the brute condescended to go on to the road and so to

Shorncliffe, where I got well rattled in the Mess, as we had both 'bucked' a bit about our wonderful purchases.

The next day the horses were ridden by a rough rider, with similar results. Lawrence's grey went splendidly and he was greatly pleased.

Green, the dealer, was one of the selected 'dealers' for officers' chargers, so Benson, the Colonel, arranged for Green to send his rough rider over and if the black horse went well, my purchase was to stand, but if not, it was to be null and void. I chose the stiffest bit of country around, called 'the Lympne line' which consisted of a succession of open drains, plenty of timber and one real rasping bullfinch out of a sunken lane. I rode the best horse I had. Green's black never got out of the first field – Lawrence's grey led the field, till we came to the sunken road and bullfinch, which he got through, but the grey left his off fore foot fast in the branches. The horse had been unnerved by Green for navicular and so Lawrence's three rides had cost him £35, as he had bought the horse without a guarantee and Dibben, our vet, had passed both horses as sound. I now had the laugh over the Adjutant, Lawrence, and got my money back. This Lympne day was a source of amusement for years afterwards, for Harry Fortescue, at that time a captain in the Regiment, was, although he was married, a great favourite with the ladies.

We had arranged a select tea party with the prettiest Folkestone ladies in Hythe village through which we had to pass after hunting. Harry Fortescue had been given a magnificent chestnut hunter by his father and took the trouble to 'parade himself' and horse at a lunch he gave in Folkestone before the hunt.

To shake off the crowd of officers who came from the School of Musketry at Hythe, I arranged the Line, so that everyone had to jump the Hythe main open sewer. H.F.'s beautiful chestnut refused this (one of the first obstacles) but an officer named Gubbins, who hailed from Cork, caught him full broadside and knocked horse and rider into the sewage. Harry 'F' was almost asphyxiated by the stench. As he did not turn up at the tea he was providing in Hythe, I walked with two of the girls back towards Lympne line and saw Harry coming through the outskirts of Hythe. As he passed everyone held their handkerchiefs to their noses. When he came up to us, we realised why they did so, as I could never imagine a worse stink than this Hythe sewage produced. His (H.F.'s) beautiful ladies only screamed with laughter!

The first winter the Regiment was in England, 1890, I accompanied Prince Dolly on a round of shooting visits during our winter leave, including Warwick Castle, Berkeley Castle and Thoresby, and finished leave at Eaton (the Duke of Westminster's) where we had a fortnight's hunting and shooting. It was our second visit there. Old Corbett was hunting the Cheshire hounds and we had excellent sport. The old Duke was a great sportsman, the *beau idéal* of a perfect gentleman.

I spent Christmas at White Lodge – and subsequently every Christmas – where I frequently met the Duke of Cambridge, till we went to Ireland in 1896. Ava and I with some other officers who were keen on boxing got up some good fights in London. Somehow the Duke heard of this and intimated that he and the Duke of Teck would like to attend a special encounter we had organised with 2 oz. gloves. This fight was arranged to take place in a hall near Willis's Rooms and HRH with the Duke of Teck and about twenty officials from the War Office came. Just before the fight took place, we heard that the police had got wind of it and would probably raid the hall, so some ten of us were told off to hold the entrance to the hall against all intruders. The entrance was down a narrow passage and when seven rounds of the contest (a really good one) had taken place, the signal was given that the police were coming, so we rushed to the passage, which we successfully held till the celebrities had escaped by a side door. I got floored in the mêlée and on coming to my senses slipped out and walked towards Covent Garden. It was dawn, so I took a hansom to drive to Bury Street where I had rooms. Almost the first hansom going towards Covent Garden which I met contained my late guardian, Uncle George Tilney, and his wife!

People often used to go to Covent Garden Market in those days to buy fruit very early in the morning and in the evening some people went to Greenwich for the fish dinners.

I drove on to Hounslow with Ava, with a change of hansoms at the pub near Syon House and arrived at Hounslow Barracks a few minutes late for Adjutant's Parade. Dolly Teck and Noel did not turn up till midday, the latter having been taken by the police. The Colonel, Belford, asked for our reasons for being late in writing. After an unpleasant interview we gave a true statement, which was lucky, as the next day Evelyn Wood, who was the Adjutant or Acting AG, sent an officer from the War Office asking Colonel Belford for a full explanation of our disgraceful behaviour! As Evelyn Wood had been in attendance on the Duke of Cambridge at the fight, we sent Dolly Teck to explain matters at the War Office, but never told Colonel Belford or any one that these celebrities had been present at the fight and had escaped with difficulty when the police raided the hall.

LIGHT SOLDIERING AND SERIOUS HUNTING

In 1892 the 17th were sent to the Cannock Chase Manoeuvres and it is interesting to remember that our manoeuvre kit was tunics, dummy lance cap and all the paraphernalia of a full dress parade.

The old Duke of Cambridge, as he was Colonel-in-Chief of the Regiment, often came to lunch after the morning's work, which consisted of trotting over the moor. The day finished with a charge. A great change was introduced into our kit at these manoeuvres, for blue serges were issued for ordinary parades, but when the Duke was present we all wore the full kit. Camp arrangements were nil, and soon most of the officers and men were down with chills, which dampened the ardour of the authorities.

We were suddenly ordered to Preston for the coal strike. My two chargers were a horse named Cross Question – which had run well in the National a few years before and a four-year-old named Boric by Ascetic, which I had just bought. My prospects were not rosy. Boric was entirely unbroken and nobody could hold Cross Question when he got out of a hand canter. On our arrival at Preston, a squadron was ordered to Derby – Jack Purvis's squadron was selected. The subalterns were Noel, Jessel, Burdett and myself, with Coventry, the late Adjutant, who had risen from the ranks, as second in command.

We arrived by train at Derby in full kit, white plastrons (breast plates), shabraks (cavalry saddle cloths) and the rest. Jack Purvis, who had recently returned from the yeomanry, was the very last man to be sent on any sort of active duty, for he was one of the old hard-drinking, hard-swearing type of officer and very keen on his food. The Mayor and Corporation of Derby met us as we were detraining, and Jack welcomed the Mayor with the following – 'We will soon settle the b———s. Shall I order my men to use the butts of their lances or the bloody points?'

The Mayor's face was a study, for he happened to be the Congregationalist Minister, so this was a bad start. Jack's first charger had seldom been on parade, being fully employed since he joined the Regiment in pulling about his brougham. It was in appearance and shape very much like Artaxerxes (Jorrocks's famous horse), and you could hang your hat on his hip bones. We paraded in front of the station before a great crowd, and started to march to our various quarters in the town. Jack, bursting with pomposity, would insist upon what he called with strongest language 'frightening the populace', so we started to march to the Market Place by the narrow street north-east of Derby station.

On approaching the canal, a woman upset the worst class of house sewage bang on the top of Jack's head, to the delight of the crowd. I was with the leading troop riding the old steeplechaser, Cross Question. When the crowd, who were screaming with laughter, began to throw brickbats, my untrained charger took the bit in his mouth and bolted down a narrow side street, where a woman with a perambulator and baby were watching the fun. Cross Question jumped the baby and perambulator in his stride and no one was hurt.

These regrettable incidents curtailed Jack's military ardour and we went to our respective billets and had no more marches through the city.

As there was no work or military duties after 1 p.m. I used to ride over to Lord Harrington's at Elvaston to play polo. The Peats and Lord Harrington had been teaching me the game since 1890 and finding them all at Elvaston with Denis Daly and Gerald Hardy, we had great fun.

I saw a great deal of Cecil Paget for he was an apprentice at the Midland Works, Derby, and used to lunch at the Midland Hotel, but slept at Sutton Bonington, his home. To do this he had to start every weekday at 5.30 a.m., returning 7 p.m. I managed to get some weekends at Sutton Bonington to see Hylda, Cecil Paget's sister, whom I had first met at Folkestone in 1890, when we were quartered at Shorncliffe. I little realised at that time that the heavenly being would eventually be my wife. She was in 1890 known as the Lily of Leicestershire, and a prettier or nicer girl never stepped the earth.

As there were no serious riots in Derby, we had little to do, so I spent a lot of time at Elvaston. We always rode to the meets, which were then at 6 a.m., some of which were fifteen miles distant. This meant starting from Elvaston about 3.30 a.m. I well remember one particular day in the Uttoxeter district, when we started at the regular time on a miserable September day, rain and bitterly cold for that time of year. The meet was at a place on the banks of the River Dare, and soon finding a fox, hounds swam the river with Lord Harrington at their tails, cheering them on. The river being very high he had a good swim and had some difficulty in climbing the opposite bank. All the other people crossed higher up only girth deep, but when we got over there was no trace of old Harrington or hounds and we only picked them up again on our way home. He had swum two rivers in one of the best runs he had for years, so he said, and killed in the open. We all rode back to Elvaston. Tom Hone, a celebrated polo player and tough man, rode with me, and we all implored Lord Harrington to gallop on and change his clothes.

On our arrival, he remarked, 'Now we will shoot some partridges before polo', so off we went. He had changed his boots and coat. We got back about 3 p.m. and had some lunch and played polo till tea-time, when he went off for a bath. After dinner he always played billiards, but if the light was good enough, he challenged me to a fencing bout. He was the strongest and most energetic man I have ever come across and a great gentleman.

Jack Purvis's squadron was now ordered to Rotherham, then Leeds, and we finished up at Birmingham. When we arrived at Birmingham, Jack Purvis suggested to Joe Chamberlain that we should have a full dress parade for him and the fashionable of Birmingham. Only a field of about six acres was available, but this did not deter Jack who ordered a ceremonial parade.

All went well until we trotted past with Jessel as the leading troop leader. Being a very bad horseman, he got too near the boundary railings. When Jack gave the command 'Left wheel in to line', Jessel's troop, being behind the audience, failed to respond. Jack shouted, 'Couldn't you hear the word of command, Mr Jessel?' His answer 'No' brought out the following remark from Jack, just as he was in front of Joe Chamberlain, the Mayor, and other dignitaries: 'Why the bloody hell don't you clear your ears out then?' This ended the only mounted parade we had in Birmingham.

I was hunting with the Pytchley from Rugby at Fitzjohns, Sir S. Maryon-Wilson's house. Lord Spencer was Master of the Pytchley. I purchased a horse named Willoughby at Tattersall's for £30. He had belonged to a Horse Gunner named Morley Knight, who told me the horse would jump anything, but no one could hold him. One day with the Pytchley at Scotland Wood this horse got clean away with me. As we descended the hill, I saw Lord Spencer standing in the gateway, and catching him broadsides, knocked him over and over.

He got up and instead of cursing and possibly ordering me to go home, he said, in the politest manner, 'Young man, how far have you come to do this?'[9]

9 This event and the remark have passed into Pytchley Hunt folklore.

I hunted from Rugby for three years and saw a good deal of Bay Middleton. One day, after a good hunt, I was riding home with him and as we were passing Reggie Loder's house (Maidwell) Reggie came out to ask me to order some fish in Rugby, since he had a large party for the Market Harborough Ball. He had calculated the exact amount required to half a pound. When we rode on, Bay Middleton told me what a frightful scrooge Reggie was and said 'Now order all the fish procurable in Rugby to be sent to Maidwell at once, and I'll be responsible for payment.' This being done, cartloads of fish of every description began to arrive at Maidwell far into the night.

I had been Reggie Loder's fag at Eton and no man could have been more hated by the Lower Boys. He was a very good runner, and one day accused me of cutting his running shoes. I told him I had not, but he gave me a good caning all the same. When my elder brother, Monkey, heard about this he went up to Reggie's room and gave him such a good hiding that he had to go sick for a week.

POLO WITH WHITE GLOVES

When I was elected captain of the 17th Lancers' polo team I asked the advice of the Peats and John Watson. Our chief rivals were the 13th Hussars of which Regiment John Watson had been a member some years before, and they had, under 'Boy' McLaren, an excellent team. The Peats' team was the best in England and they told me that the great difficulty in any team was to make the players keep their places and not to hunt the ball. I introduced numbered belts, 1, 2, 3, 4, for the players to wear during the game to keep them in their places. I had the belts 'registered' and made at Holboro's, Duke Street, St James's. We in the 17th wore them regularly until Toby Rawlinson, who had left the Regiment, ridiculed the idea in the polo and sporting papers.

This numbering of players was the origin of numbers being placed on players of all games such as polo, football and on racehorses. I made nothing out of the idea for Holboro said truthfully that I could not patent an idea.

At the beginning of 1893 I was chosen for a team to go to Paris to teach the Frenchmen the game of polo. Lord Dufferin was ambassador and Ava, his son in the 17th, had been asked to bring this team over, all expenses being paid. We had the most wonderful time. The team was Ava, Renton, Lawrence and myself, and Fortescue and George Milner as extras. We were all put up by different hosts, mine being the Duc de Rochfoucauld for part of the time and then du Val.

The first time we played, most of the Frenchmen turned out immaculately dressed with white kid gloves. The whole of fashionable Paris turned up and at the end of the game we were each presented with beautiful presents. The captain of the team, Renton, was publicly kissed by the 'Queen of Beauty'. It took us sometime to persuade the Frenchmen to discard their white gloves and beautiful clothes, but one named Rodier would not hear of such a thing, and when we asked him the reason he said that if his hands were rough he would not have the same success with the ladies.

I had bought in London a hackney for my dogcart, and Renton suggested that this would be a great chance to get rid of this useless animal by selling it in Paris. One day I brought it to the polo ground and trotted it past the pavilion. One of the Rothschilds, and another Frenchman, at once asked if I would sell it. He was delighted and whenever we had a match the new owner trotted it up and down in front of the ladies. We were in Paris for six weeks and had a wonderfully good time.

When the Regiment was at Leeds there was no polo ground, so I was authorised to secure one and got a promising field near Roundhay Park. George and Stanley Jackson, Soapy Watson (afterwards Lord Manton) and some civilians came to our help and to get the field fairly level we loaned the corporation's heavy roller. One day when we were on parade a message arrived that the corporation's roller had almost disappeared into an old sewer. This finished our polo, for the exertions required to extricate it were long and expensive and the ground was ruined. Watson made a huge fortune by inventing floating soap and after the above mishap he provided us with an excellent polo ground at his own expense.

As my grandmother's sister married a Gott of Armley and I had heaps of Yorkshire cousins, I had a grand time at Leeds, shooting and hunting.

MISCHIEF AT THE GAPING GOOSE

One day Dolly Teck, Ricardo and myself were going to shoot with Humpy Fawkes at Farnley and as I had an excellent – though vicious – pony, we agreed to drive there in my trap. Luckily Dolly Teck could not leave at the last moment, for as Ricardo and I left barracks the guard 'recovered lance' and this frightened the mare. She bolted down the hill leading up to the barracks and deposited us through a plate glass window into a milliner's shop. Ricardo was knocked out and badly cut. He was taken back to barracks with the pony which was itself cut to pieces. I landed in the shop at the bottom of the counter. I escaped, however, with a few cuts and bad shaking, and proceeded to Farnley. Humpy Fawkes was a cousin of the Cradocks and all three were shooting there that day, Shell, Monty and Kit (who became the famous admiral and lost his life at Coronel in the Great War). Humpy told us on no account to shoot any white or albino pheasants, but just before lunch Kit brought one down and to avoid a row buried it in a rabbit hole. The ladies came out to lunch and whilst we were in the middle of the meal, Humpy's dog brought Kit's white pheasant to him. The little man bubbled with rage and interrogated all of us to find out the culprit and refused to go on shooting unless he found out. Kit made a complete confession. To punish us he ordered the beaters home and the next day we were sent out grouse driving.

It was one of the worst December days with half a gale and blizzard, so when lunch came we struck. Unfortunately Humpy turned up with two theatrical ladies. We had an excellent lunch at a partly ruined inn on the Farnley Moors called the Gaping Goose; whereupon Humpy ordered us to go on shooting and remarked that he would count the shots fired and that he did not want us to take the last drive – adjacent to the Gaping Goose – till 4 p.m. since the ladies wanted to see a grouse drive. When we got outside the inn, Kit said, 'Well, we won't be bothered with Humpy and his girls!' He locked the door and put the key in his pocket.

About 3 p.m. a real blizzard made further shooting impossible, so we made our way towards Farnley, which we reached about 5 p.m. On arrival, Lady Fawkes and the other ladies met us to say that Humpy had not returned from the moor. (She was unaware that the theatrical girls had accompanied him to the Gaping Goose.)

There was great consternation. Kit said in a heroic tone, 'Tilney and I will go to look for him', well knowing that having locked them in and put the key in his pocket, we had all completely forgotten about them. So after a terrible walk in a blinding blizzard, we discovered Humpy and the two girls in the pitch dark of one of the old rooms at the Gaping Goose, very nearly perished with cold. Kit had had the forethought to order a hill cart and pony to wait for us at the bottom of the hill, which we reached at about 9 p.m. As there was plenty of hot drink, Humpy regained some of his senses and good will. He drew Kit aside and had an earnest conversation, at the end of which Kit said that he and I would take the ladies to the hotel at Otley. This we did, and had a pleasant evening since they proved to be two charming gaiety girls who were playing at Harrogate.

After this episode Humpy was very kind to me. Kit and I remained fast friends and had many a good laugh over this incident. Neither Humpy's wife nor any of the ladies found out about his affair with the gaiety girls.

At this time there was supposed to be at Farnley the finest collection of Turner pictures in the world, together with a great many Guy Fawkes relics, including the coat Guy Fawkes wore at the time of the Gunpowder Plot. There was also a collection of old armour.

One weekend during the summer, Humpy asked me over to fish. On arrival I found that Lady Fawkes was away and that he had asked a Harrogate theatrical party to stay. After dinner one of the men dressed up, or tried to dress up, in Guy Fawkes's clothes. Others tried the armour, but it was all too small for the men.

Whenever the Duke of Cambridge came to inspect troops in the north, he frequently stayed with the Vyners at Newby Hall, Ripon. As the Vyners were almost fairy-godparents to me, I came in for some excellent shooting. Lord de Grey was then in his prime and he taught me all there was to know about shooting. He was Bob Vyner's brother-in-law so I met him at most of the big shoots.

A QUESTIONABLE BAG

Bob Vyner's moor at Askrigg, though small, was exceptionally good. One season, wanting to get a thousand brace in two days, he asked the best team of guns he could muster, including Lord de Grey, Digby Cayley (died 1917), Harry Beaumont, Mossop and myself. It was a very interesting party for John Osborne, the old jockey, Teddy Welsh, an old pugilist who used to do much of the commission work on the turf, and Jack Parker (the original James Pigg of Jorrocks fame) were there. Digby Cayley had got 'James Pigg' to load for him and I stayed with them and Teddy Welsh in some rooms opposite the village hotel.

After dinner there was a devil of a row and we saw James Pigg and Welsh having a first class fight in the street. When I went to bed, Pigg was very drunk and remarked to me 'I'll go to see how that old b—— Digby is getting on.' He stumbled over to the hotel and into Digby's room. Digby jumped out of bed and threw Pigg downstairs, waking up the whole establishment. The language was of the Billingsgate variety on both sides and Digby told Pigg to get out of the place by the first train.

Getting up early the next morning I was surprised to meet Pigg looking none the worse for his night's adventures, carrying Digby's things to his room.

The first evening, after a very good shoot, there was a heavy discrepancy in the number of birds claimed by the guns and the actual bag, so Bob Vyner arranged that in future a checker would visit each butt, take down the number of birds, and that the same should tally with the keeper's record.

Some of Bob's friends in Wensleydale came to dinner that night and as four of the guns were supposed to be about the best in England, someone said 'Let us get up a selling sweep for the highest scorer.' After dinner, John Osborne, James Pigg and Welsh came in with a lot of people from the village, and Lord de Grey sold for the highest price and Digby Cayley second. Lord Grenfell, who had arrived that day, and myself, were well at the bottom. When I was put up for auction there were no bidders, so I bought my chance for a sovereign. We drew for butts and I found myself between Lord de Grey and Digby, who were at any shoot extremely jealous of one another and on this occasion both were doing their utmost to be top scorer. It was a wonderful sight to see how they shot.

It was a lovely day and we did not get down to the inn until just before dinner, after which the individual scores were to be announced by the head keeper (Topham). He came in about 9.30 p.m. accompanied by 'James Pigg', who was already drunk, together with as many others as the room could hold. Outside were all the beaters, valets, and so on. I couldn't believe my ears when John Topham announced me as the winner, Lord de Grey second and Digby third. The numbers were re-checked and I led the other two by five birds.

The evening before, after the sweep had taken place, James Pigg had asked me to sell 'half myself' and he gave me ten shillings the morning of the shoot. I told him it was throwing his money away, so after the result had been announced, Bob handed me over £46 and when I got to my lodgings over the way I handed Pigg his half, £23. Pigg and his companions kept the whole village awake for most of the night, but he was the first up the next morning.

Two years afterwards when shooting at Askrigg, one of the pony boys said to me, 'You will miss Parker this year on the moor.' He said it very pointedly. I asked him 'Why?' He replied that Parker had bribed him to bring some of Lord de Grey's and Digby Cayley's birds to my butt when the village sweepstake took place two years before as Parker had backed me to be top scorer!

Old Skidmore, who kept an antique shop in Askrigg, collected some extraordinary old English furniture around Wensleydale. Some of the best pieces at Newby came from him. Skiddy was looked upon as being the cleverest fisherman in Yorkshire. He would get a good dish of trout when nobody else could catch a fish. After much persuasion he showed me an antique book, *Anglers' Secrets*, in which all the poachers' dodges were told. Here are two: – To catch fish without tackle. Take *cocculus indicus*,[10] pulverise it and mix it with dough. Scatter a few handfuls in still or eddying water, when the fish will seize it and become intoxicated, turning belly upwards. Catch them and put them in a bucket of fresh water, where they will revive. When fly fishing for trout or salmon – point your hook with a small piece of worm and then dip the fly into a bottle of oil of rhodium or oil of ambra and rhodium (equal parts) when the fish will be attracted from afar. These old Chinese secrets are said to date from circa 1100 and are still used in the Chinese rivers. Oil of rhodium is difficult to get, but when I tried it the results were wonderful.

On this occasion Skiddy told me that he always fed his worms on salmon roe and laughed at the professors who said salmon did not feed in fresh water. I subsequently proved him right in Ireland, Scotland and Norway. On the Namsun in August 1933, I got 47 salmon, average 24 pounds, in 11 days, and one day played 24 salmon but only landed 2 as the river was at record low and I was using an eight-foot trout rod. Erik Moum of Moum House, Norway, was with me when I hooked with the rod what the Norwegian papers described as the biggest salmon that had ever been taken with rod and line.

About this time the Prince of Wales (later King Edward) came for a week's shooting at Newby and I was asked by the Vyners to be one of the party as the 17th Lancers were then at York. The company was select. At the first day's shoot I was put between Lord de Grey and the Prince of Wales, and to my astonishment shot better than I had ever done before which put me in very good fettle. That night I joined the others at baccarat and lost a good bit. I had stood out the night of my arrival and two of the guests remarked that my attitude was very unsociable. So the third night I had another try and began to lose much more

10 A South East Asian berry, very poisonous.

than I could afford. Just as I was almost *in extremis* Bob Vyner said to the Prince of Wales (Bob Vyner was looking on as he never gambled), 'Sir, I think we will all go in to the drawing-room'. There was a roar of dissent, but Bob was obdurate and as host insisted. Off we went and there was no more gambling during the week at Newby.

The next summer I stayed with the Hillingdons for Ascot. They had a house on the course and the first night there was pretty high gambling. A lieutenant in the navy named Tufton was among the party, also two men who had 'gone for me' at Newby when I declined to gamble the night of our arrival. One of these two was Lord William Nevill (Bill Nevill). Tufton came into my room the second day of the races and said he was broke and could not gamble any more. Would I stand out with him? I said I certainly would, so when gambling began after dinner, Tufton and I stood out and positively refused to join in. Bill Nevill and his pal were extremely rude whilst players were taking their seats, but we were not to be drawn, for Tufton who was much younger than myself had arranged that I should be spokesman. After the ladies had gone I went up to Bill Nevill and calling him every name I could think of asked him to step into the garden. He was a 'drooping lily' sort of man, but much taller and bigger than myself. When he declined to 'have a round' in the garden, I said as quietly as possible, 'I see you are a coward, cur and blackguard.' I naturally left the next day and was sorry I did, for the dirty swine at the same party took over £500 from a lady friend of mine. When shooting afterwards with Bob Vyner, I asked him why he had stopped the gambling when the Prince of Wales was at Newby, and told him my experience at Ascot the summer following the Newby shoot. He quite beamed with delight and said that he had seen Bill Nevill and his confederates with a certain lady (the old Duchess of Devonshire) deliberately swindling. This evidence finished my card-playing and I never gambled again, but it was an expensive experience to have gone through.

When the 17th Lancers were at York I was nominated for service with the Egyptian Army. Broadwood, commanding the Egyptian Cavalry, wrote to our Colonel specifically asking for me. Le Gallais, Mahon and Legge, all in Egypt, were great pals of mine, and knowing most of the officers I was most anxious to go.

Colonel Belford was then in command with Lawrence (afterwards Sir Herbert Lawrence, Chief of Staff to Lord Haig) as Adjutant. I thought the 17th authorities would be very pleased at this honour that had been done to me. But when I presented myself at the orderly room to get the CO's approval, I got a good wigging for preferring the Egyptian Army to the 17th Lancers. He refused his consent, a refusal which thoroughly disheartened and disgusted me, for such a nomination was one of the sure ways to distinction in a military career.

THE CASE OF THE DISHONEST VALET

I happened to be captain of the polo and cricket teams at the time, and all of a sudden, it seemed to me, found myself senior subaltern, for a great many officers had recently left the Regiment. I had been 'boots' of the Regiment for four years. Lawrence told me that this was the reason why the Colonel would not allow me to go. In addition to running the polo and cricket, I was made mess president during the latter period we were at York. The Duke of Cambridge, who was still Commander-in-Chief, came to inspect the Regiment. The Colonel, who dreaded any form of inspection, fairly got the wind up and asked me to see that the Duke had pork chops, which he was known to like, and the best claret procurable.

I asked Bob Vyner to help me to get the wine for the ducal lunch and he gave me six bottles of Napoleon claret. When I was arranging the drink with Harris, the mess caterer, this old stager said, 'Six bottles is no good, as once they know it is Napoleon claret all the officers will want it, so I'll get some at 2/6d per bottle from the grocer outside the barracks and put it into the Napoleon bottles when they have been decanted.' Of course we gave the Napoleon claret itself to the Duke and his staff, but all the other officers had the half-crown brand from the grocer's served in the Napoleon bottles. The wine went down extraordinarily well, and by the end of the lunch the grocer's stock was exhausted. The assembly never found out the hoax till their mess bills were paid, when I was mercifully away from the Regiment on Lord Cadogan's staff at Dublin.

Before the Regiment left York a most unpleasant incident happened at Newby when the old Duke was staying there. Bob Vyner was now a bosom friend of mine and one day he and Watson (his secretary) asked me if I was certain that my soldier servant was strictly honest, to which I replied in the affirmative, as he had been with me for a long time and I had had no reason to think otherwise. They told me that a great many valuables had disappeared from the house during the last three years, especially valuable books and *objets d'art*, and that they had had a Scotland Yard detective in the house as a waiter. When the old Duke was leaving one afternoon, Bob took me with Watson and the detective to search the valet's kit. We found he had selected some almost unique books and a quantity of *objets d'art*. The detective said that he might have packed a lot more in the Duke's bag. We were on our way to the Duke's room when we heard the lunch gong and thought it dangerous to search any further. Now what was to be done? The Duke, not only holding the highest position as C-in-C of the Army and a member of the Royal Family, was going away about 3 p.m.

We therefore had a hurried consultation in the library. It was agreed that nothing could be said to the Duke, but Bob naturally did not want to lose his valuables, especially one particular sporting book that was unique. The detective wanted to arrest the valet forthwith. Watson rather lost his head, but Bob settled the matter thus: 'We will meet here immediately the Duke and his entourage have gone.' When we met about 4 p.m. in the library, Bob said to the detective: 'You will go at once to London, find out where the valet is staying tonight, search his kit and room and I will be responsible for any unpleasantness with the Duke that may ensue.'

At the time it struck me that this was pretty drastic, but Bob was right.

Detectives from Scotland Yard visited Mr B's (the valet) room about 3 a.m. in London, found he had gone to bed without unpacking and that he was in possession of hundreds of pounds' worth of valuables he had stolen from various houses whilst visiting with the Duke. Bob had told Scotland Yard that no action was to be taken without his consent and that he would be in London to claim his treasures the following day. When Bob arrived, Scotland Yard said Mr B. must be arrested, but Bob just put his eye-glass and said, 'If he is arrested we shall never recover or trace these stolen goods, so tell Mr B to come to Combe Hirst [Bob's London house near Richmond Park] tomorrow.'

When Mr B. came (the Duke happened to be staying at White Lodge, Richmond Park), Bob interviewed him with three detectives dressed up as footmen and told him all the facts of the case, to which he gave a flat denial. Bob replied, 'The three footmen here are detectives and unless you give a full detailed list of all the articles you have stolen during the past three years, you will be arrested at once. If you give this list and the names of the owners of the property you will be allowed to remain in the Duke's service as long as he keeps you and nothing will be said.' Mr B in about a week disgorged hundreds of pounds' worth of stolen property, much of which was returned to the original owners with no explanation, except that it had been recovered from a thieves' receiving depot.

PIONEERING THE BALLOON

When the Regiment arrived at York, there was no polo ground. As I was in charge of the Regimental polo, I was authorised to find somewhere to play. We began in a small field towards Escrick – Guy Palmer being very helpful – but this was useless when the grass began to grow. So I approached the Lord Mayor with a view to getting the centre portion of the Knavesmire.

It transpired that this land belonged to the freemen of York, and had it not been for the kindly help of Sir Edward Green I could never have started polo at York. After a lot of negotiations we were given permission to play three days a week. This made all the difference to our summers at York, as the racecourse committee allowed us to use the grandstand as a pavilion. Soon after we had got polo going at York, I was asked to help form a polo club at Hull and this ground was opened on Easter Monday, during our second year at York.

Since the Hullites were ignorant of the game, I took a team over. The ground was packed to its utmost capacity. All the Hullites had surnames beginning with H, such as Hodgson and Hartley, but they hadn't an H in their voices. They were really good sportsmen and we had a nice outing except for one unpleasant incident. Obby Beauclerk (Lord Osborne Beauclerk) was one of my team. The Wilsons of Tranby Croft, who were very keen on members of the peerage, asked to be introduced to him. Obby got one of his subalterns to impersonate him and on our way back to York, I said to Obby, 'I thought you were going to stay at Tranby Croft.' 'No,' said Obby. 'So-and-so took my place. I could not stay with the old snob for anything.' The next day I was sent for by the Adjutant. He showed me a letter from Mrs Wilson, who had been foolish enough to write to the Colonel protesting against the imposture ... and was rude enough to kick Obby's substitute out of the house the next day. The 17th gave a great ball at York and none of the Wilson family were allowed to be asked.

Shortly after the Colonel's refusal of my request to join the Egyptian Army, an army order came out asking for volunteers for the aeronautical section of the Royal Engineers. In went my name. I was thoroughly sick of the humdrum life of regimental soldiering.

I soon found myself at Aldershot in the RE barracks, seconded for six months. The CO of the Balloon Section was Colonel Templer, an extraordinary man in many senses; in his way a genius, for he was the inventor of the goldbeater's skin envelope for balloons. He was one of the earliest pioneers of aviation, and his enthusiasm was unbounded when the Balloon Section was recognised officially by the War Office and eight army volunteers turned up. Nothing at that time was known about 'the air' so it was laid down that to get a certificate as a balloonist you had to learn all about the construction of a balloon, make thirty ascents, and take charge of three 'free runs', i.e. in a loose balloon.

The first day of training took place adjoining the Farnborough Hotel near the canal. Each volunteer was let up 'to observe' for half an hour, whilst the others were lectured on technicalities on the ground. About noon we had taken cover from a very hot sun near the Farnborough Road canal bridge, when the balloon (whose basket was then occupied by a subaltern belonging to the Essex Regiment) burst. The officer mercifully fell into the canal, otherwise he would have been killed.

This was a terrible blow to old Templer's enthusiasm, and the propaganda that he was pushing – 'that balloons would be of the greatest value in a European War'. There were only two gas-bags left so we had our practical work very much curtailed. When it became known that one of the balloons in which we had to make a daily ascent had been condemned as unsafe two years previously, the volunteers began with one accord to make excuses to rejoin their regiments. I had been asked by the 17th to remain on as captain of the polo team and when the first burst took place, I asked Templer's permission to have three afternoons off every week to play polo at Hurlingham, where I had four good ponies. The volunteers dwindled down to a boy in the RE named Mellor[11] and myself.

When Mellor and I were the only ones left of the original aeronautical class, there was little to be done in the afternoon, so I brought two ponies to Aldershot to play polo there, as well as at Hurlingham. Winston Churchill was then a subaltern in the 4th Hussars, and one day

11 W.A.T notes: 'Mellor was an enthusiastic photographer and always insisted upon taking snapshot photographs from the captive balloon and then we used to decipher them with magnifying glasses. Mellor bored us all by jawing about the wonderful uses this aerial photography could be put to in war. One day in the Long Valley he took photographs of troops at rest and in movement and showed how valuable the information would be if this branch of aeronautics was properly developed. I will refer to this man's genius when we come to the South African War and how his enthusiasm ruined his career as a soldier. He was the very first man to realise and practise aerial photography and was its greatest protagonist till the commencement of the Great War. He was rewarded by a grateful country by losing his commission.'

asked me to give him some tips about hitting the ball. The 4th Hussars had at that time a good team and Winston had been provided with two first class ponies by his mother. Being a beginner, he was not in the team but his ponies were used in regimental matches.

He brought them down one day to knock the ball about and I happened to remark that any old pony was good enough to learn how to hit the ball from and that these first class ponies were often no good for a beginner. He replied, 'I'll sell them and get four old crocks, so as to become ball perfect.' He did just that, much to the disgust of the Regiment. Colonel Brabazon was commanding the 4th Hussars at the time and there was a lot of unpleasant ragging in the mess. One fine afternoon Winston did not turn up for polo and when we went to his room to fetch him down, we found him in his shirt sleeves and dressing-gown reading Gibbon. He got unmercifully ragged, but he took it very well and told me that he always read the best English literature for two hours every day.

I had every afternoon off, which suited my plans perfectly and I had a first class season's polo. This made me stick to the nerve-wracking business of going up in rotten balloons; for the only alternative was to rejoin the Regiment which had an Adjutant, Sandeman, whom I could never get on with and who discouraged polo. The first 'free run' I had with Gerry Heath, RE, almost ended in our deaths.

It was an ideal day with a light breeze that took us towards Portsmouth from Aldershot. When we neared the sea, Heath ordered me (I was in the net) to pull the valve cord to make our descent, which I did, but instead of coming down we went up to 3,000 feet and as it was hazy, out of sight of the earth. The next orders I got were in quick succession – to pull the ripping rope; then (in headlong descent) throw overboard everything we could lay our hands on, including our boots. To ascertain the rapidity of the descent Heath threw out handfuls of torn paper, which whizzed past me in the envelope of the net. One did not realise the rapidity of our fall until looking downwards I saw a shining spot in a green park and then felt a terrible crash combined with a miasmal stench of manure.

When I temporarily regained consciousness I found myself in bed with a doctor and two ladies standing alongside it. The place was Rowlands Castle owned by Mr Christie (the hatter). It appeared that when we got into the whirlwind and Heath ordered me to pull the ripping rope, we had fallen like a stone. The shining thing I saw was the butler's bald pate, and we providentially ricocheted off a tree into the manure pit, which saved our lives. Heath had got off with a few bruises and scratches.

I slept the night at Rowlands Castle. Realising that I was dining the next night at the Zetlands' in London, and being much in love with a certain girl, I insisted on leaving the Christies' most hospitable house. It does not say much for the doctor in letting me go, but go I did and arrived at the Zetlands' feeling all right, except for a very bad head. In the middle of dinner (it was one of the huge old-fashioned dinner parties) everything became clouded, although I had been careful to drink no intoxicant, and the next day I found myself in hospital and remained there a fortnight. On arrival at the Zetlands' I had fortunately told my love-bird what had happened the day before and about the marvellous escape we had had, so they knew I was not the worse for drink and Lady Zetland could not have been kinder when I was in hospital.

The next free run was pleasant enough and very beautiful as the wind took us up a great part of the Thames Valley. We landed near Swindon. This made me quite keen on free running and I tried to go whenever possible and did twelve free runs in all and only had one further mishap.

Now that I was a qualified aeronaut, Templer ordered me to take a new man for a short free run. When the mouth of the Thames was visible I looked out for a landing place. I put out the anchor in some flats near Tilbury, but unfortunately caught the roof of a shed, which was torn off and the next thing hooked was an outside closet with a woman occupant. She must have had the surprise of her life, as she with the closet was lifted some feet before the anchor gave way and she was dropped in the mud alongside the river.

As the escape valve had been open for the descent we had no lift. Just missing Tilbury Fort we landed on some mud flats – the tide being out – on the other side of the Fort and about half a mile from land. I made signals of distress in hope that I might be rescued by a punt when the tide came in. Soon two men came from the shore skating on the mud with mud skates and told me that we would have to wait for an hour before being rescued. When a light punt came down the river I had sunk in the stinking mud up to my waist. We were landed at a margarine factory, given a change of clothes by the foreman and went to London by train from Tilbury. I had arranged for the salvage of the balloon with the foreman of the factory and reported this misadventure at Aldershot the next morning. I imagined that old Templer would be pleased at my escape but to my surprise he was furious and said I should have waited to rescue the balloon and bring it back to Aldershot. He berated me as an unworthy balloonist and sent me off to bring everything back. Now, although there was no code of laws regarding aeronautics in those early days, I felt certain that the lady who had been hooked from the commode and deposited in the Thames mud would make herself nasty on my return. I therefore asked Templer for a party of men to accompany me: thereabouts the wharfingers and bargees are a rough crowd. I had not heard if the woman had suffered any injury. Templer having stipulated that I should defray all expenses, I arrived with three men at the margarine works. Soon a somewhat hostile crowd assembled. They would not permit us to pack up the balloon until I had been confronted by the woman. I was taken to the scene of the accident. She certainly weighed a good fourteen stone, a real good sort, the wife of a fisherman, and treated the incident as a great joke saying, 'If I had not been a bit stout, I might have been taken to heaven, like Elijah!'

The crowd then roared with laughter and when I gave her a fiver she begged me to return as soon as possible and give her a ride in the balloon, saying, 'I expect it is more comfortable in that small basket, than the ride you gave me on the closet seat.'

A TOUCH OF LUNACY

Soon after this I rejoined the 17th, who had been sent to Ballincollig under the temporary command of Harry Fortescue. By the regulations I had to put in three months annually with the Regiment. Fortescue was very nervous and frightened of the authorities, especially of the Inspector-General of Cavalry, General Luck.

When the Regimental dinner took place more than half the officers went to London to attend it. They were only given three days' leave because the inspection by the general was imminent. When the officers from London were due to return, a wire arrived to say that they had been given an extra day's leave by the Duke of Cambridge. As I was then the Assistant Adjutant I pointed out to the Colonel that some would have to return almost immediately after their arrival and could not possibly stay till the end of dinner, for the train for the short leave officers left Euston at 10 p.m.

The CO however was in such a funk that he would not extend their leave, so when the Duke of Cambridge, who was then C-in-C, heard of this at the dinner, he said, 'What nonsense! The officers who have attended the dinner will have a week's leave', and instructed Sir Evelyn

Wood to advise the GOC Cork, who was General McCalmont, of his decision. To my consternation the CO ordered the officers to be placed under arrest on their return to Ballincollig for overstaying their leave. I politely tried to show Fortescue the impossibility and enormity of the order, but he was obdurate and about ten officers were put under arrest.

This was not a good start, but it was soon forgotten as a most amusing hoax was played upon us all by the Irishmen.

The resident magistrate at Ballincollig told Fortescue that the Mayor of Cork was giving a ball and hoped as many officers as possible would attend. Fortescue told me to warn the subalterns to go in full kit. On arrival we found everything well done, and some extraordinarily pretty girls and women. When supper came in I was seated at the same table as Brin Sheridan and Reggie Wyndham and we all had nice pretty girls as partners. Suddenly Brin's partner seized a fork and stabbed him in the leg, which he took for a joke, but Reggie's girl became hysterical and we all left the supper-room. I went to smoke a cigarette, and saw Tom Donovan the horse dealer, Feard the vet, and a batch of Corkites roaring with laughter, so asked what the joke was. Their reply was that the ball was not given by the Mayor, but was a charity ball for the lunatics and the girls we had been dancing with were the inmates of the lunatic asylum. I must say it was extraordinarily well got up and organised for the Irishmen had a lunatic dressed up as Mayor and the pseudo Mayoress – a very handsome woman – was a criminal lunatic.

I took the Danesky water on the River Lee. One day Fortescue asked if he might have a day's fishing; I was happy to oblige the Colonel. As it happened that day I had nothing to do in the afternoon so rode out to see how he was getting on. When approaching the river I saw the Colonel sitting on the bank with a lady alongside him and another man coming over the hill from Macroom. As I got nearer the Colonel seized the rod and almost at the same moment the lady screamed and held her behind. The other man from Macroom started to run towards them. When I got up they were having high words. Harry Fortescue still held the rod and was virtually 'playing' his lady love, who was hooked in the tenderest part of her anatomy. What had happened was this. Harry Fortescue had taken a very beautiful wife of an officer in the Fusiliers for a 'honeymoon' trip into the country, unbeknown to her husband who had started off in pursuit immediately he heard of his wife's indiscretion. When Harry Fortescue saw the husband coming over the hill, he at once seized the rod, pretending to fish, but unfortunately she had been sitting on the worm hook, which took a firm hold. The husband would not allow Harry or myself to extricate the hook so we proceeded to the doctor's at Macroom, Harry holding the rod, the husband the lady's skirts and John Barry, the fisherman, and myself as rearguard. The lady was in pain but nobody thought of cutting the line, so she was 'played' at the end of the rod as far as Macroom.

Soon after this incident I joined Lord Cadogan's staff in Dublin. He was Viceroy of Ireland. The ADCs were Frank Wise, Ath Lumley, (Anthony Weldon was there when I first came and then retired), Child Fielden (the Greys), Jerry Cadogan, Herbert Featherstonehaugh, George Scott, John Keane, Bunny Dundas and myself.

Shortly after my arrival at the castle, Lord Cadogan told me that part of my duties was to look after the house party when hunting. As there was a different house party every week, I made a host of new friends, and had the best of times, yet it was a very strenuous existence. There were balls during the season almost every night, and when the meet was with the Meath in the Thursday country, the special train started about 8 a.m. I found it impossible to burn the candle at both ends without going into strict training. I gave up smoking and had only a glass of wine at dinner and nothing afterwards and never felt the worse for the hard life. When I was ADC-in-waiting, Lord Cadogan said I could look after the party out hunting but had to arrange the dinner party.

One Thursday, when the meet was the far side of Navan, I asked George Scott to make all the arrangements for an extra large dinner party – about 200 people – that was to take place that night. He promised to do so. However, about noon he joined the hunt and as the hounds had just found, I had no opportunity to ask him if all was OK for the evening's dinner. We had a grand hunt and got back to the castle just in time for dinner, when Pogson, the old butler, came up to say that no arrangements had been made and that the guests were already arriving. These big dinners took a lot of arranging and organisation, for in Ireland at this time there were innumerable feuds and animosities. For instance, the RC Bishop had not spoken to the Protestant Bishop for years, so when the guests arrived, no one knew whom they had to take into dinner. George Scott, a man of initiative, said, 'I have arranged a novelty, sir, that every lady can choose her partner, but they must have the same coloured eyes.' Lady Cadogan quickly realised what had occurred, but there was a scramble for partners. It so happened that the RC and Protestant Bishops sat alongside of one another, the first with Mrs Atkinson, the wife of the Solicitor General, and the latter with Mrs McCalmont, the wife of the General Commanding at Cork. I was at this table and things were going very badly, until the sweets were handed round when unfortunately – or perhaps fortunately – the footman upset a large piece of ice onto and down Mrs Atkinson's bust. She was a well-known Irish wit, but disliked the Bishop. With the sweetest smile to the Bishop, she said, 'Would you not like to be where the ice is?' Doctor Mahaffy added some nutty remarks and both the Bishops roared with laughter. The dinner was the greatest success.

When I first hunted in Ireland with the Duhallow, Muskerry and South Union, I brought six English horses straight from the Pytchley, hunted them hard all over Ireland and got the name in Meath of the man who never had a fall. This was due to a conversation I had with Dick Norcott of Cork, who was the finest horseman I have ever seen over a country. He said, 'If a good horse is left alone by the rider and is allowed to jump his own way, he will never fall.' He could ride any brute and when going across country the reins were literally dangling on the horse's neck, but he steadied the animal well before the fences, just like John Watson used to do.

I had bought a dangerous 'man eating' horse at Leeds from a Captain Ryder, 3rd Dragoon Guards, when the Regiment was quartered there, just before going to York. Chrome Yellow was one of the best-looking thoroughbreds I have ever seen. Owing to its vice it had a special box provided with 'escapes'. The price was only £70. My having paid this, the question was how to get it to my stables at York.

At that time I had the most extraordinary man as groom. He drank nothing during the day, did his work well, but by 10 p.m. was always blind drunk. I had been told by old John Osborne (the jockey) that really vicious horses go quietly at night, so sent Fielder, the groom, over by train to Leeds with an old trooper mare, told him to couple Chrome Yellow to her and ride all night to York.

He gave me his word of honour that on this occasion he would keep sober. When I went to my stables the next day about 11 a.m. I found Fielder sound asleep in Chrome Yellow's box with the old trooper mare. Beside Fielder lay a bottle of whisky half empty. It transpired that none of the other grooms dared go into the box to wake Fielder since the horse went for them at once.

When I returned to the stables in the afternoon, Fielder had groomed Chrome Yellow and suggested I should ride him on to Knavesmire. He said he had come quite quietly (when coupled) from Leeds. When I approached him to mount, the horse made a sudden rush and bit me on the nose knocking me down with his forelegs. It was about 4.30 p.m.

Remembering John Osborne's remark about training vicious animals at
night, like hawks, I came down after dinner and rode him for two hours
and every now and again gave him a lump of sugar. Until the beginning
of the hunting season we exercised him only at night. The first meet I
took him to was the Middleton. We had a good run, and Chrome went
A1 and was much admired. Unfortunately, I took a toss at a drain. The
first thing I realised after falling was that the horse, which only had a
snaffle on, was savaging my behind. By the time I gained my legs the
seat of my breeches had gone. On my way home I called at Sand
Hutton for a fresh pair of garments. Colonel Neeld, who was then
second in command of the 17th, witnessed the incident and it gave
great amusement in the mess for some time. I make this digression
because Peard, the Dublin vet, always says that Chrome Yellow was the
best hunter he had ever known. I rode him in Warwickshire, Leicestershire, Yorkshire, Duhallow, Limerick and Meath, and he never again
gave me a fall. Peard had him in Meath whilst I was in the South
African War, and then I gave him to Hylda when we married in 1902,
and he carried her at the top of the hunt with the Quorn until he died in
1909. He won point to points in Yorkshire, Limerick and Cork.

After the incident when the officers returned late from the Regimental dinner the Colonel decided that a polo team could not be sent to
London for the Regimental tournament.

We had a good, though new and inexperienced team, consisting of
Obby Beauclerk, Carden, Alan Fletcher and myself, and we got leave
to play in the Irish Champion Cup and Irish Inter-Regimental. In the
first tournament we were beaten by the Inniskilling Dragoons, who had
won in London, and we played them again in the final of the Inter-
Regimental.

A curious incident occurred in the Champion Cup Match. There was
a huge crowd in Phoenix Park. When we went on the ground Obby
became completely crowd-struck and, as a player, quite useless. I
rearranged the team after our defeat – Carden No. 1, Self 2, Fletcher 3,
and Portal back. This team was never beaten.

During the Champion Cup the team stayed at the Gresham Hotel
which was full of Irish Americans who had come over for the Wolfe
Tone celebrations.[12] At dinner on the night of our arrival a girl friend of

12 Wolfe Tone (1763-98) – Irish rebel – a founder member of the Society of United Irishmen. They wanted political union between Irish Protestants and Catholics to secure par-
liamentary reform. When this was seen to be unattainable by constitutional means Wolfe
Tone advocated armed rebellion against Britain. His principles were drawn from the

Maud Gonne's made my acquaintance and we walked together after-wards. Nothing immoral was possible as the members of the team were in the strictest training, so we went to bed early. About 11 p.m., just as I was beginning to undress, a priest followed by two men entered my room and 'went for me'. Carden had the room next to me and he soon appeared on the scene. At their first rush, I seized the hand lamp and got a wonderfully good shot in, hitting the man behind the priest full in the face. Except for the light in the passage we were now in the dark, but the door being open I could see them. After a few moments, when I was getting badly mauled, Carden set about them from behind and they fled. The next day, before breakfast, the manager told us he could not be responsible for our lives, so we spent the remainder of our time at the Viceregal Lodge.

Immediately we were beaten in the Champion Cup we were recalled to Ballincollig, as General Luck was going to inspect the Regiment in a fortnight. We returned, however, for the Regimental Tournament, which we won. The inspection being unsatisfactory, especially the officers' ride, we were ordered to attend riding school until the autumn. Being Assistant Adjutant I was sent to Major Herbert's detachment at Cork, for it was handy for Youghal where the musketry training took place.

The Holroyd Smiths asked some of us to stay for a dance they were giving at Ballynatray Park. On the afternoon of the dance I drove over with Brin Sheridan, arriving about teatime to find not a soul there, except the old gardener and his wife, who were the caretakers.

We waited till about 6.30 p.m. when Lady Holroyd Smith and her three daughters arrived in a shay and we all set about putting the house in order for the dinner and dance. Two of the girls did the cooking, the other the bedrooms, and as the guests arrived they were told of their various jobs. I have never seen more beautiful cut glass than that we used at dinner and some lovely old plate, cleaned by the guests. We had a most amusing and thoroughly happy evening, the dance being kept up till dawn amid great revelry. Except for the old gardener and his

---

French Revolution. Tone drew up a paper on the state of Ireland which he described as ripe for revolution but Jackson (a fellow United Irishman), who was negotiating with the French for an invasion, was betrayed. Tone fled to Philadelphia in 1795. In 1796 he accompanied the French expedition of around 15,000 men which sailed from Brest for Ireland, but the fleet was dispersed by a storm off Kerry. When the 1798 rebellion broke out in Ireland, Napoleon had started for Egypt. Tone urged the Directory to send help to the Irish rebels and he accompanied a small French force. He was captured, court martialled and after being condemned to death cut his own throat.

wife, I didn't see a servant in the house and I must say the whole thing was wonderfully done and thoroughly Irish. Brin and I decided it was not worth going to bed, so we drove home.

General McCalmont and his wife were very kind to me when he was commanding at Cork. One day at dinner, someone remarked that a lot of grouse had been seen on the forest land north east of Cork. So, very early on 12 August, Brin and I sallied forth to try and get some grouse, and for Ireland we had a really great day – fifteen brace – and got back to Cork after dark. When we were coming up the hills to barracks, I left two brace at Government House for Mrs McCalmont. The other birds were divided between the mess at Ballincollig and the 60th Rifles at Cork.

Two days afterwards I was summoned to the orderly room and on entering saw a staff officer, Major Haking, with the CO and Adjutant, all looking very grave. The Colonel gave me a proper telling off for shooting the grouse because first of all the birds belonged to the General and headquarter staff as they had taken the shooting, and secondly the grouse shooting season in Ireland did not begin till some time in September. After a real good wigging, I went to apologise to General McCalmont who, instead of cursing me, treated it as a splendid joke and asked me to dinner to enjoy the grouse.

When the hunting began I kept two horses at Mallow with Castlerosse to hunt with the Duhallow. From Cork we hunted with the United, South Union and the Regiment and the Muskerry with Tom Nickalls as Master. One day the General asked me to escort Mrs McCalmont to a good meet of the Duhallow and I explained that on that day I had to attend an officers' ride at Ballincollig. He replied that hunting was much better training for officers than riding school, and that he would tell Fortescue where I had gone.

We had a magnificent day. Mrs McCalmont, who was one of the best sportswomen and went extremely well, charged a perfectly unjumpable place and was badly knocked out. We got back to Cork about 8 p.m. and to my surprise found the Adjutant Sandeman on the platform. He said, 'Captain Tilney, you are placed under arrest for absence without leave from riding school.'

We went up to the barracks, where I handed over my sword to the Adjutant, and was told that my meals would be sent up to me in my room. I felt my inexplicable situation extremely for I was very keen on my profession and was at that time working for the Staff College. Colonel Riddell and Prince Christian, both of whom were in the 60th, came to my room and said the General wished to see me. I thought all was lost and that I would be kicked out of the Army. On arrival at Government House, the little General met me with a smile on his face and said, 'I suppose you have not had any dinner? Come in.' I found Mrs McCalmont having dinner and the General told me that he had completely forgotten to tell the Colonel that he had given me leave to go with Mrs McCalmont, and that the whole thing of my arrest was a mistake. I remained under arrest until the following morning when I was summoned to Ballincollig.

The Colonel was one of the best fellows, but unsuited by temperament to command a regiment. When I appeared before him, I was charged with breaking my arrest by dining at Government House. This was a real facer. After lunch Harry Fortescue sent a message that I was released from arrest and I heard no more, for shortly afterwards we had a new CO.

When I was at the Castle, Dublin, the Prince of Wales visited Ireland and there were great rejoicings and festivities. The royal procession through the City was the source of laughter for years. Sir Arthur Vickers was Ulster King of Arms. He with Wilkinson, who married Lord Pembroke's daughter, Lady Beatrice, had to supervise the procession from the heraldic point of view and rode at its head with glorious tabards. Sir Arthur was an extremely bad horseman, so Lord Cadogan asked Fielden and Herbert Featherstonehaugh to find the quietest animal possible. A good-looking grey from the livery stables at Balls Bridge was selected. Sir Arthur looked magnificent when mounted in the Castle yard on this supine old wedding horse, and off we went via Stephen's Green, the grey at the head of the procession. When we came to the Shelburne Hotel the old grey walked straight through the crowd on to his stables at Balls Bridge with the magnificent herald, tabard and all, still on his back, the procession continuing without him.

I don't give many details of Sir Arthur as he was most brutally murdered by the Sinn Feiners at his Irish home in 1917, but a rumour was spread that he was responsible for the theft of the Crown Jewels in Dublin.

During the Dublin season there used to be a fresh party at the Castle every week. One evening I heard the Ladies Cadogan, Londonderry and Ormonde discussing a certain High Church parson, who called himself 'Father', and had taken lodgings just outside the Castle Gate. As I recall it, his name was Dillon. Every Friday some of the ladies went to him to confess their shortcomings during the past week. It became a regular scandal, for some of the girls thought they could go on anyhow during the week and be whitewashed at its end. Lady Cadogan told me that this was the first extreme churchman to practise in Dublin, and that some of the girls really believed that by this act of confession they could start afresh with a clean slate. This had had a sad demoralising effect on many of the ladies. He apparently specialised in ladies for, as far as we could find, not one man went there.

When not actually in attendance on His Excellency I spent much of my time with the Ormondes at Kilkenny and they were more than friends, for they allowed me to stay whenever I liked. On one occasion when the Viceroy visited Kilkenny we had a great hunt, Hurkey Langrishe being Master, and in the evening there was a banquet for the chief notables in the South of Ireland. Buldo Bryan (Lord Bellew) and Hurkey Langrishe were among the guests. The wine being excellent these two took full advantage of it and when the ladies left the dining room, Buldo missed his chair and sat on the floor. When we joined the ladies in the picture gallery Buldo stumbled and fell over a lion's head and skin at the entrance to the picture gallery where the chief ladies of Ireland were assembled. Hurkey who was following in Buldo's footsteps, fell on top of him, staggered up and said, 'Couldn't you see the bloody lion in the way, Buldo?' Lord Ormonde never asked either of them to dinner again.

Lord Roberts was commanding in Ireland at the time. I got to know him very well in a curious way. I was in attendance on the Viceroy at the Army Athletic Meeting when Lord Roberts remarked to Lord Cadogan that the field in the 120 yards hurdle was a very poor one. Moloney suggested 'Tilney can run, for he won two events at Aldershot.' So Lord Roberts asked me to make a fresh entry for the event which was done through Streatfield. I had no running kit, being dressed in a top hat, frock coat and patent leather boots. So, taking these off, I ran and won the race and a beautiful cup.

Lord Roberts was the *beau idéal* of a perfect Christian gentleman, and as he always came out hunting and went at the top of the hunt with the Meath, Kildare's and Ward, I realised what a splendid man he was, in addition to his quality as a soldier. His son, Freddy, who was killed at the Battle of Colenso (South Africa) whilst endeavouring to save the guns from capture, would have followed in his father's footsteps in life. Lord Roberts often discussed with me the possible role of aeronautics. I took every opportunity of telling him what Mellor had done with a Kodak's series of photographs at Aldershot and how we learned to decipher them with magnifying glasses, but that no one on the staff at

Aldershot or the War Office saw the slightest value in them. They could not realise that you can see more from the top of a steeple than you can from the bottom of it! This nowadays seems incredible, but it was not until the commencement of the Great War that the value of balloons and aircraft was recognised to be of paramount importance.

I also told him how Colonel Templer had been repeatedly snubbed by the War Office, and made him laugh when I told him that this genius contemplated the construction of a balloon cigar-shaped, with motor power (the Zeppelin idea in England 1896), and that the War Office had sent him a primitive Darracq motor engine weighing tons. In fact, old Templer did construct two or three cigar-shaped balloons known as Gamma and Beta, but never received the slightest encouragement from the authorities.

I think it was in 1891 that the first motor car appeared at Hurlingham; anyhow I happened to be playing polo in an important match, England v. Ireland, one Saturday, when a man with a red flag followed by the car entered the ground. Ponies fled in every direction, the pigeon shooting stopped and everyone went to see this novel machine which had been brought on to the ground by Lord Shrewsbury and Toby Rawlinson. I was playing for John Watson's team at the time and remember the discussion after the game with Lord Shrewsbury and Rawlinson as to the utility of the vehicle. Most of those present averred that such a thing would never be allowed along the public streets in England.

THE TALK OF THE TOWN

In the winter of 1898 I was invited to shoot woodcock at Lord Ormonde's Tipperary shoot, which at that time was considered to be very good, and it certainly was a most beautiful place. At the last moment one of the guns could not come, so Lord Ormonde asked the Canon of Kilkenny who was a keen sportsman. On the first day the keeper, who was dressed in green with gilt buttons, came to announce the bag whilst we were at lunch. One side of his face and neck was covered with blood and when Lord Ormonde asked him how it happened he replied, 'I am only one of those shot by the Canon.' The Canon had bagged three beaters besides the head keeper, so Lord Ormonde most politely sent him home.

About Christmas 1898 there was some function in London and Fielden, Dundas and myself were in attendance on Lord Cadogan. We three were walking down Piccadilly about tea-time when an extraordinarily pretty girl accosted us near Down Street, asking us for money. It was a really bad December evening with snow, sleet and half a gale. As we were approaching the Bachelors' Club, which we were aiming for, the girl, in her surprisingly well-born voice, said, 'If you don't come home with me or give me some money I shall be turned out of the house.'

As we came round the corner of Hamilton Place she remarked or, I should say, cried, 'You don't believe me, then why don't you come and see?' As Dundas and I had no engagements that evening we walked with the girl across St James's Park to the vicinity of Westminster Abbey. On the way Dundas remembered that he had a good deal of money on him and thought the girl was a decoy and that we were in for some foul play. I showed him the umbrella that I had and told him that I could deal with three or four men with my fists, the savette, and a pointed stick, which was the umbrella. It may not be fair fighting, but in a brawl with roughs, a combination of the three is extraordinarily effective, as I had learnt at Bruges in 1888. So we followed the girl, till we arrived at a chandler's shop of the poorest description. When the girl entered, a bullyman with one leg said, 'Well you have brought two this time' but in the strongest language and demanded money from the girl in advance. As both of us went up the rickety stairs with the girl, he made the most obscene remarks and suggested that one of us should remain in the shop until the other had finished. The girl however went on and we entered a room like a common lodging house.

There was no fire in the room and some of the windows were broken. One girl lay on the mattress on the verge of death, three others – all stark naked – were huddled together on a sort of palliasse, and on the floor lay a man of about forty, dead drunk. (I am trying to narrate the facts exactly as we saw them.) How any of these poor creatures survived this bitterly cold night without any clothing God only knows. I have never appreciated the advantage of self-defence more than I did on this occasion, for when we came downstairs, two bullies met us at the foot of the stairs demanding money. We made very short work of them, and all I remember is the terrific language. We had arranged to meet Fielden at the Bachelors' Club and getting there about 9 p.m. we consulted as to what should be done to relieve these poor creatures from some of their suffering.

Fielden knew Lady St Helier and we arranged to get this particular girl away and into a home in Soho. The other women we saw had been (or so we were told) prostitutes for a long time. This girl (here called Amy) had only recently started on this mode of life and had fallen into the power of this one-legged Jew, who before the girls fell ill had had a prosperous brothel. Lady St Helier through her matron (in charge of the Soho Hostel) recovered Amy from the Jew's clutches. Amy appeared to be happy in the home. We three men, however, got unremittingly chaffed by our pals for keeping the girl and as we had to find her clothing and other needs, it became very expensive. We eventually got her a job at Whiteley's and all said goodbye and wished her the best of luck.

Just before the South African War, Fielden and I were walking in Hyde Park when we came across Amy walking with a good-looking young fellow who turned out to be in the Marines. We pretended not to notice her, but she stopped us and said how grateful she was for all we had done for her, but that she had gone wrong again and that we had better forget all about her.

We found out afterwards that she had been seduced by the manager of her department at Whiteley's and after that reverted to her previous profession. When Amy was at the hostel I looked up some of my detective friends who had taken me round the lowest haunts of London before I joined the Army. My purpose was to find out if there were many common brothels like the one kept by the Jew in Westminster, and also get some first hand knowledge of the white slave traffic. One of the detectives had become an enthusiastic salvationist (the Salvation Army was much despised at this time) and I saw the wonderful work the Salvation Army was trying to do in the lowest haunts of London. The professional procurers did a very good trade in those days, for the girls they captured were sold to European, Indian and Egyptian brothels and harems for big figures. There must have been a master brain organising the whole business, for at a receiving depot in the vicinity of Dog's Island in the East End, one saw plump and fat girls who were selected for the Turkish and Eastern markets, whereas the depot in Seven Dials contained the smart stylish girls for European markets. All tastes were catered for and the procuresses were amazingly cunning in their methods of capture. Men, chiefly foreigners, took an active part in the trade and were employed either as bullies or seducers.

One Sunday afternoon two of us were on our way down Shaftesbury Avenue to see the matron of Lady St Helier's Home We met in one of the side streets a subaltern of the Rifle Brigade who had been skinned of everything valuable he possessed on him by bullies in a house in Church Street, Soho.

What struck me most about the white slave traffic was the general unwillingness of its victims to resume a decent life, when they were given the chance by the Salvation Army or some of the other societies for the reclamation of fallen women. Some even thought it good fun to be sent to a brothel in foreign parts and only about five per cent made good when given the opportunity. For instance, a pretty, well-spoken girl turned up one day at the receiving depot in Seven Dials and everything possible was done to try to induce her to abandon the life of a prostitute and the misery it entailed. She was only nineteen and had just been seduced at Plymouth, close to where her father lived. The parents being very respectable people were, so she told me, brokenhearted. In the end, owing to her immoral behaviour they turned her out of the house. One of the white slave traders soon got hold of her and she was brought to London by a procuress who undoubtedly got a good sum of money for such a beautiful girl. She frequented the Corinthian and Gardenia night clubs for some months, then got diseased and was sent to Port Said, which was at that time one of the sinks of the world. For the few months she was in London the traffickers provided her with nice rooms in the Fulham Road, also dresses and other finery. The landlady of the house, herself a procuress, took half of the girl's immoral earnings. I am glad to be able to say that I never came across an English man or woman in charge of these disorderly houses; they were all foreigners.

A ROAN IS SWITCHED

I had a bad toss riding in the Farmer's Race at Punchestown, being deliberately knocked over as I was riding the favourite. One of the horses following put his hoof on my head, cutting the scalp badly. Townsend, the surgeon at Cork, operated and I made a good recovery in a month owing to his skill in stitching up a three-inch cut from my nose to the top of my forehead.

The Regiment did well at polo in 1898–99 with the same team – Carden 1, self 2, Fletcher 3 and Portal back – that had won in Dublin. We had been one of the first to start a regimental polo club and had trained many ponies from the raw. At that time one could buy at Cahirmee and other fairs in Ireland a first class raw pony for £50 and frequently at a considerably lower figure.

About this time an amusing case came on in the Law Courts between John Watson and Alexis Roche. John had bought an extremely high quality strawberry roan hunter – for an extremely high price – through a priest at Cahirmee Fair, and asked Roche to ride it and take it out hunting until it was conditioned to go to England. I knew the horse well and had tried to buy it before the fair took place. When hunting began Alexis Roche was riding a strawberry roan and asked me how I thought the horse was looking, assuming, I suppose, that I thought it was the one belonging to John Watson. I replied that I did not think much of it and that it was a common-looking brute. Sir T. O'Brien was with me at the time. About the end of the season a firm of Dublin solicitors asked me to give evidence, as John Watson had brought a case against Roche for replacing the Cahirmee roan by another of very inferior quality, the latter being sold to a nobleman in England for a prodigious sum. This I knew to be the fact, for the genuine roan was subsequently hunted for many seasons in Leicestershire and had been hidden away in the Irish mountains for a year, before being sent over to England by Roche.

I was very fond of staying with Lord Bandon at Macroom. He had excellent fishing and shooting, also a good pack of otter hounds When out with the latter, I saw on different days: 1 The arrival of a flight of woodcock from overseas, some of which were so dead beat that anybody could pick them up. They were just skin and bones. 2 A stream of elver (young eels), as we were going from one branch of the River Lee to another. They looked like a black stream five or six yards wide and extended from one branch of the river to the other – just millions.

Lord and Lady Bandon were greatly loved by all the people in South Ireland. Wherever we went their praises were sung with enthusiasm. The castle was almost medieval, both inside and out, and contained things that any antiquary would covet. Little did one realise in those happy days that everything belonging to Lord and Lady Bandon would be destroyed by the Sinn Feiners and Irish Bolshies.

In the year of the South African War the Regimental polo team was undefeated by any regiment. In 1899 I met many fellows who had been in the Jameson Raid. Ava (17th) had begged me before the Raid took place to accompany him to South Africa on what, I was told, was a secret mission, but we could not get leave from the Regiment. We knew most of the actors.

Whilst I was grouse driving at Scar House in Yorkshire a messenger boy came across the moor (much to the annoyance of the guns) with a

War Office telegram for me. On opening it I found that I was ordered to proceed to South Africa in two days.

When soldiering I carried about to our various quarters some of the best pictures and bric-à-brac which I had inherited. Because of having to depart so quickly I asked my soldier servant to collect all my belongings from Dublin and Ballincollig and to store them at York, where I also sent my guns from Scar House. I naturally left the shoot at once and in two days was on a Union Castle liner bound for the Cape.

I had been appointed a special service officer for service with the Balloon Service (a funny position for a Cavalry officer). Just before sailing from Southampton I got a receipt and letter from the firm at York acknowledging the receipt of some of my property, guns and so on, and so thought all my penates were safely stored. On my return from the South African War in two and a half years' time, I wrote to the storage company and had no reply, so went to York in person and found they had removed their premises. I put the matter into the hands of the police and the only memento of my belongings that was recovered was the stock of a Wesley Richards gun. All the remainder of my property had been stolen. One item of my property, however, was excluded from this misfortune – I had bought a young mare named Good Example from a Limerick farmer, after riding it in the Farmers' race at Punchestown in 1893. The mare who was then only four was one of the best bred in Ireland and showed great promise. The conditions of sale were £80 down and half her winnings up to the age of ten. When I was ordered to South Africa at a moment's notice I lent the mare unconditionally to Charlie Crighton of Mullaboden. On my return from the South African War, I learnt that the mare had been most successful chasing and had won over £3,000 in stakes. I soon got an unwelcome demand from the farmer, for a sum over £1,500, his half share of the mare's winnings. As Charlie Crighton was on his death bed, I had to pay up out of my own pocket as it would have meant very unpleasant and costly litigation to have recovered that sum from his estate.

Part II

BALLOONING AT LADYSMITH

On our arrival at the Cape, some officers were sent to Kimberley, the others including Dr Jameson and Frank Rhodes, Colonel Brocklehurst, Willoughby, Struben, and other well-known men, were sent to Durban. Colonel Howard (Rifle Brigade) was in charge of the troops on board, with Charlie Fortescue as his staff officer. Just as we were disembarking at Durban, Struben, who had been appointed chief intelligence officer to Sir Redvers Buller, spoke to me on the deck. 'Are you any relation to George Tilney who pegged out Johannesburg with my grandfather in the 1880s? He discovered the Crown Mine and owned miles of the best country until the last Boer War.' I told him he was my first cousin, and he then shook me by the hand saying 'He [George Tilney] was the whitest[1] man South Africa has ever known. I would like to do you a good turn. Buy Geduld Mines now and they will pay you well.'

As I had never had a word with Struben before and when he said this we were on the gangway, I had my misgivings as to whether I should take his advice, but did so, and bought at a pound, selling them three years later at six pounds. So he did me a really good turn.

He told me subsequently that when the first Boer War broke out, Kruger sent for George Tilney and said, 'Whose side are you going on?' George Tilney replied, 'I am an Englishman and proud of it and will fight for the English.' Whereupon Kruger replied, 'I shall confiscate all your property.' George Tilney was married to Agnes whose daughter Enid married Frank Mann.[2] Struben always told me that he, George Tilney, would have been one of the richest men in the world if he had not been so patriotic and had everything confiscated. At the end of the first Boer War, thanks to Sir Evelyn Wood, the loyal Britishers were all let down by the English government and lost everything.

We stayed only a day at Durban, the officers being rushed on to Ladysmith. When we had travelled a few hours Charlie Fortescue ordered me to report to Colonel Howard in his compartment. Frank

---

1 Meaning straightest.
2 Their son was George Mann who captained England at cricket.

Rhodes, Colonel Brocklehurst, Dr Jameson and Willoughby were also there. Colonel Howard told me that they had heard the driver of the engine was in league with the Boers. As I could drive a locomotive, I was to be on the engine for the remainder of the journey and if I suspected treachery my orders were to blow the driver's brains out and drive the engine myself. (Some four years previously I had gone through a long course of engineering at Chatham. The knowledge I then acquired was most useful to me during the South African War.) It was a thoroughly unpleasant task. The situation was explained to the engine driver and I stood at the back of the tender, revolver in hand. I was relieved from this uncomfortable post at dawn. I will never forget the pangs of thirst I underwent – I had been foolish enough to fill my water bottle with whisky and water and by dawn it was all I could do to keep awake.

We reached Ladysmith just at the conclusion of the Battle of Elandslaagte (21 October 1899). Feeling thoroughly done in, I was sent straight off to join the Balloon Section. Heath,[3] with most of the paraphernalia, had preceded me.

The day of the Battle of Nicolson's Nek (28 October) the balloon was up before dawn. There were only three who had telescopes in Ladysmith: Colonel Brocklehurst, the Naval Contingents and myself. When visibility was sufficiently good, I could see through my telescope men, horses and guns scampering down the southern slopes of the nek. Colonel Altham, Chief Intelligence Officer, Major Reid, Intelligence Officer, Frank Rhodes and Dr Jameson (Dr Jim) were down below, but on my descent neither Altham nor Reid would believe a word of my account of what I had seen. So Mellor went up, took a snap with his Kodak and had the print developed by about 10 a.m. Even after we had deciphered the photo-print, Altham could not be convinced and remarked that what we had said were men and guns was only dirt.

I begged Frank Rhodes and Dr Jim to let Headquarters know what had happened. While Mellor was up in the balloon, they went to Sir George White to advise them of the disaster. Frank Rhodes, when he realised Altham's stupidity and pigheadedness, remarked to Dr Jim and myself: 'Fancing sending a B.F. like that as Chief Intelligence Officer!' The Balloon Section had not shifted its original position and was far too close to the firing line. We had to retire speedily. Almost as soon as

---

3 Major G. M. Heath, CO of the Second Balloon Section. Three balloon sections were sent out to South Africa. The Second Section was the first to see active service. 'The Boer War was the first conflict in the British Empire in which aerial reconnaissance formed an integral part of operations.' *Aeroplane Monthly*, October 1998.

we had begun to shift our position the infantry began to pour past us towards Ladysmith. Troops were at once dispatched to reinforce Nicolson's Nek and if necessary effect their retirement, but by noon the disaster was complete and that night saw the beginning of the siege which lasted for four months (2 November 1899–28 February 1900).

For the first few days the confusion in the town, especially at night, baffles description. The stores, hotels and pubs were full of scallywag soldiers who knew no discipline. Had the Boers followed up their victory they must have taken the town. Fortunately they waited over the weekend and on the Sunday had excursion trains from Johannesburg, Pretoria and other places to impress on the people what great deeds their men had done. Not a shot was fired on Sunday for the first few months of the war. On that day parties of ladies in landaus and barouches, accompanied by Boer horsemen, picnicked within rifle range of Observation and Bells Kopje Hills and, as neither side fired a shot, it was all strangely peaceful.[4]

Incredible as it may seem, there was no plan of defence prepared in the case of our troops being repulsed by the Boers. Sir John French, his Chief of Staff Colonel (now Lord) Haig and his personal staff got out of Ladysmith after the Battle of Lombard's Kop. They had a really wonderful escape. When the Boers saw the train leaving the station, instead

4 The Boer War (1899–1902). The Transvaal Boers had been granted their independence by Gladstone in 1881 but there was still smouldering dislike and suspicion. Cecil Rhodes, Premier of Cape Colony and chairman of the British South African Company, was pushing forward with the development of native territory, which prevented the extension of Boer land. The discovery of gold in the Transvaal (1886) led to many Englishmen going to Johannesburg to seek their fortunes in the mines. Within ten years half the male white population in the Transvaal was British. Paul Kruger, President of the Transvaal, was a lifelong opponent of Britain. He denied the large British mining population all political rights and levied on them a special mines-tax, which paid almost the entire expenses of the Boer Government. Rhodes sympathised with the 'outlanders'. He hatched a plot with the British in Johannesburg, who were to rise in revolt against the Boer Government; at the same time an armed force crossed the frontier in their aid. Dr Jameson, who led the raid, crossed the frontier before the outlanders were ready (29 December 1895). The raid was a complete failure – Jameson and his men were surrounded and captured. Rhodes had to resign. Kruger, congratulated by the German Kaiser and encouraged by Rhodes's resignation, began to believe that in a contest between the Boers and the British, the Boers could win. The Boers began to buy massive amounts of armaments from the Krupps factory. At the beginning of 1899 Sir Alfred Milner (British High Commissioner for South Africa) warned Chamberlain that the situation was becoming unsustainable. In September the British Government sent extra troops to South Africa. Kruger then delivered an ultimatum and war followed. The Boers began by invading Natal and after early successes laid siege to the important town of Ladysmith.

of sending a few men to damage the line, they brought their guns to bear on the train and line. Mercifully they did not hit the train. Caesar's Camp and Wagon Hill were the key positions of Ladysmith and these were occupied by our troops only at the last moment, after the disaster of Nicholson's Nek.

The Balloon Section was at first camped near the Imperial Light Horse lines in the town, but whenever the balloon was seen, the Boers shelled us. We were therefore sent to camp in a river-bed between Caesar's Camp and the town. One of our amusements in this horrible place was to catch scorpions and tarantulas, with which the bed and bank of the river swarmed. We had prize fights between a scorpion and a tarantula in a basin. Soon our camp became a very popular resort, for it was near the path from Caesar's Camp to the town and both officers and tommies used to drop in to bet and see the fun. It was far more exciting than cock-fighting. This place was insanitary from every point of view, as we had about forty REs and thirty natives with the Balloon Section and they all bivouacked in the riverbed. My teachings from the old African explorers at Newstead came home to me, and I implored Heath, who was in command, to enforce strict sanitary discipline, but to no effect. General Hunter, Chief of Staff (later Sir Archibald Hunter), sent for me. He asked me to get up some sports for Christmas and they duly took place. We had a polo, football and cricket match, also an athletic meeting. Unfortunately the Boers got wind of it and began shelling. Our polo match was in full swing when one of the first Boer shells knocked over one of the opposing team – the rider escaped unhurt. We stopped the game and went over to see how the football match was getting on. Three shells had landed on the ground – one man had been wounded. But the tommies insisted on finishing the game, which they did. On 'time', a big shell almost decapitated the goalkeeper, which caused great amusement.

General Hunter sent for me one day before Christmas and made me Chief Observation Officer in addition to my other duties with the RE Balloon Section. During this interview, at which Sir George White, Colonel Hunter and Colonel Sir Harry Rawlinson (later Lord Rawlinson) were also present, I pressed the tremendous importance of our aerial photography. I told them that when visibility was good one could see for twenty miles from the balloon, including movements of the larger bodies of the enemys' troops, and that our intelligence reports had been very accurate. I suggested that a Staff Officer should go up in the balloon to see for himself the value of aerial reconnaissance.

THE DEATH OF AVA

A few days later Harry Rawlinson, Dr Jim and Frank Rhodes turned up and I let up Harry in the balloon. I had warned him that he would probably be very seasick. The others were just chaffing him about how he felt when a small shell from Bulano went bang through the gasbag. Luckily the envelope formed a parachute and he was not hurt, but there were subsequently no volunteers for the balloon from the Staff. Of course it was not pleasant when the Boers got the range, as every time a shell came near the balloon jumped into the vacuum created by the shell. I was very pleased at Harry Rawlinson's experience, since about a week previously I was up with Sergeant Birkinshaw when there were a lot of air-devil clouds in the sky and suddenly we were struck, at about 1,000 feet up, then bumped on to the top of Caesar's Camp. When Birkinshaw jumped I was precipitated in the balloon to the original height with a tremendous jerk. Fortunately the rope held. Soon afterwards a Staff Officer arrived to ask why the balloon was not up taking observations and insinuated that I was a coward not to go up. He would not listen to my explanation that these air-devils were extremely dangerous and that it was impossible to make any reliable observations when struck by these terrific gusts.

By 6 January half the men and all the officers at Caesar's Camp were in hospital, with the exception of Heath. On that day's dawn attack on Caesar's Camp and Wagon Hill, Heath was a very sick man. I was ordered to act as Staff Officer at Caesar's Camp on that vital day, the officer commanding being Colonel Curran, Manchester Regiment, with Colonel Sir Ian Hamilton on Wagon Hill. No proper defences, communicating trenches or field works had been erected, although our troops had been there two months and the advance contingent under Altham for over a year. The consequence was that when the Boers occupied the perimeter of the Hill our men had to cross open spaces to endeavour to drive them out.

About 3 p.m. one of the worst thunderstorms it was possible to imagine broke out. I had been sent to Hamilton with a message from Curran that the Boers had captured the whole front of Caesar's Camp, and requesting troops to reinforce the Manchester Reserves who were still holding out. Hamilton had lost half of his men and was also hard pressed. He ordered me to run (all the telephones being cut) to advise Sir George White as to the situation.

Just as I was entering the town, I met poor Ava (the eldest son of

Lord Dufferin), my best friend in the 17th Lancers, as he was being carried to hospital. He had been shot through the head. After I left Headquarters, I was with him as he was dying in the hospital. I got back to Caesar's Camp about 5 p.m.

The thunderstorm was now at its height. Some men were killed by lightning, which literally ran along the ground. Fire from the enemy was simultaneously intense. The fighting was confused and bloody. We had collected small reinforcements from the riffraff in Ladysmith and on their being ordered to retake the outer fringe of the Hill the fire from the enemy suddenly died down, just as Colonels Curran and Hamilton thought that all had been lost. No one understood why the Boers had not pressed home their attack and captured the key to Ladysmith. Next morning an armistice was declared and I was ordered to remove and bury the dead.

For this gruesome task, I collected all our available natives and on the night of 8 January began our work. In addition to some Boers on the perimeter of the Hill, we found a large number in the surrounding bush, who it appeared had been killed by lightning. This sudden onslaught from heaven so terrified them that they relaxed the attack and Ladysmith was saved.

As I had collected these natives, I asked Colonels Curran and Hamilton if they might be employed in future putting Caesar's Camp and Wagon Hill into a proper state of defence. The former readily agreed and drew out plans, but the latter was furious and said that it was gross impertinence for a junior cavalry officer to suggest how a senior infantry officer should defend the position entrusted to him. However, Sir George White sent for me and laughingly said that Hamilton was very angry with me for making the suggestion and that he had therefore ordered him to draw out a defence scheme. When it was received, Headquarters would send an officer to supervise the work. As Colonel Curran personally asked me to get on with the defences on Caesar's Camp, I worked with the natives every night and when the work was completed the Chief of Staff (General Hunter) ordered me to report to Hamilton. When I did this Hamilton completely lost his temper and gabbled a lot of rot, saying that as his men had repelled the attack on 6 January they had no need for any further defence works.

A day or so afterwards I was called to Headquarters, Lieutenant-General Sir George White, General Hunter, Colonel Sir Henry Rawlinson and Colonel Ian Hamilton being present. The latter expressed his resentment at my being sent to improve, or should I say make, defence works on Wagon Hill and said that his men preferred the natural cover. I pointed out that without communicating trenches between the front and back lines no messages could be sent and we had suffered heavy casualties through our men having to advance over open ground to the attack. I laid special stress on the endeavour of the Rifle Brigade to reinforce the front of Caesar's Camp on 6 January.

Sir George and General Hunter thoroughly approved of what had been done at Caesar's Camp and politely suggested to Colonel Hamilton that he should draw out his own scheme of defence lines. He replied that he would get his own men to do it. Nothing was done till the end of the siege. Ian Hamilton never forgave me and according to what Sir Archibald Hunter told me subsequently he had my name erased (for he was a bosom friend of Lord Roberts) from all Dispatches and Honours Lists.[5]

THE SIEGE INTENSIFIES

All the other officers and most of the men of the Balloon Section were in hospital by the middle of January; food was now getting very scarce, and we had started eating horse and mule flesh. I had pointed out to Heath, CO Balloon Section, from the first day of the siege, the vital necessity of having everything as hygienic as possible. When he did not agree, but allowed Cape boys to cook and wash up for us, I asked to draw my own rations and cook for myself. About the beginning of February, Colonel Ward (now Sir Edward Ward) sent for me. He said he had heard that I knew about fishing, and Sir George White was very anxious to get some fish as food for the men in hospital. I told him that as I was SO on Caesar's Camp, Chief Observation Officer, and in command of the Balloon Section, I had no time available, except possibly on Sunday, which the enemy generally observed as a holiday. In a day or so, I got orders to be the Official Fishing Officer, with about twenty natives as assistants. We systematically blew up the Klip river with dynamite, and twice per week provided all the hospitals with fish. Colonel Ward and

5 Thomas Pakenham in *The Boer War* says of Hamilton: 'Lord Roberts's speech-writer and protégé, White's friend, the veteran of Majuba, Hamilton was a poet and wit, debonair, excitable and brilliant, if somewhat effete. No doubt he found the job of digging trenches a dull one. He was rarely to be seen on the Wagon Hill sector. He messed in the comfortable house in the town where Colonel (Frank) Rhodes dispensed champagne.'

Colonel Stoneman, the food providers, were delighted, and Sir George White sent for me and was very warm in his thanks.

At the first day's blowing up of the river, I noticed a Chinaman watching us very intently and when we had finished our evening's work he begged me to give him a fish in return for a gourd. Any vegetable or vegetable food at that time was worth its weight in gold, so I agreed to make the exchange. When I got to his house I gave him a good barbel and he gave me a gourd, which I believe saved my life. At that time our men were suffering terribly from scurvy, due to lack of vegetables and diuretic food, and I had begun to get cramps and terrible pain in the stomach, with veldt sores on my face and neck.

The next week I visited my Chink, and he gave me some veldt berries, as well as a gourd and some wild spinach, which he said grew in profusion round the town, and which had never been made use of for the troops. As I was leaving, he asked me for my word of honour not to divulge to anyone where I had obtained these precious vegetables. My servant Bardens (17th Lancers) was down with dysentery in the hospital, and I went to see him. I found him lying in the Dutch Church between two dead men, and he implored me to take him away to die, as he described it, 'in the open'. Contrary to all regulations, I went that evening and brought him back to our camp.

Stanley, Webb, Baker and other explorers, at Newstead Abbey, had told me that rice water and starch were a good antidote for diarrhoea, so I gave Bardens nothing but Colman's starch, mixed with rice water, slightly flavouring it with essence of lemon. My Chinaman gave me some berries, rather like bilberries, that he collected on the hills. Captain Milner, RAMC, who was in charge of the Dutch Church Hospital, found out that I had taken away Bardens, and I had to explain everything to Harry Rawlinson. Unfortunately, Colonel Stoneman (Sir Edward Ward's understudy in ASC) was there and he asked me how Bardens was fed, as his rations were being drawn at the hospital. I blurted out that he was getting nothing but starch and vegetable soup. By the middle of February the authorities discovered my Chinaman's hoard of vegetables, commandeering the whole lot. I begged Colonel Ward not to be too severe on my Chink, as hoarding supplies was a criminal offence, and I am glad to say he survived the siege.

My duties as Chief Observation Officer entailed my being at my post on Observation Hill before daybreak, and I had to remain behind two rocks till after sunset, and was supposed to report every movement of the enemy.

By early February in the Balloon Section, all officers were still *hors de combat* – except myself – and only about ten men fit for duty. Every night on returning to camp I collected my rations – ¼lb horse flesh, 2 biscuits – put them in a pot with some Colman's starch, adding chopped wild spinach and the Chink's berries, and let the pot simmer through the night. This 'mess' I took up every day about 3 a.m. to Observation Hill, together with a bottle of boiled water, and this kept me alive and well, though a skeleton, till the end of the siege. When visibility was good I could see the enemy's movements, especially during the battles of Spion Kop[6] and Vaal Krantz.[7] I was now under Harry Rawlinson to whom I had to send my reports, and I had further to check all the other reports that were made from elsewhere. As I mentioned before, my post on Observation Hill was behind two rocks, and to approach it one had to go over fifty yards of open space.

A SNIPER SNIPERED

One morning I was late, and a sniper almost got me. I determined, however, to get him; so every day subsequently I took a beautiful rifle with telescopic sights, lent me by Colonel Howard of the Rifle Brigade. One morning I saw my sniper approaching his post. Captain Blackadder, of the Leicestershire Regiment, was commanding the company that held this Observation Hill position, and he sent me the best shot they had in the Regiment. Together we made out the distance to be 1,000 yards, and that evening, when we had seen the sniper depart, I got some explosive bullets and successfully hit his lair.

I waited a week until he took no trouble, just walking to his post, reaching it regularly by 2.30 a.m., leaving it at 12 noon to return at 2 p.m. Blackadder told his men not to frighten 'the bird', as I would do the trick when I thought it was a certain kill. One day Harry Rawlinson and some of the Headquarters Staff came up about 11.30, and I told them to watch my sniper leave his lair, as his time had come. The sniper that day just sauntered from his post, and with the first shot I got him, as far as we could see, stone dead. This was a red-letter day for me, as I was invited to dinner at Headquarters, and ate the best meal that I had had for over two months.

The conversation turned on the shooting of the sniper, and I

6 24 January 1900.
7 5–7 February, captured then evacuated.

remarked that this event had kept me awake and relieved the monotony of remaining behind a rock from 3 a.m. till the following nightfall. It was more exciting than deer stalking. After dinner Sir George White, General Hunter and Colonel Howard asked me if I would go with an officer named Watson to try to find out where the Boers were camping on the north side of Bell's Kopje, as the Rifle Brigade had suffered a lot of casualties from dawn attacks. We started on this night reconnaissance two nights afterwards and were more successful than we could have possibly imagined, for Watson and I got within listening distance of their bivouac, and the former made a very clear report, with sketches of their positions. If ever a man earned some recognition for his work, Watson did, but at the end of the siege, when I was in control of the Mapping Section, I found Watson's work had been signed and credited to a certain staff officer, who is now dead, so I won't give his name; and this staff officer had signed Watson's reconnaissance as his own work.

By mid-February things were getting desperate in Ladysmith. In the balloon section there were only five men fit for duty, and one sergeant (Birkinshaw). When I returned to camp every evening it was a pathetic sight to see these skeletons of men, who had little to occupy their minds, getting thinner and thinner. There was a grand-looking Basuto among our natives named Isaac, who took the greatest pride in being a Christian.[8] To this man I entrusted my servant Bardens, and he nursed him like a mother would her dearest child.

As rations were now crawling with maggots, I begged the remnant of our men to make a *ragout* with the additions of Colman's starch and the Chinaman's wild spinach and berries. But they would not touch my 'stew', Sergeant Birkinshaw remarking that he had heard that starch was very bad for the bowels.

---

8 W.A.T. notes: 'Isaac and Jacob were two of the finest Basutos one could see, and both almost fanatical Christians. One evening after my return from Observation Hill, I found them both on their knees praying aloud. When they had finished, I called and asked them simply if Christianity had been a help, comfort, and pleasure to them?

'Isaac replied: "Before Mr — visited our country, some of us worshipped a tree, others stones or stars, and we were all like animals. Mr —taught us that there is a real living God, who will watch over us and help us throughout life and in every way act as a most loving father. We were taught to ask Jesus for everything we wanted and Mr — told us that if we did our best to follow Jesus we would go to the same place after death as the white man, and live forever in wonderful happiness. When we became Christians it was as if we had been blind before, with no hope in life, but now we see and know that we have just the same chance of being with Jesus forever as the white man. Many of the headmen are Christians now, and it has completely changed our lives." '

THE SIEGE IS LIFTED

One day I was sent for by Headquarters, to be told by Sir George White that the Colenso attack was about to take place and that if it was unsuccessful I had to make a 'free run' with the balloon and all-important papers, and try to reach the British lines.

Since the beginning of January I had been advised of all movements and attacks by our troops to enable me to follow from the balloon the Battles of Spion Kop and Vaal Krantz[9] and the second Battle of Colenso. As I was leaving Headquarters, General Hunter told me to get the balloon ready; immediately the secret papers were sent I was to be off. I explained that there was only enough gas to fill the balloon once, and if the wind was from the south I should be carried into the enemy's country, to which he replied that I must use my own judgement and do the best I could. So we filled the balloon with all the gas available, and I cannot describe my feelings when I saw our infantry take Green Hill, Hlangwane,[10] and the positions guarding the Tugela. That night I dined at Headquarters and heard that Sir Redvers Buller had gained a great victory. I was up in the balloon before dawn the next day and sent a message to Headquarters that the Boers were in full retreat from all their positions and that they were retiring in complete disorder. I suggested that if the cavalry pursued via the Newcastle road, the rout would be complete. It had been the custom, since we were besieged, for the Boers to have weekend parties to come and see the 'Rooinek' prisoners in Ladysmith. When the last Battle of Colenso took place (prior to the relief of Ladysmith) the Boers sent their families northwards, accompanied by ox wagons, sheep and cattle, and when the main body had to retire they found the roads blocked with this paraphernalia. I told Headquarters every detail over the telephone and suggested that Sir Redvers's cavalry should pursue for all they were worth.

Soon Harry Rawlinson with other members of Headquarters staff came to see for themselves what the situation was. Harry Rawlinson explained that we could not pursue from Ladysmith as over 50 per cent of the garrison were *hors de combat*, and the remainder too weak to march over five miles. When I pointed out that there was nothing to hinder Sir Redvers's cavalry from pursuing, Altham remarked that the country at the foot of Bulwana was impossible for horses to traverse; to which I replied that I would ride to Bulwana and back if the authorities

9 27 kilometres west of Ladysmith
10 15 February.

gave me leave to do so. Leave being given, I rode to the top of Bulwana, brought back four hand grenades and a Boer flag, besides two wallets full of correspondence. These I handed over at Headquarters to Harry Rawlinson.

Had the British Cavalry made any attempt or even threat at pursuit around the flanks of Bulwana and Lombards Kop, pincer fashion, they would have captured the main Boer force, which I could see struggling in the greatest confusion on the road some few miles to the north. I described the *sauve qui peut* flight to Headquarters on my return from Bulwana: how the family wagons, guns, cattle and loose horses were completely blocking the main road northwards, and that as far as could be seen from the top of Bulwana the enemy retirement had become a rout. Nothing, however, was done, although Sir Archibald Hunter urged the necessity for Buller's cavalry to pursue. Had they done so, I believe the war would have soon terminated.

That night the vanguard of our troops was in Ladysmith,[11] and the first officer to greet me was George Paget (brother to Hylda), accompanied by Vivian Henry, 7th Fusiliers. George's first remark was 'Good Lord, what a sight!' and as I was a walking skeleton I suppose his remark was apt. He produced a tin of preserved sliced bacon from his haversack, which I devoured, and soon afterwards I was taken violently ill. At the beginning of the last Battle of Colenso we only had one sergeant (Birkinshaw) and nine men fit for duty in the Balloon Section. When the relieving force had crossed the Tugela river, I rode back to Balloon Spruit (our camp) to cheer up the men with the good news. Birkinshaw remarked: 'Thank God, I shall see my wife and family again', and as he was then suffering from diarrhoea, I begged him to eat some of my starch stew, but he would not touch it. He was dead the next day.

Instead of pursuing the routed enemy, every man available was called upon for a ceremonial parade of welcome to Sir Redvers's army. It was a pathetic sight to see the skeleton men who had been defending Ladysmith standing in the streets on a sort of ceremonial parade. That evening the relieving force took over our posts.

I was put in charge of the mapping section for ten days and discovered that there wasn't one reliable map of the country from the Tugela to the Mahlesburg mountain range. In the Colenso section, Hlangwane and Green Hill were put on the wrong side, i.e. south of the Tugela River.

---

11 On 28 February 1900 Buller relieved Ladysmith.

It was arranged for me to proceed home to attend the Staff College, which was the summit of my desires; but a wire arrived ordering me to the Western Transvaal as ADC to Lord Methuen. The promise was made that I could go to the Staff College when the war was finished, which the authorities thought would be in six months at the most. Sir George White sent for me and he and General Hunter thanked me most heartily for the work I had done. On arrival at Durban I got a message from Lady Sophie Scott asking me to stay aboard Sir Samuel's yacht in Durban harbour, and this saved me from collapse, for I only weighed 9½ stone and was a weak man

A week after this I was in Cape Town, where I found the Mount Nelson Hotel turned into a fashionable resort for the riffraff of the London and Paris smart set, and every sort of iniquity going on. I only stayed a day or two, and reached Lord Methuen's headquarters at the beginning of April 1900.

ENTER COUSIN CECIL RHODES

Soon after my arrival I received an invitation from Cecil Rhodes to visit him in Kimberley and, as I had to get some kit, I went there for three days. Only Willoughby and Robert Williams were there, and as the controversy between Cecil Rhodes and Kekewich was in full swing, I had to listen to a lot of acrimonious discussion.[12] In the midst of all this Rhodes discussed the future development of Matabeleland, Mashonaland, and what is now Rhodesia and Tanganyika. Mitchell, the engineer, and one of the pioneers of the Cape to Cairo railway, arrived the second day I was there, and they began to discuss the feasibility of the scheme. Rhodes treated me as his cousin, and told me to come whenever I could get leave, and was in every way most kind. When I told him how much he reminded me of my uncle, William Rhodes of Hennerton

---

12 Colonel Kekewich of the North Lancashire Regiment was the commander of the Kimberley garrison but Rhodes the real power in Kimberley. For four months the town held out in spite of the acrimonious dispute between Rhodes and Kekewich. Kekewich commanded the Kimberley garrison (though having to defer to the highest military authority outside Kimberley), but Rhodes was de Beers and de Beers controlled Kimberley. Rhodes wanted the relief of Kimberley to be the prime objective of the British force. Half the white population of 20,000 were Afrikaaner who, it was reported, wanted to surrender the town. It was vital from Kekewich's point of view that those Boers should not have sensitive information. Rhodes excited public opinion through the newspaper he controlled in a way Kekewich believed to be the detriment of the military position. The situation provoked personal loathing on both sides.

(for he was in many respects a striking likeness), he laughingly said: 'I thought that I was much better looking.'

We used to play whist every evening, and as I was practically an invalid – I had not recovered from the effects of Ladysmith – I became almost comatose after dinner. Rhodes took me as his partner, and at the end of my visit I was told that my winnings amounted to £20. Since I never seemed to win a rubber, I suspect this was a present from Rhodes. He admired Lord Methuen and was truly sorry that he had been so abused over the disaster at Magersfontein; he always ascribed these disasters to the rotten training that the troops had received in peacetime at Aldershot. They won't realise the power of the modern rifle, he frequently said.

When I returned to Lord Methuen's I found my baggage laden with good things from Cecil Rhodes; also to my great joy the Provost Marshal told me there were two Basutos who wanted to see me, and that they told him they had been with me in Ladysmith. They, Isaac and Jacob, were overjoyed at seeing me and begged me to allow them to continue in my service. They had apparently trekked from Basutoland to Kimberley, then followed me up to Lord Methuen's headquarters.

Preparations were now in full swing for the relief of Mafeking,[13] and we were pushed up to the Vaal river, from which base Mahon had to make his dash.

Colonel Douglas was CSO, Colonel Benson DAAG, with Streatfield, Lord Loch, and myself as ADCs. The preparations were most amusing, for Mahon requisitioned for what his men wanted (they were mostly Colonials), whereas the authorities were intent on fitting his column out as laid down in War Office regulations. Mahon pointed out that their equipment must be as light and mobile as possible and that the ordinary four-wheeled service wagon was useless.

FORMING MY GANG

To my surprise I was called to the conference, and asked if I would take a reconnoitring patrol as far as Taungs, to report on the roads and country, for Mahon insisted that the only way that he could reach Mafeking was by outflanking the main Boer force. As I was far from being fit, I did not look forward to such an outing, but the CSO insisted

13 Relieved 17 May 1900.

on my going, for he said I was the only available cavalry officer who had a military sketching certificate.

With twenty-five Colonials and five Kaffirs we started off about 9 p.m. to swim the Vaal river. We were mounted on the best the Remounts could provide, and there was not a bad animal amongst the lot, including eight led horses. At dawn, the first day out, we took five prisoners, whom I sent back, with five Colonials as escort, to Lord Methuen's camp. I selected the escort from the men and horses that appeared to be most tired: the men – mostly Kimberley Light Horse – took this duty an insult and were most insubordinate.

Two days afterwards, when we were in the hills above Taungs, these men turned up again, and a half-caste named Chapman (whom I had put in charge of the five prisoners) reported having handed over the prisoners to the Provost Marshal, so I congratulated the escort on their expeditious journey. When I got back to camp on the Vaal and my report was received, the CSO had heard nothing about the arrival of the five prisoners, so the Provost Marshal was sent for. He said they had never arrived. Chapman, the half-caste, produced a receipt from the Provost Marshal's office, but the prisoners were never found. Almost a year afterwards I was out with Chapman on a long-distance night patrol, when he was mortally wounded, and he then confessed that he had killed the five prisoners, so as to return quickly to the Baas (myself). I always had him with me, as he was an extraordinary scout, and could talk all the Kaffir dialects.[14]

Soon after I joined Lord Methuen's staff, we captured Villebois de

14 W.A.T. notes: 'All the men of the reconnoitring patrol were picked from the Colonial Division, some of them most desperate characters, and this was the cadre from which I formed my troop of scouts, which is described as "Tilney's Gang" in some of the books dealing with the South African War. When the Australian and New Zealand contingents arrived for service in Africa, I had one hundred men, who were not only brave as lions, but also amazingly clever in scout craft. One Australian named Pym had been a member of Kelly's gang in Australia, and when this gang of bushrangers was caught, after they had held up South Australia for a considerable period, Pym, owing to his youth, was imprisoned, whereas the remainder of these bandits were executed. Pym then became a professional soldier and served in every war from Lord Wolseley's Red River Expedition to the Russo-Japanese War. Before the latter war had commenced, he came to London and asked me to get him enlisted into a fighting unit. As I knew Shiba, the Jap military attaché in London, I approached him, but Shiba said that a man with a red beard (he was exactly like "Captain Kettle") would be a marked man and certainly killed in the Japanese ranks. Pym was very despondent when Shiba would not enlist him, so he asked me to approach Levcravich, who was the Russian military attaché and also a pal of mine: they took him. He wrote frequently to me from the Russian front, but his letters suddenly ceased, so I assume he was killed.'

Mareil's force of European foreigners. Lord Chesham's yeomanry had recently joined our force, and as I had many friends in it I was sent to advise them on their best lines of attack. I found myself not twenty yards from Villebois when he was killed (5 April). Mrs Patrick Campbell's husband was killed close to Villebois – he was one of Lord Chesham's yeomanry, and a good fellow. Villebois's European contingent consisted of every nationality, including German, French and Italian, and I was ordered to take charge of the prisoners and have them searched.

The French, Belgians, and some of the Italians had the most immoral and disgusting photographs in their inside pockets, and as far as we could judge they had been recruited through a German agency. The Germans whom we took prisoner from time to time were of a very superior type to those from any other country. The authorities realised at that time that many Germans were fighting against us, but they never dreamt that most of these men had been sent by the German Government to learn the rudiments of modern warfare.

Soon after Lord Methuen's successful coup against Villebois de Mareil, we moved eastward against a strong commando under De La Rey. When we arrived at Schwartz Kopje Fontein, I was ordered to take my 'gang' on a long-distance night reconnaissance to ascertain De La Rey's strength and exact whereabouts, as Mahon had started for Mafeking and the High Command wanted to prevent the Boers from attacking the Mafeking relief column in flank or rear. We pushed off about 6 p.m., accompanied by Warwick and some of his best South African Scouts and my gang of about fifty picked by me, all of the bandit type with murky pasts – some of their life careers were amazing to hear. We covered some thirty miles during darkness and as daylight approached one Basuto scout spoored Boers that had lately traversed the veldt. It was amazing in the semi-light how these men could read the road, and we followed their track till we came to a high kopje with a flat top, just as the sun appeared. I was a mere child in the hands of those experienced scouts, and after a consultation with Warwick and Beranger we decided to rush and if possible surprise the Boer pickets on the top of the kopje. Three Basutos and five Colonials stalked the picket, whom they found fast asleep. When we all arrived on the summit I found five dead Boers, and not a sound made.

The top of this kopje was crater-shaped, so our horses were completely hidden, and when Warwick, Beranger and I crept to its edge, we found the whole of De La Rey's Commando bivouacked around a large farmhouse near its base not half a mile away. After posting reliable sentries, we all went to sleep in the crater, and I had every reason to think that this would be the last sleep for most of us, as the Boers were certain to relieve the picket we had slaughtered. We therefore told off five extra stalwarts to lie in ambush on the path to the top of the kopje, placing them in a tope of trees near the base, with orders on no account to fire but to kill the reliefs as silently as possible. The five dead Boers had English bayonets, captured at Magersfontein, and one a naval sword, so these were given to the men who were to lie in ambush.

About noon a Basuto scout woke me. As I couldn't understand him, I took him to Warwick, who could talk all the native languages. He, the Basuto, had completely disobeyed all our orders and had gone to the Boer bivouac for food and water, but came to warn us of the arrival of the relieving picket. He told us the Commando was marching at 2 p.m., and that a new picket would arrive about 1 p.m.

I'll never forget that hour we waited in a blazing sun: nothing to assuage our or the horses' thirst, and our survival depending on our ambush being able to kill the relief in absolute silence, which seemed an impossibility. Warwick told the Basuto – a huge fellow – of our plans, and he begged to be allowed to take the naval sword and join the ambush party, which he did. I had taken whisky and water, chocolate, meat, biscuits, and some lozenges for this night affair, and had realised by 9 a.m. what a real tenderfoot and fool I was, for they were useless to relieve one's thirst. By 12.30 I felt so bad that I did not mind what happened.

We waited and waited in the crater of the kopje, smoking and talking prohibited, until Jacob, the Basuto, appeared stripped naked, except for a loin cloth, whirling the naval sword, which was covered with blood. He reported that the relief of the picket had been killed, and that the main body of De La Rey's Commando were commencing their march.

Warwick immediately sent orders to our ambush party to dress up in the slaughtered relief party's coats and hats and rejoin us on the top, for were the Boers not to see their picket they might have suspected something and sent another batch of men to occupy this commanding position.

All however went splendidly, and we watched the force of some 3,000 men march past us at the foot of the kopje, with their guns, Cape carts, ox wagons, and a great many women and children. One specially smart Cape cart, drawn by two beautiful bay horses and containing two smartly dressed women, returned to the farm below our kopje about 5.30 p.m., with three men riding good horses, so I decided not to retire till dark.

Leaving the half-caste Chapman together with Jacob and ten men to act as rearguard, we moved at nightfall down to the open veldt, and rode as fast as our weary steeds would carry us towards Schwartz Kopje Fontein. Approaching this at dawn, we were received by fairly heavy rifle fire from the direction of the British camp.

Taking cover at once, we saw in behind us a mounted party with two mule-wagons and the smart Cape cart with the two bay horses, and for the moment we thought they were Boers. Sending out reconnoitring parties towards our camp and to our rear, I was much relieved to see one of our men – a wonderful type of adventurer named Schofield[15] – returning with Jacob the Basuto. Then the rearguard with the Cape cart and the wagons rejoined us. We were now being properly attacked from the direction of our camp, so Beranger offered to advance with a flag of truce towards the attackers, probably about 300 men.

I had given orders that on no account should any man return the fire, when the whole force of four squadrons (two yeomanry, two regulars) under the Chief Intelligence Officer, Colonel Altham, advanced towards us..[16] After asking me a lot of stupid questions, he informed us that he was making a reconnaissance to ascertain the direction of the Boer advance, and that he had taken us for Boers. When I asked leave for my

15 W.A.T. notes: 'Schofield was one of the few Englishmen who was ever a member of my reconnaissance gang. He had been to a first-class public school and university (both English) and was a record athlete. Getting into serious trouble when he left his university, he emigrated to Pretoria. After the Jameson Raid the Boers set a price on his head. During the year and a half he was with me, he changed his name according to the country in which we happened to be operating. Curtis, Smeeth, Sandison were all names he used. It was not until the Battle of Klip Drift (Tweebosch), when we were wounded and made prisoners, that I knew of the Boers' anxiety to capture him dead or alive. He had been one of Kruger's private secretaries, and when war broke out with England he escaped, taking with him many of his chief's most secret and private papers. He was badly wounded at de Klip Drift (with myself and about 300 other prisoners of the Boers), and thinking he might be identified, he told me his story and that his proper name was Curtis. The Boers, however, never recognised him, and he eventually got a good job in Cape Town when he recovered. He was the most extraordinary runner I have ever seen or heard of. Sometimes when we were in very difficult situations, I used to send him back with any important information, on foot, when a horseman would not have a chance of getting through the enemy's lines, and he never failed me once; sometimes he travelled thirty miles in the night. He always carried an orange coloured cloak, and once when I asked him why he did not have an ordinary overcoat, he told me that the orange colour was practically invisible at night, especially in moonlight.'

16 W.A.T. notes: 'Altham afterwards got the nickname, with the Yeomanry and British Troops in the Western Transvaal, of "The King of Fools". I am only giving his red tape

men to go to camp, as we had been out for two days and nights with scanty food and water, he ordered Warwick and myself to report everything to him, and getting out his notebook he began to interrogate us.

Warwick, who was a Colonial, blurted out that we had to report to Colonel Benson, DAAG 1st Division, and to nobody else; so, as I would not say a word, Altham lost his temper and said that he would report us on his return to camp. Colonel Benson (then Major) was one of the most brilliant, bravest officers in the British Army, and would have risen to the very highest positions had he not been killed in a later period of the South African War. He was just dressing when I reported at his tent, and having given him a verbal report, he ordered me to send in my written report after I had had a good rest.

In the afternoon I went round to see my gang and found them having a Lord Mayor's dinner with the poultry and foodstuffs they had brought back in the two wagons. On my asking the half-caste, Chapman, why he had allowed this looting, he replied that the men wanted to give 'the Baas', Lord Methuen, the two bay Cape cart horses, so as they left the kopje they raided the farmhouse and brought away all the horses, carts, food and other loot. As I was the newest arrival on Lord Methuen's staff, I did not know how this raid would be looked upon by the authorities. An Army order had just been published threatening death to anyone convicted and that everything 'commandeered' must be paid for. I knew that Altham would report everything in the blackest form on his return. The two bay horses were real beauties, so I went to Benson and suggested that they would make perfect chargers for Lord Methuen. When after dinner I called to make a verbal report to my written one on De La Rey's strength and the enemy movements, I made a clean breast of everything that had happened. The next morning Lord Methuen told me that he had recommended me for a DSO, and I asked whether I could send in the names of the men who had formed the ambush party, as by their actions they had saved the whole party. Our information proved to be of immense value and two days afterwards I was sent for by the CSO and told that my name had been sent in for a DSO, but that none of the men of the ambush party could be recommended. I thereupon told Colonel Douglas, the CSO, that I would

---

and stupid acts in some detail to show how Lord Methuen and the other British Chief Generals were hampered by such officers holding the most responsible and important jobs – in this case that of Chief Intelligence Officers – thrust upon them by the War Office. After Altham had blundered on for a year, he was sent home and Warwick (the Scout) put in his place, after which all went well.'

accept no honour if the names of the men I had recommended could not be sent in, for our success was due entirely to them. Lord Methuen heard what had happened, and from that moment was almost like a brother to me. One of the bays he took as his charger, and the other was sent to Lord Kitchener.

Altham, when he returned, reported that he had been engaged with the enemy three miles north of our support line, but had had no casualties. I had to disclose the fact that 'the enemy' had been my men, and that we had five casualties, none very serious. This caused much comment and amusement throughout the 1st Division.

When nothing was done to reward those men of my gang who had done such excellent work, I personally gave the Basuto Jacob a present of £5, which he refused to take, saying that Chapman's rearguard, of which he was a member, had done very well out of the raid on De La Rey's headquarters (the farm alluded to being that at the bottom of the kopje). He showed me a gold watch and chain which was his share of the loot. He told Warwick, who acted as interpreter, that when I retired with our main body, Chapman, with the rearguard, surprised the occupants of the farm and when they left, with the three vehicles cram full of loot, there were only women and children left alive in the vicinity. He said the Cape cart and the two bay horses belonged to De La Rey.

When Lord Methuen heard this, some months afterwards, he sent a cheque to De La Rey in payment for his horses. Lord Methuen also did every possible honour to Villebois de Mareil, for which he received severe censure from the British public, and questions were asked in Parliament as to why Lord Methuen had had a memorial stone erected on Villebois's grave.

When in 1900 Lord Methuen's troops fell back westwards, the Imperial Yeomanry Brigade under Lord Chesham formed the rearguard. Our retirement from Schwartz Kopje Fontein,[17] when De La Rey attacked our flank and rear, was the first serious fighting the Yeomanry took part in, and everyone was loud in their praises, for they behaved in a most admirable manner.

After the Relief of Mafeking (17 May 1900) the 1st Division moved northwards and gradually pushed into the Marico district and the Mahalesburg mountains.[18]

This is only a general narrative of my life – Lord Methuen's column

17 Koffiefontein, south of Kimberley.
18 West of Johannesburg.

was seldom inactive, for we were trekking and fighting almost every day in the western and northern Rhodesian countries, and as far as German West Africa.

FREE-LANCING UNDER METHUEN

When the Australian and New Zealand mounted troops came under Lord Methuen's command, we were kept busy incessantly. Some of these were almost uncivilised, having come straight from the Australian bush and never having seen the sea or a railway before they sailed; yet they were grand fighters. I acted as Staff Officer to the Australian and New Zealand contingents for about four months, and also as Military Tactical Adviser when they went into action. They were the wildest, most undisciplined troops imaginable, and for the first six months quite uncontrollable, but I never experienced any unpleasantness or unfriendliness; we got on splendidly together. Most were magnificent horsemen and when opportunity offered they lassoed the wild horses from the veldt, of which at that time there were any number, and had a rodeo. Whenever they went into action they took everything lootable, and sometimes returned with excellent led horses. I suggested to Lord Methuen that it would simplify the question of remounting our columns if we instituted a travelling Remount Establishment, with my gang as roughriders, to break in the wild horses for the less experienced men of the Regular Army and Yeomanry. Lord Methuen jumped at the idea, as at that time we were miserably mounted from the Kimberley Remount Depot. The Australian and New Zealand contingents provided me with some excellent roughriders. On Sundays, or any day when nothing particular was on, their schedule of riding feats gave great amusement to the troops. A man named McKenzie was particularly good, and backed himself to ride anything.

One day a particularly dangerous and vicious grey mare was brought in, so we had a rodeo on the veldt in the vicinity of the Vaal river. Lord Kitchener and most of the 'big bugs' of the Army happened to be there and saw a wonderful feat of horsemanship. The mare twice bucked herself clean out of the saddle; the second time landing McKenzie on the ground seated in the saddle. Having sent a party to lasso her, he jumped on to the mare barebacked and disappeared into the Vaal river. In about an hour's time he returned with the mare ridden to a standstill, and then saddled up what seemed to be a quiet animal.

I received orders to make a reconnaissance northwards from Ottoshoep, and to order the chiefs and headmen to attend an indaba, so as to allow them to give their allegiance to Queen Victoria. This became necessary as the Boers were forming hostile native commandos who had been giving our troops considerable trouble. I took my gang of about sixty Colonials, but without transport, our rations being carried on led horses. All goods commandeered were to be paid for by official chit. These were the orders I received, but we soon found that the chit system was a veritable paperchase for the Boers, who could follow our movements exactly. We moved only at night and lay doggo all day. The ingenuity of the Colonials and natives in laying false trails and information was wonderful, and although we had a hostile Commando on our heels for seven days we shook them off in the bush veldt of the Marico District. Having learnt that the official chit system had given our movements away, we devised a much simpler system for repaying commandeered goods. One of the Australians wore a cash-belt with some £20 round his waist and we used these coins as tokens, so that when the natives came to the indaba they could be recognised and paid in British cash. A strict list was made of all things commandeered and we lived on the country in this way for the six weeks we were on the mission.

When we reached the Rustenburg district, I was told that a certain George Rex was a very influential personage and had refused to fight for the Boers, claiming that he was an Englishman. Warwick, Schofield, myself and the bushmen made a forced march from some thick bush near Olifant's Nek and arrived at Magato Pass to find it occupied by a strong Boer Commando. We lay in a donga all day and visited George Rex (just south of Rustenberg) at dawn, finding him delighted to see us. After a wonderfully good breakfast, he took us up a spruit to a good water hole, surrounded with thick bush, and told us to stay there till nightfall, as the Boer commandant always visited him about noon. In case of danger a bonfire was to be lit in front of his house. About 2 p.m. two native girls arrived at the water hole with a note from George Rex to say that the Commando was marching southwards that night and it would be quite safe for us to sleep in his house. When we returned he treated us right royally and showed us his pedigree to prove that his grandfather had been the illegitimate son of George III. He had many relics in his house of that period. When he arrived at the indaba, he not only brought his pedigree but also many of the family relics for Lord Kitchener to see, and we all agreed that his story was true. He was of the greatest assistance to me on this mission, and lent us two natives who knew the country north of Johannesburg up to the Crocodile river.

Avoiding all inhabited districts, we were unmolested by the enemy, except on one occasion when some bushveldt Boers, clad in skins, ambushed us, and we lost seven men. The women of this party took us in properly, for as we came to an opening in the bush we saw two women sitting under a large umbrella made in vierkleur (Boer Republic flag – orange, green, white and blue) colours – a most unusual sight. Apparently they were friendly, but when the youngest retired into the bush, without saying a word, I sent two men after her, and almost immediately fire was opened on us.

On this six weeks' trek from the Vaal to the Zambezi I was lucky enough to see Africa in its virgin state. One evening we bivouacked at the top of a hill overlooking a huge plain, with the River Zambezi in the distance, the plain being covered with wildlife.

On going down to get some meat, they allowed me to get within easy rifle range and showed no sign of fear. The Australian bushmen got completely out of hand on this occasion, for they had acquired some very potent native spirit during the day's march. When they saw these herds of wildebeest, zebra, kudus, and many species of antelope congregated around a water hole in the evening, they poured lead at them. Half my men were incapably drunk that night, and I had to remain in the same place for two days till they recovered.

We returned to the Marico district about a fortnight before the indaba took place, and when the headman and chiefs did appear, they were the most extraordinary lot of human beings it is possible to imagine. Some grand-looking natives, others half-castes, and some of white extraction but clothed in skins. George Rex seemed to be 'Baas' of the lot, and created a fine impression among the British staff.

I will only give one more account of these outings, to show how impossible it would have been to carry them out with any troops except the ones I always took, real Australian and New Zealand bushmen, some native South African whites, or halfbreeds such as Chapman, and Basuto scouts like Isaac and Jacob.

Among such men, discipline as understood in the British Army was impossible and could never be enforced. I tried it when we commenced operations in the Taungs reconnaissance and at Schwartz Kopje Fontein. They simply would not have it, and gave me the best 'Billingsgate' in return. It was only by turning a deaf ear and blind eye to their many excesses that these forty-seven long-distance night reconnaissances were so successful.

As my men generally came back to camp laden with loot, the authorities on one occasion ordered me to take out a squadron of 9th Lancers and two squadrons of yeomanry. I protested as vehemently as I reasonably could, pointing out that these men, not being 'at home' in the dark at night and ignorant of tracking or spooring, would soon get lost. General Headquarters was adamant, and off we went.

Our objective was the house of a Free State Senator named Theunissen, some twenty miles distant. We had to deliver a communication from Lord Roberts relating to the Peace Terms proposed by the British Government. Before leaving camp I had had an interview with Lord Methuen, when I explained how hopeless it was to send English cavalry (who could not read the heavens as a compass as my men could) on such a mission. I begged that the Senior Officer of the three squadrons, Major L., should be responsible for the success or otherwise of the outing, and that if we arrived at Theunissen's house my job would be confined to delivering the message. Lord Methuen gave orders accordingly, and granted my request that I should take my two Basutos, Isaac and Jacob, with Major L. conducting the night march.

When around 1 a.m. I suggested that the column should halt for half an hour to close up, it was discovered that the rearguard was missing. Scouts were dispatched for the lost troops, and when dawn was breaking I suggested that we should push on towards Theunissen's house, the proximity of which we reached about 7 a.m. Not wishing to alarm the inhabitants, I rode up with Isaac and Jacob, leaving the 9th Lancer squadron in a spruit about a mile distant.

I found Theunissen to be a delightful man of the old Boer stamp, and having delivered Lord Roberts's letter, bade farewell to the household. As I was mounting outside the dorp, my pony fell dead riddled with bullets, mercifully knocking me into a donga that ran alongside the entrance road. Almost immediately Isaac appeared shouting 'Jump up, Baas', and getting up behind him we escaped to the spruit held by the 9th Lancers. It was only by a miracle that neither of us, or Isaac's horse, were hit, for Jacob, who had been in hiding, saw that the enemy numbered well over fifty. Our retirement home to camp was most unpleasant. Being peppered all the way, we lost half of our men as the Boers, shooting from the saddle, galloped to within a hundred yards of the rearguard and took most of them prisoners.

The day following our arrival in camp, Theunissen sent a letter to the

GOC to thank the latter for the gift of a hundred rifles and said that he would return the wounded and prisoners the next day. When they arrived, the unwounded were naked, except for their shirts. They brought a note from the Boer Commandant to thank the GOC for the excellent clothing supplied, asking that more reconnaissances should be dispatched at an early date, as they were in need of arms, ammunition and clothing.

Benson was still with the 1st Division as DAAG, and was recognised as being the rising soldier of the British Army. After I had been interviewed by Lord Methuen, I went to see Benson, who was always so full of common sense and understanding. I told him the secrets of the successful night-raids I had conducted with my gang hitherto, summarising as follows:

1. The men should be born bush trackers, who knew their direction at night and were as much at home at night as in the day.
2. They should disperse if attacked by superior numbers, rendezvousing at a prearranged spot – e.g. a kopje five miles S.W. of Krugersdorp.
3. Their knowledge of direction at night should be enough for me only to tell them, when moving off, for example 'N., twenty miles from here, we come to a camel-shaped hill where everyone will halt', and for every man invariably to turn up.
4. With English troops we were absolutely dependent on the guide, and should expect no individual soldier to be competent to act for himself at night.

Benson then told me of his experience during the Magersfontein attack. He described how when he was leading the attack by compass bearing several shots rang out. The Highlanders then fired at the Guards column and the troops, having completely lost sense of direction, fired at one another, thereby creating chaos in the three columns. He said that if our men could be given the same sense of direction at night as that possessed by bushmen, Basutos and the natives, the night fighting power of the British tommy would be vastly increased and night operations revolutionised. I therefore questioned the men of my gang how they got this pigeon-like instinct. They all assured me that it was by the stars at night and the sun by day. They explained how easy it was, for if one was going north, then naturally south took you home. They pointed out to me the various fixed stars by which they got their bearings so the dome of the heavens became for them a compass. In all our raids and expeditions a compass was never produced. We never had a casualty through a man losing his way.

SERGEANT GELL, MAN OF GOD

Towards the close of 1900 there was a lull in the operations, when peace parleys were taking place. There was a big concentration of mounted troops in the Krugersdorp District including Lord Chesham's Yeomanry Brigade, the Australians, New Zealanders and the Colonial Mounted Division. To keep the men amused and fit, excellent race and sporting meetings were held, as well as a boxing tournament for the championships of South Africa. In one of the races McKenzie, the wonderful rodeo rider and member of my gang, entered the big race on his own horse, in a field including some very good horses which belonged to the rich men of Johannesburg and had been sent down specially for this race of £500. McKenzie's horse started at the longest odds and all my gang and many Colonials backed it. No one could understand how he won, for we had been unable to watch the race on the far side of the course owing to a thickish mist, but everyone saw that he made a very bad start and was a good last first time round. The distance was twice round, just over two miles. The officers backed the well-known horses. Most of the rank and file had their money on McKenzie. They won a packet for McKenzie's horse came in first – no one could understand how. There was a lot of money available for drink and hilarious times among the tommies.

Sometime afterwards, when I was DAAG[19] of the 1st Division, I took a reconnaissance through the lead mines in the Zeerust district, and to accompany me had collected many of the members of my original gang, of which McKenzie was one. One night we bivouacked adjacent to a native village on a river in the Mahlesburg mountains – a particularly nasty, dangerous spot, but my trackers assured me there were no Boers in the vicinity. After I had posted sentries – the rest of us being all dead beat – not a sound could be heard till dawn when I was awakened by a drunken chorus of bellowings from the bed of the river. Going down, I saw McKenzie with five Australians lying dead drunk in the bed of the river, surrounded by kegs of alcohol which the natives had distilled from oranges. Two of the men never recovered, and we had to tie McKenzie and his remaining pals on to pack saddles before we could

19 DAAG October 1900. Promoted Major June 1902.

march. When he came round, which was in about two days, I had him up for disgraceful conduct, and thought it would be an opportunity of solving the mystery of his win near Krugersdorp. All these splendid fellows had become pals of mine, and we were on the most friendly terms. Any man who was not up to the highest standard in scout craft, pluck and stamina they would not work with, categorising him as 'white-livered', or 'white-livered cur' or indeed in much stronger language.

McKenzie on this occasion replied: 'If you let me off a court martial I'll tell you.' I assented, and he told me that he had purposely hung well back in the race till they passed a tope of trees on the far side of the course, where he pulled in and hid till the field came round a second time. He then joined in at their tail on his fresh horse, and naturally won the race. He jauntily explained that owing to the bad visibility, no one could have seen his ruse. In this he was mistaken, for at the conclusion of hostilities he rode a winner at Johannesburg, and was recognised by some natives as the man who had hid in the tope of trees and fraudulently won the £500 race some months before. He was warned off all racecourses for life.

At this sports gathering there was some especially good boxing for the various championships. The heavyweight final was between a huge Australian and a yeomanry sergeant named Gell. Up to the tenth round it was a hard hitting, bloody affair, and then Gell, much to the British tommies' joy, landed two hooks to the jaw that staggered the giant Australian. It was not until the fifteenth round that Gell was declared the winner, and deservedly so: he could have knocked his man completely out at any moment. The result was received with the greatest enthusiasm, for the betting was 3 to 1 on the Australian and you could get almost anything against Gell. At the conclusion of the fight Lord Chesham beckoned me to come and speak with him, and said: 'Sergeant Gell is one of the men whose names have been forwarded to headquarters as a clerk in Holy Orders, with a view to being made one of the chaplains to Lord Methuen's mobile columns.'

Most of the chaplains who had been sent out from home were of the ritualistic High Church order, and we had had real trouble with two, who insisted upon tommies and officers confessing before they administered Holy Communion. Anyone who wasn't on their list they passed by when administering the sacrament. Feeling ran so high that Lord Methuen sent both of them home and any qualified clerk in Holy Orders who was serving among the troops under his Command was asked to send his name to Headquarters as a potential replacement.

There were over fifteen in the Yeomanry alone. As I was DAAG I told Lord Methuen, who was present at the fight, what Lord Chesham had said about Gell. He replied, 'That's the very man we want; send him to me tonight.'

After much trouble, I unearthed Sergeant Gell and ordered him to accompany me to Lord Methuen's tent. It was a good hour after Lights Out, and poor Gell begged me to allow him time to wash and dress properly, but I told him the General's order was to come as he was. So, putting on a great coat, I ushered Gell into Lord Methuen's tent. It was a good minute before the General looked up from his Bible, which he was intently reading, and then these two magnificent men discussed the evening's fight like two enthusiastic young pugilists, without the General even alluding to the purport of the Yeomanry sergeant's presence until I chipped in to say he was one of the candidates for the Divisional Chaplaincy. 'I am quite delighted,' said Lord Methuen, clasping him by the hand, 'and we will have Holy Communion the day after tomorrow' – this night of the fight being a Friday. 'Put Gell in Orders as officiating from tomorrow' were his final instructions. So three services, at 8, 11 and evening, all naming Gell, appeared in Command Orders.

About midday on the Saturday Gell came to ask if he might be given a few days' leave to allow his face to recover from the mauling he had gone through in the fight – both eyes were black and swollen, and his left ear badly torn. As it was lunchtime at Headquarters, I took him in with me, and after a good meal handed him over to our dear PMO, Townsend, whose breast was covered with war medals – a real tough old nut. He returned Gell, swathed in bandages, saying he would be fit to fight again tomorrow. The next morning I walked with Lord Methuen to the early service which was being held on the open veldt. As we approached the spot he said, 'You must have put the Parade Service at 8 a.m. instead of 11 a.m. Go forward and see what has happened.' Gell, with a beaming face, announced that they were all communicants. The service was indeed the most impressive that anyone could possibly see. There was every description of manhood assembled as communicants, over 600 in all, from the officer to the Colonial scallywag – many of the latter had never been to a service of any description before and consequently had not the vaguest idea of the procedure.

Lord Methuen and some of the senior officers partook first, and the service proceeded in the most fervently reverent manner. Half way through, the parson who was assisting Gell asked me to get more wine, so I ran down to the camp. No wine of any sort was procurable, the remaining wine bottles being filled with beer. This made no difference to the broad-minded Gell. At the conclusion of the service I talked with three members of my gang who were present, Pym (our 'Captain Kettle') being one of them. He had apparently come out of sheer curiosity, and comically remarked that Christ hadn't come his way in life and that it was beyond his understanding how a splendid man like Gell could be a Christian, since the few professing Christians whom he had known had come from towns and were white-livered softies. 'Tell me, Captain,' he said, 'what and who is Christ? I think the only time I heard of him was when I was in prison at Sydney before my friends of the Kelly gang were hung. I was too young for hanging, so remained in prison until this war broke out, when I escaped and joined the 6th Bushmen. Yes,' he continued meditatively, 'before the hanging day each of us was visited by a man in a black coat or gown who talked for half an hour about Jesus Christ, but what was the – good of that? It didn't save my pals from being hanged. That is the only time I particularly heard of Christ.'

That afternoon I told him briefly the story of the Cross, and that through Jesus Christ we can treat God as Our Father in Heaven, and if we trust him as our very best friend he will help and care for us in innumerable ways, and never fail, and that Jesus whilst he was on earth asked his followers to commemorate his death by holding the service we had this morning, by eating the bread, such as Gell had given him, and drinking the wine. Jesus Christ was the personification of all that is noblest, bravest, heroic and lovely in men's lives, so we think ourselves most fortunate in having him as our Counsellor, Adviser and Friend. 'Well, I'm –,' was his rejoinder. 'It is worth coming to Africa to have learnt this, for all the men I knew at this morning's service were good chaps, including the General. Do you think I could be one of Christ's followers?' So the next day I took him to see Gell, who after a talk gave him a Bible, which Pym read very assiduously thereafter, on all occasions. When we were out raiding – whenever opportunity offered – he could be seen poring over what he called 'the wonderful book', and when his comrades chaffed at him he replied: 'I am reading about the Kingdom of God; would you like to have a look?' He was a demi-god among the men, especially in the canteen, where he narrated his experiences with Kelly the bushranger, and with Wolseley in the Red River Expedition. He lived for war and adventure and, as I have narrated elsewhere, he was killed in the Russo-Japanese War whilst fighting for the Russians.

Gell remained chaplain of the 1st Division till the end of the war, when Lord Methuen asked him to become rector of Corsham. He did splendid work there until the outbreak of the Great War, when one day he went to Lord Methuen and begged to be relieved of his duties. Lord Methuen was much upset by this demand, for he had rebuilt and furnished a very nice house for him and Gell was very popular in the parish.

Lord Methuen told me that he begged Gell to stay, pointing out that he had a wife and three children who were dependent on him. All Gell said was that he must go and serve Jesus at the front. He would not listen to any arguments or entreaties, even from Lady Methuen. He enlisted at Aldershot as a private, was wounded on three occasions, rose to command his battalion, and was twice selected to command a brigade, with promotion to brigadier-general. The latter he declined, for as Sir Herbert Lawrence told me, Gell said his work was for Jesus, with the men. I am informed that his is a unique case of a man rising to commissioned rank from the ranks in two separate wars.

ZIP

I will only describe one more of these exploits by my trained band. Up to the time of the Cape Rebellion,[20] we were out most weeks raiding, collecting information, horses, oxen, cattle and other provisions for the troops. When the Cape Rebellion broke out we were in the Lichtenburg District (due west of Johannesburg), and orders were received from Headquarters for a force to be sent to destroy Christian de Wet's house. I was DAAG of the 1st Division and pointed out that an English force of all arms would only too easily be rounded up, as de Wet was scuppering all isolated posts and forces with lightning suddenness and rapidity. When Frankie Maxwell of Lord Kitchener's[21] staff arrived to make final arrangements, I volunteered to carry out the job with some of my gang. Approval being given by Headquarters, I selected fifteen of my men, including Bloody Bill (the Australian bushman), Pym (the bushranger), Schofield, McKenzie (an Australian bushman), my three Basutos (Isaac, Jacob and a half-caste Basuto named Skin-the-Goat – a wonderful tracker), and the half-caste South African, Chapman. The remainder were Australian or New Zealand bushmen.

Pushing off at dusk, we covered the thirty-five miles and arrived at de Wet's house about 1 a.m. Bloody Bill, Pym, McKenzie, and three other

---

20 10–28 February 1901, de Wet's invasion of Cape Colony.
21 Created Lord Kitchener following the victory of Omdurman in the Sudan, 1898.

Australians formed the advance guard. Never shall I forget, as we approached the house, the noise made by a flock of geese on a pan [pond] in the vicinity of the house. When those geese started squawking we galloped the place, and completely surprised its occupants.

All the Boers who were sleeping in an adjoining building were quickly disposed of by Bloody Bill & Co. When we had got the females and children into an adjoining barn, and I had collected some valuable documents, we burnt the place to the ground.

I had given as our rendezvous a sugar loaf kopje ten miles westward (an unusual shape in South Africa, as the hills are mostly blunted at the top), and we were to move away from there as soon as the sun appeared full up from the horizon.

At this time, and until the end of the battle of de Klip Drift, I had a most wonderful Basuto thoroughbred pony, chestnut, about 14.2 – it would jump anything and stay forever, even over the worst country in Africa. I called it 'Zip', and always rode it on special excursions. On this occasion I arrived at the sugar loaf hill with Isaac and Jacob, who were my personal attendants and bodyguard, but found not a sign of anyone else. As the sun rose the Australians turned up. When the sun was well up I spied a party of ten men riding through the scrub in a disorderly manner and I gave up ourselves as lost, since Isaac and Jacob were both certain they were Boers. As they approached, the two Australians who were with me 'coo-eed'. To our delight they 'coo-eed' back, making enough noise to awaken the whole countryside. On their arrival at the foot of the kopje, I saw that all were drunk, some almost incapable, and their horses and persons were festooned with loot of all descriptions. Since it was hopeless to try and march back in broad daylight with this drunken gang, I dismounted them in a riverbed, with a fervent prayer that the Boers would not discover our whereabouts, and we all laid down and slept till the afternoon. I arranged with the two sober Australians that we should each take turns of two hours to watch, and that if the Boers arrived we should surrender without resistance. Thereby some of our lives might be spared, for if anyone resisted we would all be slaughtered, most of the party being completely *hors de combat* with drink.

I took the first watch, and about 10 a.m. woke up one of the two sober Australians to take his watch. I found Schofield, the English runner, wide awake, and he asked if he might be allowed to push off at once to camp on foot, some thirty miles distant. Knowing his great running powers, I had no doubt that he would reach camp by nightfall, so

I entrusted him with a message saying where we were and what we had accomplished, and asked them to send out a suitable party to meet us halfway on our return journey.

Being dead with fatigue, I didn't wake till dusk, when I found the remainder of the party ready to march and what seemed an excellent dinner ready for me. Some of the Australians had lassoed some sheep and done the cooking in a hole on the river bank, and as they had brought from de Wet's home some Vermouth and a very potent orange wine and Dom liqueur, we had a good dinner. When we got on the march they told me how the finding of de Wet's cellar had been their undoing, and that three men had to be left behind as they were incapable of movement.

As we approached the British lines, the party sent out to meet us greeted us with rifle fire and wounded one of the Australians. Bloody Bill asked me to take a gold ring as a memento of our expedition. It was not until two days afterwards that I found it was Christian de Wet's ring which de Wet had left at home for safe keeping, and which Bloody Bill had collected with other loot. I gave it to Hylda when we married, together with a wonderful sjambok (rhino-hide whip), from the same raid.

Schofield had reached our camp at midnight. When I saw him the next morning he reported that he had been chased by Boers up to our outpost line, and had eluded his pursuers by crossing some country impassable for horses, concealed under his orange cloak in moonlight. Unwittingly he had acted as a decoy. We did not encounter a single soul, let alone any Boer during our return journey. It was also fortunate for me that we did not meet the relief party, as my men appeared to have relieved C. de Wet's house of all valuables. The unique sjambok was handed over to me by Chapman after we had reached camp.

I was allowed to rest till the evening, when I was told that Frankie Maxwell had been sent by the Commander-in-Chief to take a verbal report of our raid. I was, indeed, in a most difficult quandary, for I could not give anything like a true version of the men's behaviour and their many iniquities, so just factually reported that the job we had been ordered to do had been completely and satisfactorily carried out. Some time afterwards I was ordered to go to Headquarters, and was closely questioned about the conduct of the raid by Lord Kitchener. I shall never forget this interview. Before appearing, I made a clean breast of everything to Frankie Maxwell and Birdwood (both ADCs), and they advised me to narrate everything to 'Great Man' as I had done to them. I was relieved when the C-in-C received me in the nicest manner and asked me to sit down, with Frankie and, I think, Birdwood still in the room. He said that questions had been asked in the House of Commons about the disgraceful manner in which de Wet's house had been raided and burnt, and that he had to send an explanatory answer. So I gave him a version that was fitting for the occasion.

He asked me to dine and sleep and I had a very pleasant evening, and found on my return to the 1st Division that I had been confirmed as DAAG 1st Division, vice Benson, who was given command of a column. The fighting and ubiquitous trekking of Lord Methuen's column are now a matter of history, and I know that he has kept an accurate and minute account of all the phases of the campaign.

When the new Yeomanry arrived, I was sent down to take charge of their camp and superintend their training on the Vaal river near Warrentown. An Irish Brigade held the railway bridge over the river, consisting of some Dublin Fusiliers, Connaught Rangers and Irish Fusiliers.

About Christmas time the Yeomanry asked leave to have a dance in the Station Restaurant, and having assented, I went there about 11.30 p.m. to see everything properly closed up at midnight. The woman in charge of the refreshments was a hugely fat cook from Kimberley. On closing time heavy firing broke out, just as most of the men were leaving the premises. Shouts were raised that de Wet was attacking the outpost. The old cook shouted: 'It's those bloody drunken Irish.' Outside of the station there was a very brisk fusillade and it continued – in spite of the Yeomanry trumpet sounding 'cease fire' – until dawn. Making my way to the Irish camp, I found they had had eleven casualties, and that the fight had started between the Dublin Fusiliers and Connaught Rangers. The new Yeomanry, thinking they were being attacked, had fired into the Irish camp, to which the latter replied, with the result that we lost three dead and several wounded.

It was a week or so before the Yeomen's saddlery arrived. When it came, the stirrups were too small for the men's feet! Most of them had been 'trained' at Aldershot, and many of them had not been through any musketry course. Doing our utmost with the arms and saddlery available, we used the best horses and men on reconnaissance duty just outside the perimeter of camp. Progress was satisfactory, until one day a swarm of horses stampeded into camp, some dragging their riders. It appeared that during 'Riding School' some few Boers had opened fire, when there was a *sauve qui peut*.

Most of the old Yeomen, however, were with us for the de Wet chase, and they covered themselves with glory. Lord Methuen's troops were on the left flank with Kitchener's column in the centre, the right extending to the Basuto border. When we were approaching the hills from the south, with Olifant's Nek and Magato Pass in the far distance, Lord Methuen became very worried because nothing had been heard of the Kitchener columns for two days. All forms of communication had failed; our native dispatch runners and riders refused to make more attempts, as those who had been engaged in the communications hitherto had been captured and killed. Warwick of Warwick Scouts, who was now Chief Intelligence Officer, gave a very doleful account of our prospects at a conference we had about midday, and rightly pointed out that the Boers might attack in the broken bush country and try to defeat us piecemeal after severing our communications (which had apparently been effected). Lord Kitchener's columns were estimated to be about forty to fifty miles eastward, but no one knew for certain their whereabouts or exact line of march.

Knowing the marvellous staying power of my pony Zip, I volunteered to try and carry a dispatch through to Kitchener. Warwick said that it was impossible for me to get through without any knowledge of the country, and told Lord Methuen so. I insisted, however, upon going, and made my preparations to start whilst the dispatch was being coded in the most secret code. In a way I cannot explain, I felt that the dear, kind God who had brought me through so many hazardous adventures would be my mainstay in this 'do or die' job. So having retired to a spruit, I earnestly entreated him to allow me to get through, and then having said goodbye to Lord Methuen, I started about 3 p.m. on my beloved chestnut Basuto gelding Zip. Our mounted troops occupied a hill from which one could see down a valley leading eastwards for at least ten miles, intersected with spruits and mostly covered in bush, except near the base of a mountain to the south east where the country was covered with veldt grass.

Just as I was setting off, an orderly from Lord Chesham galloped up saying that two natives were to go with me and that I had to wait for them. Soon my dear Basutos, Isaac and Jacob, cantered up and implored me to take them, as the Baas would assuredly be lost without anyone to guide him. It was really pathetic to see their grief when I refused to take them, both men bursting into tears and making heartrending lamentations, and I don't know what would have been the outcome had Lord Chesham not arrived and promised to look after them whilst I was away. The only arms I carried were two Mauser pistols and fifty rounds of vega ammunition. Isaac and Jacob told me to go north east on a V shaped cluster of stars and only travel by night.

A reconnaissance of Yeomen accompanied me for about two miles until I could reach the grass veldt (mentioned above) at the foot of the large mountain lying to the south east. Zip's best pace was a very slow canter, so when I left the reconnaissance we started at this pace, going about eight miles per hour. I chose a line that would keep me about a mile away from the base of the mountain, the foot of which was covered in bush. When the sun was just above the horizon I heard the familiar *ping-pong*, *ping-pong* on my right, and saw five Boers emerge from a farm at the gallop. A few minutes appeared to elapse before bullets were whizzing past me, and looking back I saw the Boers were shooting from their horses almost 300 yards away. The ground was criss-crossed with spruits but I realised that this alone could save me from being captured. The pony seemed to take in the situation at once. When the pursuit had lasted over three hours I had got out of rifle distance, but five men were still on my track.

It was now getting dusk and to my dismay I saw a deep donga [land crevasse] crossing my path, which as I approached seemed absolutely impassable. As its banks were perpendicular, there was no chance of going in and out. Making a very fervent prayer, I rammed my beloved Zip at this seemingly impossible place, and to my amazement got over with a scramble. When one realises that high veldt grass was growing up to its very edge and the going was as bad as any pigsticking country in India, it was only one of God's miracles that we got across. It was the broadest open space that I have ever seen jumped by any horse. My pursuers now began to fire with unpleasant rapidity until they reached the donga, where they were pounded, and turned down the spruit where I imagine there was a crossing. I therefore called upon Zip to make a supreme effort and – the going being much better – I soon got out of sight of my pursuers. I was still far from being safe, for there were two farmhouses to my front, the lights showing that they were occupied by Boers. It was now quite dark and I was steering my course by the stars that Isaac and Jacob always used, I couldn't risk going on, however, for had the farm dogs, which the Boers always keep, started barking, my fate would be sealed.

I therefore dismounted in a bush-covered donga, gave Zip a good feed and fell fast asleep. The pony treading on my foot woke me with a start, and I saw from his alertness that there was something in the vicinity. Looking over the bank of the donga, I saw several mounted men silhouetted against the light of the farm, and as the lights in the farm soon afterwards went out, I presumed they had returned from a reconnaissance, probably trying to find me. As it was past midnight, now was the time to be off. I had no chance of reaching the British columns in daylight, surrounded as they would be by Boer reconnoitring parties. Just as dawn was breaking, Zip pricked his ears and became quite lively and I thought we were in for more trouble when I saw a column of smoke ahead to my half right, some distance away north east. Knowing from past experience the marvellous sagacity of Zip, I laid the reins on his neck, trusting him implicitly. The country was almost unrideable, being covered with scrub and intercepted with dongas and spruits. He soon brought me to a large pan where to my joy I saw fresh hoof marks of English horses, cigarette ends and some empty MacConachie tins. I knew the British columns could not be far away.

After watering and feeding in a tope of trees, Zip was much refreshed, and on the reverse side of a gentle slope I came across the flank guard of an English cavalry brigade, who told me that the 17th Lancers were with the main body. Pushing on, I reached them just as the column had halted to camp for the day. They gave me an excellent breakfast, after which I proceeded on to the Headquarters camp on a good pony lent me by Anstruther, who promised to look after Zip until I sent for him. Lord Kitchener and his staff gave me a warm welcome and overwhelmed me with kindness. They insisted on my staying the night and Frankie Maxwell sent for Zip and gave me his best horse to ride the following day, at the same time promising to send Zip to be well cared for at the Remount Depot until he could be returned to me.

I was sound asleep when Birdwood woke me to say the C-in-C wished to see me before the column marched. The CSO had given me a dispatch for Lord Methuen. I contemplated making an attempt to ride back on Maxwell's horse, but when I saw the C-in-C he would not hear of it. He ordered an escort of Colonials to take me back. It was not until then that I realised that I had ridden about sixty miles through a Boer-infested country. Birdwood was the Acting Military Secretary, and Kitchener turned to him and said, 'Ask Tilney what he wants', and thanking me very heartily, said goodbye. I told Birdwood of my Ladysmith experiences, and how none of my gang with Lord Methuen had as yet received any honour or reward, and he agreed that it would be most invidious and seemingly unfair if I were to receive some honour and none of the men even mentioned in dispatches.

He explained that the present mode of distribution all came from the War Office in London, and that they did not recognise special unofficial units. Regular units, wherever they were, had one CB, two DSOs, and so on allotted to them. This was red tape *in extremis*, so the result was that at the end of the South African War many officers who had never seen a shot fired and had done nothing but stay in a camp or hotel, got DSOs and CMGs. It was a rotten and iniquitous system.

As I was preparing to leave on my return journey, Lord Kitchener showed me a beautiful bay that my gang had captured in our raid at Schwartz Kopje Fontein, and which I have explained formerly belonged to General De La Rey. Lord Methuen had the other of the pair, which Chapman drove back in De La Rey's barouche, and he handed the pair to Lord Methuen. I got back to Lord Methuen's column in two days, before they reached Magato and Olifant's Nek passes.

We knew these passes were held by the North Lancs Regiment and other details; they had been placed there before the start of the great de Wet drive had been begun, and the success of the drive depended entirely on these passes being securely held. The pursuing columns had been marching day and night for a week, driving the whole Boer force before them, and a day before we reached the passes it seemed certain that the enemy would be completely defeated, for all the prisoners we took told the same tale: they had no ammunition and were very short of food.

Imagine our consternation, when we arrived within sight of Magato Pass and Olifant's Nek, on seeing a huge caterpillar of wagons and horsemen ascending the passes. I was with Warwick the scout well in advance of our troops, and having my telescope, could see this swarm of ants ascending the hill. We at once galloped back to inform Lord Methuen. We presumed that our garrisons had been scuppered by the enemy, but no shots had been heard. The column pushed forward to the base of the mountain. It was then we learnt that Ian Hamilton had recently returned from England and had been given command of the Krugersdorp District. Hearing that de Wet was to strike a blow in force at the isolated detachments (as he called them), Hamilton on his own authority withdrew all our blocking troops, and never said a word to either Lord Kitchener or Lord Methuen. Thus, through the treachery or consummate folly of Ian Hamilton, the South African War was prolonged for a year and thousands of lives lost.

When the troops heard what had happened, feelings ran very high, and they expected Ian Hamilton to be tried by general courts martial, but owing to his great friendship with Lord Roberts, nothing happened.

That night, when de Wet escaped over the mountains, our troops completely broke down and officers and men wept like children. It was a sight never to be forgotten, for every superhuman effort had been made to end the war. All officers and men were quite deadbeat at the unsuccessful end to the de Wet chase. My gang had been broken up and the men returned to their units.

GUERRILLA WARFARE

One day when we were bivouacked in the bush veldt, I was going round the outposts, which was part of my work as DAAG of the Division. When inspecting the section occupied by the 6th Imperial Bushmen, I came across my scout, Pym, lying behind a rock smoking: apparently no regulation outpost line had been made. I asked him why he was there and whether he was sentry or what? Without getting up, he replied: 'I am all your bloody outpost regulations turned into one,' and continued peremptorily, 'Get off and lie alongside of me, and we will have some fun' – which I did. As I have mentioned Pym (the newly converted Christian) was in appearance exactly like 'Captain Kettle', with red hair and scrubby beard. His knowledge of scoutcraft was amazing, and he had the greatest contempt for our military authorities and regulations.

When I had crept alongside of him, I inquired what the devil he was doing. All he said was: 'Wait till the fun begins. Don't speak.' The Lancers Cavalry Brigade continued the outpost line to our right, and presently Pym pointed out a small reconnoitring patrol of Boers some two miles away. When they dismounted, Pym crawled through the long grass into a kopje overlooking a ravine, some 200 yards to our right, telling me to stop where I was. In about an hour he fired four shots in rapid succession, and I saw two Boers scampering over the veldt away from the kopje. He stood and beckoned me to come up, and, within 300 yards at the bottom of the ravine, lay four dead Boers. Pym then said in a nonchalant way, 'Now I am going to have my dinner with the Squadron.' When I replied, 'Where is the sixth Bushmen Outpost Line?' he became abusive. 'Didn't I tell you I was the outpost line? I have done more than all your English "Ostrich" soldiers, and saved some of their lives – these Boers were stalking the vedette [advance mounted sentry] post of Lancers up there on the right. Look, you can see the whole of their line from here. Don't try to teach me anything about war; that's my trade. I have been in all of them since Wolseley's Red River Expedition.' And so he had.

We found his squadron dismounted in a hollow, and I tactfully asked the Commanding Officer where he was going to put his outpost line, never hinting that he had omitted to carry out orders, for they should have been posted at dawn and it was now early afternoon.

I only give this incident to show how extraordinarily hard it was to deal with these first contingents of bushmen. Some of them had never been in a train or seen the sea or any vast expanse of water before they sailed from Australia. They were entirely without discipline. Their language was terrific, but they were mighty good fellows, and quite fearless.

It was now guerrilla warfare, as all Boer Commands had been broken up. We dashed about South Africa, burning crops and confiscating anything that might be useful to the enemy. The old yeomen and bushmen were going home and being replaced by miserably trained men who could neither ride nor shoot, yet were stouthearted, decent people.

I pointed out officially to the authorities what a great risk and danger these men were, and prophetically explained that if the Boers galloped in open order at one of our convoys in the open veldt many disasters would occur. I pressed home my views to the best of my power, but without result, though Hubert Gough, David Campbell and Maxwell well realised the danger. Little did I realise then that Lord Methuen's column would be one of the victims.

We had an interesting trek through the Bechuanaland Desert towards Kuruman, starting from Vryburg. The Yeomanry asked if they might have a dance the night before we marched. Leave being granted, they had a real beano. At 2 a.m. I ordered the officers to prepare their units, and to march at 6 a.m. I was now Acting Chief Staff Officer of the column, and seeing that many of the officers had drunk far too much, the order was given that water bottles had not to be touched till mid-day halt.

The only reliable maps were Jeppes, but reconnaissances and our Intelligence assured us that there was a good pan of water some twelve miles from Vryburg, near Geluk. When we reached this pan, men were allowed to finish their water bottles, but most had disobeyed, and those officers who had drunk heavily overnight were parched with thirst.

The third day out there was only very muddy water to drink. All ranks had been ordered not to drink any water unless it was boiled. As I was passing the Yeomanry, I talked to several of the officers, including Stephen Wombwell, and they told me that both officers and men were so exhausted with thirst that they had drunk out of some of the filthy pans of water we had passed. The consequences were bad, for soon they were seized with terrible gripes and most died, including Stephen Wombwell. On Jeppes map there was a big pan marked near Rietvlei, which we reached about 3 p.m., but the pan was quite dry, with no water anywhere. The troops and animals were dying of thirst, and we were indeed in a desperate plight. This was the only occasion during the whole time I was with Lord Methuen (eleven years) that he got angry with me – and properly angry he was. We had had a long march in burning heat, so all ranks were distressed.

Warwick and I pushed forward with a patrol of Australians to search for water, and at a little distance we saw a native, with a small pot on her head and another on her huge behind. We dismounted and watched her walk over the desert to what seemed on our arrival a dry spruit.

When she started back for the native reserve, we found both her pails full of decent water. We rushed to the place, and when the engineers arrived we made a dam with sufficient to allow half a pint per man. We carried on watering all night. Many of the men were mad with thirst, and we had to have a strong-armed picket to hold the men away. Mercifully, the understream kept going and by noon the next day all men and animals had sufficient to keep them alive.

During the trek, when passing through a native reserve in the Kuruman District, the native people reported that the Great White Queen (Queen Victoria) was dead. It was a complete mystery to us all how they had received the information, for we were ten days' march from any civilised region, and the official news did not reach us till a fortnight after the natives had told us. The most uncanny thing was that the Queen had not been dead a week by the time they gave us the information. No South African or Colonial could throw any light as to how this information had reached them.

The scrub is covered with water melons, which the natives relish, but they soon give the white man colic. A deadly poisonous weed called tulp which grew in profusion was responsible for the death of a number of animals. We passed through the native reserves around Kuruman, and then trekked north to the Mashowing river and back to Vryburg.

It was one of the hardest marches conceivable, and both men and animals suffered terribly from thirst. All of us were lousy, for we were not able to have a bath or wash for over five weeks. One day I saw two yeomen sitting on an antbear hole picking at one another's backs, like monkeys. One of them remarked: 'Just fancy, me with ten thousand a year, having to get you, Sandy, to pick bugs off my back.' The speaker was Andy Coats, brother of Lord Glentanar, and the other a very rich man named Clark, a Glasgow cotton spinner.

PYM AND THE STOLEN HORSES

When the old yeomanry, plus the Australians, New Zealanders and Colonials, were about to be broken up, there was a huge concentration of their horses at Warrenton. For some time past there had been thefts of horses at various camps, particularly at night and when they were out grazing on the veldt. Lord Kitchener asked Lord Methuen to try to discover how these wholesale thefts were being carried out. On one night the Notts Yeomanry lost most of their officers' best chargers, and others suffered severely. The Australian and New Zealand horses were mostly the personal property of the men, and many of the yeomanry chargers were very valuable animals. Lord Methuen ordered me to take the matter in hand, and to report my success or otherwise to Kitchener's Chief of Staff. Altogether about 500 horses had been stolen. It was an extraordinarily difficult job, for these thefts had been going on for a long time, and many of the losses were not reported until days after they had occurred because many of the English commanding officers had the men tried by court martial when they lost their horses, making the men unwilling to admit they were gone.

I was given an absolutely free hand by the authorities. I collected the chief members of my old gang, with Pym (Captain Kettle) as my Chief Intelligence Officer, and Skin-the-Goat, Isaac and Jacob in charge of a troop of Basutos and Zulus, all picked riders and scouts. I was given authority to offer the natives £2 for every horse recovered. For some time we could not get a trace of any of the horses. Then the headman of the Vereeniging natives reported that a big mob of horses had been seen moving in the direction of Kimberley, on the east of the railway, driven by some Cape boys and a few white men.

A curiously marked 'schimmel' stallion, which was half piebald and had belonged to one of the Australian contingents, was reported as being ridden by one of the whites in charge of the mob. So we knew that they must be a part of the stolen contingent. The native troop, under Skin-the-Goat, were not allowed to carry any firearms, but they had a large assortment of knobkerries, assegais and spears, and in the dusk, when we started on this most exciting hunt, they looked like a troop of lancers. I intended to use them solely for rounding up and capturing the horses, whilst the party of thirty picked Colonials and bushmen dealt with the white men. After a lot of discussion, we decided that each white man should be armed with two revolvers and a lasso rope, which was already in use to strap a waterproof rug to the front of the man's saddle.

Secrecy being of paramount importance, the men were not fitted out for the expedition until an hour before starting, when each man was given a nosebag containing antelope biltong, three army biscuits, and two cakes of slab chocolate. Instead of attempting any military formation, I explained to the natives and picked Colonials that the former would act as a pack of hounds and the latter as the field, whilst my role would be that of the huntsman. We were all superbly mounted. I had my beloved Zip and another thoroughbred Basuto pony, and altogether we had fifteen spare horses under the charge of the half-caste Chapman. Our latest intelligence was that our 'prey' had reached Zwart Kop, some twenty-five miles from Kimberley. So there was no time to be lost. I took the precaution before starting to ask headquarters to send a plenipotentiary representative to Kimberley, and to my joy Kitchener sent Frankie Maxwell, for the General and staff at Kimberley were well-known incompetents who had spent most of their time in the Kimberley Club, his troops being nicknamed 'Settle's Circus'. I was well rewarded for the provision.

I calculated that a successful capture would entail our travelling at least sixty miles at speed, and was informed that there was good water between Zwart and Baken Kop, the latter being ten miles to the north east of Kimberley.

The natives (hounds) started at 5 p.m., an hour before the soldiers (the field), and a more exciting hunt no man ever enjoyed. I gave Skin-the-Goat Boesman's Kop as our first rendezvous, about fifteen miles from Warrenton, and we reached this place an hour before dawn to find the hounds in the greatest glee, for they had located the quarry on the northern foot of Baken Kop – hundreds of horses, as they described them. But the white escort was evidently larger than had been hitherto reported. Pym, Bloody Bill, Skin-the-Goat, Schofield and ten natives volunteered to push forward to ascertain the exact situation, whilst the remainder rested in a deep donga at the foot of Zwart Kop, twenty-five to thirty miles from Kimberley. As we had no rifles, it was futile to take military precautions such as an outpost line, which would only attract the attention of passing Boer patrols. So I gave orders that, should we be attacked, not a shot was to be fired till the enemy came to close quarters.

I chose a spot for our resting place where the spruit made a sharp zigzag bend. I plugged each end of the zigzag with white men, and the centre with natives who also provided watchmen; for it is astonishing the distance African natives can see and hear. It was midday before I awoke, to find everyone sound asleep, including the watchmen. On my having woken the latter, they noticed some asvogels [vultures] showing signs that they had been disturbed some miles to the south east of our resting place. Isaac and Jacob both thought this must portend that Boers were in that vicinity, so I woke up the men and waited for developments. I can only describe the hours that passed till dusk came as excruciatingly exciting, for nothing further was seen of Pym's party. I gave them up for lost. Just as the stars began to appear a native was seen worming himself through the high veldt grass. He was Skin-the-Goat himself; he soon gave me a detailed description of our quarry's whereabouts, and said that there were no more than five or six white men with the horses, the remainder having ridden into Kimberley. He accurately summed up the situation, at once begging me to push forward with all speed, overcome the escort, and round up the horses. We could be well on the road to Kimberley before daylight and the return of the remainder of the escort from their carouse in Kimberley.

As soon as it was quite dark, Skin-the-Goat returned with the remainder of his natives to Pym. He gave me the direction by a star, and we were soon following him at a Boer amble [slow canter]. Pym and Bloody Bill met us on our arrival at the foot of Baken Kop, and immediately I realised that something crucial had occurred, for they both gripped me by the hand and almost hugged me with joy. It was pitch dark as they took me on foot down a deep spruit – you could hardly see your hand before your face. We soon came across the natives sitting round a fire, and I noticed many strange faces amongst them. I guessed at once that these must have been in charge of our quarry. Skin-the-Goat then reported that hundreds of horses had been captured and rounded up at a farm nearby, about a hundred yards distant.

By the light of a small lamp burning in the dorp, I saw five white men lying in the front room and heard moans coming from the kitchen. The five whites had been knobkerried and were stone dead. In the kitchen were three more whites, one of whom was mortally wounded with a spear while the other two were recovering consciousness and being nursed by two half-caste women. Luckily, they soon had recovered sufficiently to give a coherent account of how they came to be in charge of this mob of stolen horses. Knowing that Pym had been a professional horse thief in Australia, I left him and Bloody Bill to make them give a detailed account of how they came by the horses, and under whose orders they were acting, and went with the others to examine the dead. They all wore army breeches and shirts. Three were certainly Irish, from letters we found in their pockets, named O'Grady, Flanagan and Collins. Having collected all their papers, I returned to see how Pym was getting on, and found he had forced them to make a full confession, which they had signed in the names of O'Hara and Schobel. They also told us that the escort men were due back at dawn, so there was no time to be lost.

Returning to where we had left the natives in the bed of the spruit, we found Isaac and Jacob with some of the other natives kneeling round the fire as if in prayer. Bloody Bill, who hated all forms of what he called 'bloody psalm singing', greeted the prayer meeting by giving Isaac a kick on his behind, shouting 'Get up you –.' In a flash, Isaac had bludgeoned Bloody Bill and it looked as if the natives were going to turn on us, when Jacob shouted something in Basuto and they all held up their right hands in submission to me, their Baas. I ordered Skin-the-Goat to parade all the natives he could find who had been in charge of the stolen horses, and to tell them that each native would receive two pounds from the Great White Queen (the Government) for every horse that was delivered to me on the railway line some twelve miles to the westward. It was past midnight when this mass of men and horses moved off, under command of the Englishman Schofield, who was the only man I could trust not to do in the two prisoners, O'Hara and Schobel, both of whom claimed British citizenship and whose evidence was vital.

I then repaired to the farm to peruse the confession of these two rascals. Briefly, it was to the effect that their boss was a man named Jeyes (subsequently we found out that he was the brother of the owner of Jeyes Fluid), with Goldstein, Donelly and Kelly, all residents in Kimberley, as his subordinates, and that they and their confederates had deserted to the enemy from the Irish Brigade during the attack on Colenso in 1899. In conjunction with native horse thieves they had systematically stolen horses from the British lines, obliterated all marks and brands, then turned them out on the veldt within the Boer sphere of occupation, and sold them either to Boer farmers or back to the British through remount agents.

Chapman the half-caste, Isaac and Jacob, my constant attendants, were the only ones with me, and as they all claimed to know the road to Kimberley – about fourteen miles distant – I decided to ride there without delay and have Jeyes and Co. arrested before they got news of our coup.

Knowing that the Boer escort would also be returning from Kimberley, I told Isaac that we must make a wide deviation to avoid them, and he replied that if the Baas did not mind swimming a river instead of crossing the drift, he could take me to Kimberley without meeting anyone. I'll admit the ride was a most unpleasant one, for the river we swam was wide, with steep banks, and very cold. However, my beloved Zip made light of everything, and when I pulled up about 7.30 a.m. outside Cecil Rhodes's house, she appeared quite fresh. I at once went to Frankie Maxwell's room, and found him still in bed. My appearance certainly surprised him, for I had a three days' growth of beard and was wet to the skin.

After he had finished laughing at 'Pongo', as he called me, I told that we must have Jeyes & Co. arrested at once. He made out an order to the Provost Marshal to have this done forthwith. I was then shown into a luxurious bathroom and while I was wallowing in a hot bath, Frankie and the Provost Marshal were ushered in. The latter then said that he could not arrest these men, who were very prominent citizens, without the authority of the GOC. Frankie showed him the plenipotentiary order signed by the C-in-C, and again ordered him to carry out the arrest without delay. Frankie Maxwell was one of the most charming personalities – having won a VC in India when a subaltern, he became Kitchener's *fidus Achates*, boon companion and friend, and would have had a great career had he not been killed in the Great War. He was a fine horseman, sportsman, very quick-brained, and there were few better men in India after a pig. He had had the foresight to bring Marker, of the Headquarters staff with him, and sent him to report the action we had taken to GOC, General Settle.

A very promiscuous kit and dry underclothing were sent to the bathroom by Cecil Rhodes. I have never seen people laugh more than when I appeared in the breakfast room about 10 a.m. – Willoughby, Dr Jim and Mitchell were there besides Cecil Rhodes, Frankie and Marker. Soon after we had finished, an order came from General Settle that he wished to see me at once. This was quite impossible in my present kit, for I had three reefs in Cecil Rhodes's trousers, and the coat and other garments were sizes too big. Frankie said he would go to explain, and that I had better go to bed until my clothes were dry. Never did a man sleep more soundly, for I had not had a wink of real sleep for three days and had ridden over sixty miles.

It was a heavenly awakening, for C.R.'s own valet brought me a tray of tea and the most luscious fruit procurable, with some new washing material, toothbrush and shaving kit. About 5 p.m. Frankie and Marker appeared, and I at once realised from their faces that trouble was on the tapis.

Frankie, whom I knew to be one of my best friends, assumed an official tone and said: 'I have had a long interview with General Settle, and he is convinced that you have made a terrible blunder, and have let us all down terribly. Do you realise that Jeyes, Donelly and Kelly are very well known people in Kimberley, and no one has had cause to question their loyalty or integrity, and Cecil Rhodes says they did their duty in the siege, and he knows them all very well. The General wishes you to go at once to explain your action, and I don't know what on earth I can say to the C-in-C.' Frankie was thoroughly perturbed and upset as we walked to the General's office.

On being ushered in, there was the General with his CSO (whom we knew as 'the Goat'), the Remount Officer, Provost Marshal, and a man in mufti who looked like a lawyer. The General began: 'I have telegraphed to Lord Methuen that there is not a particle of evidence against these gentlemen, whom you have caused to be arrested, and by my order they will be released at once.' He would not listen to any statement or explanation I had to make, and having made some scathing remarks as to my unworthiness to hold the high appointment of DAAG 1st Division, he sent me out of the room.

After dinner at Cecil Rhodes's, I asked him if I might see him for a few minutes. I told him every detail of our exploit and showed him the confession of the two survivors, O'Hara and Schobel. I also showed him the letters I had taken from the bodies of the five Irishmen. He then called in Dr Jim, who when perusing the letters exclaimed, 'Why, here is one addressed to Jeyes himself.' This, still wet through, I had mislaid in the corner of my pocket. Dr Jim and I had struck up a great friendship in Ladysmith, and he at once took up the cudgels in my favour and begged the Great Man to wire his view of the case to Lord Methuen. They were anxious moments for me, whilst he cogitated with his hand on his chin without saying a word, and then wrote out a wire to Lord Methuen: 'I believe Tilney is right.' He instructed me to ask for an interview with General Settle the following morning, and to tell him exactly what I had said to him, also to show him the letters I had taken from the Irishmen's bodies.

The same people were present at this interview, except that the lawyer brought in a colleague who stated they were representatives of the accused. The General's sanction of their presence at this stage appeared to be thoroughly unjust and wrong. However, I took the bull by the horns, showed him all the letters, and gave a full account of what had happened. He actually allowed the elder lawyer to intervene, with the remark 'You, Captain Tilney, will probably be tried for the murder of these five poor Irishmen, who belonged to the Remount Establishment. Captain Fenn [the Remount Officer] has examined all the horses you brought in, and none of them has a Government mark or brand. They were horses belonging to Mr Jeyes and were being brought from his farm for sale at the British Government's request.' This was, indeed, a nice facer and I left the Office in the deepest gloom.

On my return to Cecil Rhodes's, I met Frankie, the real true friend, who told me that he had had a long talk with C.R. and Dr Jim, and that he would do anything to help me. I asked him to wire Colonel Belfield, CSO 1st Division, to send for the captured horses without delay, with a view to holding an identification parade at Warrenton by the Yeomanry, Australians, New Zealanders and Colonials, and that I was returning that night.

On my arrival, Lord Methuen and Colonel Belfield were most sympathetic, and on the following day the identification parade took place. Over 300 horses had been brought in, but Jeyes & Co.'s legal representatives insisted upon various miscellaneous animals being mixed up with the contingent – horses direct from the veldt and from the Remount Depots. In all there were over 500 animals. Luckily, Lord Chesham, Minor Lawson, Eric Smith, Anderson and other old Yeomen had not left for home and on this occasion they were invaluable witnesses. The rank and file made blunder after blunder in claiming horses as their own that could not possibly have belonged to them. The Australians were dead certain about some fifty, and one New Zealander recognised the horse he had taught various tricks, which the animal performed before us all. Lord Chesham also recognised a horse which had belonged to 'Gaudy Wood' who had been killed near Ottoshoep, and which would lay down at command. However, not a brand or any identification mark could be discovered on any of the horses, and the schimmel stallion that any of the Australians could have sworn to was missing. As the parade proceeded, I pictured myself being tried by a GCM for the murder of the five Irishmen, the loss of my commission, and various other forms of disgrace.

At the end of the parade Jeyes & Co.'s legal representatives demanded a trial in a civil court to vindicate aspersions that had been made upon their characters, and asked that disciplinary action should be taken against me for killing five of Jeyes's employees and maiming two. Everyone, including Lord Methuen, the Yeomanry and Colonial COs was most kind and sympathetic to me after we had finished the parade, but none could bring absolutely conclusive proof that any particular horse had been his property. That night I was indeed in the deepest gloom, for I was the youngest DAAG in the Army and had envisaged a successful future. Now everything appeared lost.

Just as I was going to bed, Pym appeared and asked for a few minutes' conversation. He bluntly told me that he could prove beyond any doubt that these were horses stolen from the British lines, although none of the Yeomen in particular could recognise the animals that had formerly been their property. He demanded the sum of £500 from the Government if his evidence and help brought about a conviction of the thieves, and I told him I would give him a definite answer in the morning. He would not divulge his secret on any account even when interviewed by Lord Methuen, but replied: 'Wait till the case is tried, and I will then tell and convince the court.'

Well, the case came on for trial at Vryburg, Headquarters sending down a Crown counsel who hardly knew the difference between a horse that had been bred on the veldt, a Waler or an Arab. The first day our case appeared hopeless, and there were a host of hostile witnesses who told the court the life history of many of the better-looking animals. On the second day I obtained authority from Headquarters to be relieved of the Crown counsel's advice and help, and to be allowed to conclude the case myself. Jeyes & Co. were now the prosecutors. When their counsel had addressed the jury, to everyone's surprise I got up and told the magistrate and jury that I could conclusively prove, in five minutes, that these horses had been stolen from the British lines, if they would come outside.

Pym was in waiting with a score of the animals, and I had arranged with Colonel (now Sir Herbert) Belfield that immediately Pym had given his demonstration the GOC Kimberley should be ordered to arrest Jeyes and his confederates. On my telling the magistrate to select a particular horse at random, Pym then produced a bottle of some mysterious liquid, which he rubbed on the the horse's flank, and immediately I.Y. became visible; the others being treated in a similar manner, there was no doubt left as to the guilt of Messrs. Jeyes & Co. These gentlemen were tried in Kimberley and sentenced to two years' imprisonment with hard labour, but Goldstein and another had escaped to foreign climes. I was informed that the authorities subsequently recovered many hundreds of horses that his gang had stolen from the British and had hidden in out-of-the-way districts of the Transvaal and Orange Free State.

Pym got his £500 and, as I have related elsewhere, became a Christian gentleman, and was finally lost or killed in the Russo-Japanese War. My natives also reaped a rich reward.

At the commencement of the trial when I had arranged with the authorities to dispense with the services of the official Crown counsel, a private in the 6th Australian Bushmen, whom Oxley at the 6th Imperial Bushmen informed me was one of the cleverest horse-thieving lawyers in Australia, was appointed in his place. The trial lasted about three weeks, during which time I was the guest of Cecil Rhodes. The night after these rascals were convicted, Mrs Jeyes came to see me offering herself and everything she held dearest to me if I would get the sentence on her husband reduced. I sent for the Australian lawyer Cummins. He told her that if Jeyes would disclose the names of all of his accomplices, and inform the authorities of the whereabouts of any more stolen horses, that he would forward a recommendation for the remission of part of the sentence to Headquarters. Mrs Jeyes was an exceedingly beautiful woman, apparently of easy virtue, and belonged to the upper class of Kimberley society. Having made some bold advance to Cummins, whilst I was out of the room, she took him off to dinner. The sequel was a full confession from Jeyes, the recovery of hundreds of horses, and the capture and imprisonment of the heads of this organisation throughout South Africa.

After the conviction of Jeyes & Co, I resumed my duties of DAAG 1st Division with Lord Methuen, whilst Cummins carried on the capture and prosecution of the directors of this vast horse-thieving company. Cummins told me that the defence in these trials claimed that brands on many of the Waler horses which had been recovered could never have been feloniously obliterated, so Pym gave a demonstration how this could be effected. With a cooking salamander, heated to a certain temperature, he blistered the old brand to a bubble and then either rebranded or 'ironed' the blister flat with a hand iron. When the hair regrew, nothing was to be seen of the original brand. Most of the English horses were marked on the hoof, which quickly grew out, so the above faking was only necessary on the Colonial animals.

CAPTURE AND DEATH OF ISAAC

I pointed out to the high authorities what a danger it was to take the freshly recruited, scarcely trained men 'on trek'. But there was no better material available. So before some of the best Colonials had departed for home Lord Methuen gave them a trial outing through the lead mines north of Lichtenburg. We had plenty of hardship and excitement and heard that De La Rey had collected a Commando of some 3,000 men, who were raiding and capturing all our isolated posts eastwards.

Soon after we got back to the Mafeking-Kimberley railway lines, we heard of many disasters south of Krugersdorp and Johannesburg, so Headquarters decided to break up three Boer Commandos by converging columns. Lord Methuen's troops in Western Transvaal were reinforced by the riffraff of General Settle, who commanded at Kimberley. These troops, nicknamed 'Settle's Circus' as I have mentioned, had been employed in convoy duty for a long time and had never seen really severe fighting, although they had been allotted various honours for peaceful campaigning around Kimberley. As our column left the railway line to march towards Lichtenburg, the Kimberley Light Horse formed our rearguard.

No words could exaggerate Lord Methuen's heroic and patriotic gallantry at this time. Kitchener had explained at length to him the peril of the British situation. Before Lord Methuen started on this – our last – trek, he opened his heart to Warwick and myself about the prospect of marching with these untrained and (in the case of the Kimberley contingent) rotten troops. The PMO, Colonel Townsend, and myself were the only two remaining of his original staff. I had never missed a day since I joined his staff after Ladysmith.

That night before we marched, he called me into his room and fully explained his forebodings of disaster. 'We can't do more than our best with the material I have and K. says that it is imperative to smash up De La Rey's Commando.'

'May God be with us' were the last words, as he went to bed.

We had been going only about three hours from Vryburg when some of the Kimberley Light Horse and new Yeomen galloped back from the rearguard to say they were heavily attacked. Lord Methuen sent me back to report on the situation. I found that only a few snipers had attacked the right flank guard, who at once bolted into the main body. I noticed that some of the men were so scared that they couldn't load their rifles and some few Boers actually rode to within 500 yards without being hit. Lord Methuen, Warwick, Beranger and myself had a conference that night. As I was Chief Staff Officer, Lord Methuen ordered that I should see to it that the Yeomanry should form the rearguard. After the second day, we all realised the great peril of the situation, for the Yeomanry – gallant fellows that they were – could not hit a haystack. Lord Methuen hoped that when we reached the plateau north of the de Klip Drift, the enemy would not attack us in force, as the ground was as flat as a billiard table. Having got over the Drift, we bivouacked at the base of the plateau, the top of which we held with the infantry. My Basutos, Isaac and Jacob, were still with me and that night I sent them to a pan to get some wild fowl. They soon came back, with the report that a large body of Boers was lying in the rough country to the south.

At the conference that night, I advocated starting at once to gain the plateau. But it was then dark and the others agreed with Lord Methuen that the columns should move on, an hour before daylight, to allow the rear troops an opportunity to clear our bivouac. At dawn the next day I was riding alongside Lord Methuen, who was as usual walking on foot, when we heard firing near the site of our late bivouac. He ordered me to gallop back to see what was happening.

When I arrived almost at the edge of the plateau, I saw a swarm of mounted men galloping in open order towards our rearguard, the OC of which ordered his men to dismount and fire.

I was riding my beloved pony Zip. When the Boers were not 100 yards away, I turned back at top speed and to tell Lord Methuen what was happening. He was as cool as if on a Horse Guards Parade and ordered me to send the Northumberland Fusiliers to a kopje on our right and Colonel Paris with his troops to hold a stone kraal to our left and to get the whole column closed up.

Having carried out the first two missions, I was getting the wagons closed up, to laager, when some Boers came galloping down the line of wagons, firing, and knocked over our PMO, Colonel Townsend. Mixed up with the Boers were our riffraff troops. I reached Lord Methuen at the front of the kopje, which was then occupied by the Northumberland Fusiliers. He ordered David Mitford (now Lord Redesdale) and myself to endeavour to stop the rout. I did everything humanly possible, but the men were so terrified and panic-stricken that they paid no attention even when I held a revolver at their heads. I managed to rally some fifty men and held on to a piece of slightly rising ground, until our ammunition was exhausted, when I tried to get down to the kraal still held by Paris's men. On my way five men in khaki galloped at me and seized my bridle, which came off. Ramming my spurs into Zip, I flew towards the kopje, where Zip was wounded. I was taken prisoner with a slight wound. It was only through a miracle that my body was not riddled with bullets, for the doctors counted eleven holes through my clothing when I got to the line at Maritzani. Isaac was by my side throughout the rout as he always rode my second horse on the line of march in action, and when I was brought down and taken prisoner he stayed with me. I was taken before De La Rey's Chief of Staff and closely questioned, but managed to get through the ordeal very happily by taking Jorrocks's advice that 'bees make honey'. They questioned me closely about the raids and reconnaissances I had conducted, and asked me if I knew the whereabouts of Schofield, alias Curtis, whom I have previously mentioned several times as one of my gang and an extraordinary runner. This was a facer, for I had seen him with Warwick's Scouts when we struck camp and knew he would not be with the mob of mounted men who had bolted. I said he had gone home when my troop was broken up some months ago.

The meeting was interrupted by the arrival of De La Rey, who, much to my surprise, treated me in the most courteous manner and asked me to take charge of the wounded. He would not allow me to see him but said Lord Methuen was dangerously wounded through the thigh and was not expected to live. De La Rey promised that every care would be taken to have him sent comfortably to the railway line. He said there were no doctors, nurses or medical outfit, so I asked to see Colonel Townsend, our PMO, who had been badly wounded when the Boers galloped into the convoy. The wounded were all laid out on the open veldt. As poor Townsend was too bad to offer any advice or help, I asked the Boer Staff officer to send some men to help. I must admit that they showed the greatest kindness to our men.

It was now early afternoon and as I was organising some means of preventing the wounded from dying of cold during the night, my old servant Bardens, 17th Lancers, who had been with me all through Ladysmith and the South Africa campaign, tugged me by the sleeve and said, 'They are going to shoot old Isaac.' Bardens was helping me with the wounded and it was not until this moment that I noticed he had had his eye shot out – he was just going about as if nothing had happened. I rushed towards a squad of Boers, who had already shot a number of natives – for they had a lot more rounded up – and begged that Isaac's life might be spared. My vehemence was such that three men took me to see the staff officer who had interrogated me, and who spoke English well. I told him that Isaac had never carried arms and had only been my 'riding boy', but he only replied that all natives caught with the English were always summarily shot and that there was no hope of saving his life. So I went back to the firing party and Isaac was brought out. When I begged the firing party not to shoot, Isaac said, 'Don't stop them, Baas, for I shall see my dear Lord now', and looking up to Heaven, he said 'Goodbye, Baas, will you take this?' and gave me a tin cigarette case – which I still have. The next moment, whilst he said 'My Jesus, receive me into Thy Kingdom', he was riddled with bullets. I was thoroughly overcome at the death of this magnificent brave man, who had saved my life on two separate occasions.

On returning to the wounded, I found David Mitford with a terrible wound through the centre of his chest, fountains of blood spurting out with every respiration. As there were no medical stores, I plugged the hole with a bit of shirt soaked in permanganate which prevented him from bleeding to death. But there appeared at the time little hope that his life would be saved.

To my consternation, I saw Schofield, whom the Boers had asked about and for whom they had offered a reward of a large sum, dead or alive. He was fortunately wounded and in a coma. I was employed at the moment in making a list of the wounded, so the Boers who were accompanying me did not find out his name.

Bloody Bill, the Australian, who had been in my gang from its inception, was lying on his back perfectly calm, conscious and collected, with a pom-pom shell in his stomach. He asked me to gather round him every man who could walk, as he wanted to say something to them.

It was an awful evening and night, for all those men who had not been wounded in the fight, and those who had been in the rout, were hunted down and shot. That night I made a soup for the wounded out of horse flesh, mealies and biltong. As there were no blankets we bedded up the wounded with clothing stripped from the dead.

The next day I asked again to be allowed to see Lord Methuen, but was told that he was being sent away and that a convoy would arrive that day and take us to the Mafeking line at Maritzani.[22] When I returned to the wounded, Bloody Bill again implored me to bring every man who could walk to hear what he had to say, and as he was quite conscious, I did so. He then told us that he had scoffed at Christ and everything good all his life, and now he knew that the story of Christ was true. He had been told how Isaac had met his death and said: 'Jesus will let me live for three days, to tell you all I now know about our kind Saviour, so when we halt, come round to hear what I have to tell you.'

On the arrival of the ox wagons the next day, we started our three days' trek to the railway line at Maritzani, passing scores of our dead en route, all stripped naked. Each evening when we halted to outspan, we collected around Bloody Bill to hear his wonderful words. On the third day he was perfectly conscious, although he had had nothing but water. The remainder of the wounded had had to subsist solely on soup made from horse-flesh and mealies. By the time we had reached Maritzani we had buried half the badly wounded men including Bloody Bill, who died the evening of the third day. By then I knew that he had been much troubled when he heard that Isaac was to be shot and had asked the Boers if he might be allowed to see him before the execution. Some kind-hearted Boers brought Isaac to see the man who had always been nagging and chaffing him for being a Christian. Bardens told me afterwards that the meeting of these two men, one about to be shot and the other about to die, was most affecting. Frankie Maxwell, ADC to Kitchener, met me at Maritzani, bringing a letter from the Chief of Staff congratulating me on my behaviour at de Klip's Drift. The letter said I was to be made Chief Staff Officer of the Western Transvaal for my services, and that I was to take the first opportunity to come up and see the C-in-C, Lord Kitchener. This I did, after about a fortnight, and stayed with him for three happy days. He was most kind and questioned me closely as to how the disaster had happened. I told him that the troops supplied to Lord Methuen were in every sense untrained, could not shoot, and some had not been taught to load their rifles, and that the Boers simply galloped through them as if they were a flock of sheep. He had heard how I rallied 'some hundred men' and held the hill ground to the south of the kopje, where Lord Methuen was wounded, till our ammunition was exhausted. I claimed that with one squadron

---

22 The Boers did not keep prisoners. At this stage in the war natives were shot and whites, having been deprived of their weapons and sometimes their clothes, would be left by the railway line.

of good cavalry we could have charged from this position and routed the enemy. This projected idea seemed to please the staff very much and in the evening the Chief of Staff said that my name had been sent to London for a brevet, with a personal recommendation from the C-in-C.

An awkward incident occurred the first night of my stay in the C-in-C's house. I was given an excellent bedroom on the ground floor and much looked forward to a real rest, for I had rarely slept in a bed for almost two years. At dawn I woke after a heavy sleep, thinking that I had smallpox, scarlet fever or some other dire ailment, for I was itching all over my head and body. After lighting a candle, I looked at my face with much difficulty, for both my eyes were almost completely closed. Feeling all right in myself, I went to bed again, but not for long for the itching was impossible to bear. It was now daylight and putting on an overcoat, I slept till breakfast on the verandah.

On returning to my room, I happened to look at my pillow and saw two red bugs. Further inspection revealed hundreds of these beasts. When I came down to breakfast, some of the staff remarked on my appearance and suggested my seeing the doctor. When I said that Doctor Keating was the only one I wished to see, Birdwood had my room thoroughly disinfected and made extra comfortable. In fact they were all most kind.

HOMEWARD BOUND WITH LORD METHUEN

On reaching the railway line, I received a telegram ordering me to proceed to Vryburg as Chief Staff Officer to Sir John Maxwell ('Conchie'). The new Militia were placed under his command and put into the Blackhouse line.

In a few months 'suicide mania' broke out amongst these troops and grew to such an alarming degree that the General (Conchie) sent for all the COs and ordered that all men who committed suicide should be buried without any military funeral or ceremony. When I pointed out to him afterwards that if this got into the English papers there would be a real good row in Parliament, he said he didn't mind, and this was the only way to stop the mania. Our CO protested with the utmost vehemence, so Conchie sent him back home by the next train. The General and I became great friends and he promised that if I remained with him till the end of the war he would arrange for me to go to the Staff College, which was all I wanted. One day Kitchener's ADC came to ask if I would go to Johannesburg to see Lord Methuen, who was dangerously ill in hospital, and accompany him home, as peace would be proclaimed shortly if the Vereeniging conference was successful. So off I had to go, and found on my arrival at Johannesburg that Lord Methuen's thigh had not united and he was in excruciating agony, which he bore with admirable fortitude.

After a while Lord Kitchener sent for me to say that peace had been signed at Vereeniging and that I could tell Lord Methuen in the strictest secrecy, as the news would not be published for a week. Two days before its publication, the Dale Laces gave a magnificent ball in Johannesburg, all the big bugs of Africa being present. I was so pestered with questions – chiefly by the Jews – as to the probability of peace that I had to leave the ball.

Whilst Lord Methuen was recuperating sufficiently in Johannesburg to allow him to travel to Cape Town, I took Lady Methuen down to visit Ladysmith. We had a reserved carriage, but at one of the stations an Irishman named Cullinan got in. He was very voluble about a diamond mine he had discovered and offered us shares in the mine at 2/6d per share. We British officers had been so often swindled before that I persuaded Lady Methuen not to touch the project. Cullinan showed us a small bag of what looked to be wonderful diamonds and implored us to believe in his veracity. We parted at Ladysmith and didn't hear his name again until the great Cullinan mine had been exploited and one of his diamonds sent to the King to be put in the Imperial Crown! Had we accepted Cullinan's offer at the time, we would have made a mint of money. Such is fate.

At Ladysmith we went over the ground where the British cavalry should have pursued the enemy after the last Battle of Colenso and found it quite practicable for cavalry. Generals Burn, Murdoch and Buller were severely criticised for not following up the Boers; but it was Altham and his intelligence staff who were were responsible for this, as they reported the ground to be impossible for cavalry.

Lord Methuen was still in the severest agony when we reached Cape Town, so we stayed there a time and I had opportunities of meeting most of the key South African and Boer generals. The High Commissioner gave a dinner to commemorate the armistice and peace. I was invited and sat between Villiers (afterwards Lord Chief Justice) and Struben.

On our voyage home we touched at Madeira. Lady Methuen landed to see the cathedral, which was reported to contain the heart of St John. The head priest was a charming old fellow. When Prentice, Lord

Methuen's doctor, examined the reputed saint's heart, he found that it had been recently preserved and mummified and told the old priest so, before all of us. The priest frankly admitted that it was a fake, yet it was a much worshipped and venerated relic. The poor RCs truly believed the lies that the priest told them.

Lord Methuen was taken to Corsham, his thigh not having united. He was still in great pain and I was there for some time answering correspondence and dealing with other business until an order came for me to rejoin the 17th at Edinburgh.

A short time before I was married, I was offered second-in-command of the Aeronautical Training School at Farnborough and went to my prospective father-in-law, in high glee, to announce my good luck. He replied shortly: 'You'll either stay on the earth and marry my daughter or accept that air appointment and go to hell.' So I gave up the air and married his daughter.

About this time a conference of all the men interested in aeronautical development was held at the Agricultural Hall, Islington. There most of those the world looked upon as madmen were present, including Santos Dumont, Blériot, Cody,[23] Maxim, one of the Wrights, Templer Short and Spencer. Heath, myself, Mellor and Grubb represented the British Army. A more interesting day to look back upon could not be imagined. A Frenchman had a model heavier-than-air machine, with box-kite-shaped wings and a propeller spun with a spring. He succeeded in making it fly almost the length of the Agricultural Hall. Those interested in the making of balloons, such as the Spencers and Shorts, proved by aero-dynamics – apparently to everyone's satisfaction – that a heavier-than-air machine was an impossible project, yet within five years the Wright brothers had made their first successful flight.

23 Cody's flying machine was the first powered aeroplane to fly in Britain in October 1908.

Part III

HYLDA ENTERS MY LIFE

At the end of 1902 I was married at Sutton Bonington to the noblest and best girl in the land. We had a hunting honeymoon in Yorkshire and Leicestershire from Bob Vyner's at Newby and the Zetlands at Aske, and then settled for the remainder of our leave at Sutton. We had a great fortnight at Aske, driving to the meets in an open brake with four horses, two postilions. I shot on all non-hunting days. Lord Zetland always said this was the best fortnight's hunting he ever had, for we had a good run every time we went out.

When I rejoined the 17th at Edinburgh, the comic side of soldiering began. Lawrence, who had commanded the 16th Lancers in South Africa, was now in command of the 17th. Everyone imagined that this brilliant soldier would remain our colonel for the duration of his command. This was not the War Office plan, for Haig superseded him.[1] Lawrence sent in his papers at once in high dudgeon – naturally so, since he had done brilliantly during the South African War and had passed the Staff College, and all expected him to succeed to the command of the Regiment.

Worse was to follow for those officers who had conscientiously gone through the war. An edict went out from the War Office that those who had been promoted on the field had to pass their promotion exams at once, although we had not had an opportunity of studying a book for two or, in my case, four years. This order drove some of the best officers

---

1 Douglas Haig (1861–1928). In 1885 he joined the 7th Hussars. Nominated to serve with the Egyptian Army in 1888. During the Boer War he went to Natal on the staff and was present during the opening engagements near Ladysmith. At the conclusion of the Boer War he commanded the 17th Lancers for a year. He then went to India as Inspector General of Cavalry. Between 1906-9 he was a Director in the War Office. From 1909-12 he became Chief of General Staff in India. In 1912 he was brought home to take command at Aldershot. Knighted in 1913, at the outbreak of the First World War in 1914 he commanded the 1st Army Corps, which he led at Mons, Marne and Aisne and the 1st battle of Ypres. Following Neuve Chapelle, Festubert and Loos he succeeded French in the chief command. For his services during the war he was created Earl Haig. On his retirement he devoted himself to the welfare of ex-servicemen and united the various organisations of ex-servicemen into the British Legion and by the sale of poppies he created a large fund for the benefit of ex-servicemen.

out of the Army. When I took my papers to 'the Colonel', Haig, he wrote a strong memorandum to the War office, pointing out that I had served more days in the South African War than any other officer or man and had held the biggest staff appointments possible for my age and rank, finishing up as Chief Staff Officer, Western Transvaal. As the War Office would not relent of their folly, I went up for the exam at Berwick-on-Tweed and had the mortification of finding two members of the examining board to be officers whom we had had sent home from South Africa for incompetence, or, in the case of the board president – from one of the columns operating under Lord Methuen – for 'Mauseritis'. This disgusted me so much that I again sent in my papers. Sir Archie Hunter intervened and all was put right. and Colonel Haig put me in command of the detachment of the 17th at Glasgow.

At a mass meeting soon after this, I was re-elected captain of the polo team and interviewed by the Colonel who said, 'We must win the inter-regimental this year and I will do everything I can to help.' I asked him if he would not be captain as this was the officers' wish and that Pope and others had promised to buy some first-class ponies. He replied in his blunt way: 'If you think I am good enough to play, I will. You are responsible for winning the tournament and don't hesitate to curse me.'

Hylda and I lived in the Gordons' mess at Glasgow, Maryhill Barracks. McLean commanded the Gordons. When King Edward visited Glasgow, the Gordons had a great show in the mess, the pipers playing round the room all through dinner, so when the 17th had a similar big evening in Edinburgh we had our trumpeters, much to the amusement of everyone, but the Gordons did not relish the joke.

The Lord Provost of Glasgow happened to be a teetotaller. When the King was in Glasgow he gave a ball to which our officers went. At this ball Obby Beauclerk, who was a captain in the 17th Lancers, told one of the junior subalterns, Bunny Walmesley, to get some whiskies and soda. 'You see that man with a chain round his neck?' he said. 'Go and order three whiskies and soda.' So off went Bunny to this man, who was the Lord Provost, and said, 'The officers over there want some whiskies and soda.' When the Lord Provost showed hesitation – he was dumbfounded at the affront – Bunny said (just to show the man he was), 'Off you go and get them damned quick.' About a week afterwards, the Colonel summoned me to Edinburgh, as the Lord Provost had made an official complaint against the officers of the 17th. Having concocted an abject apology, we all enjoyed the joke for a long time and no one more than Colonel Haig.

Marching or Flying by Night Without a Compass

WITH

Time·Table of Directional Stars

COMPILED FOR
LATITUDES 40° N to 55° N

Tables for the same stars for India,
N. Africa and United States (Lats.
20° to 35° N), also for the Southern
Hemisphere (Lats. 0° to 35° S) have
been published.

by

Col. W. A. TILNEY, F.R.G.S., F.R.A.S.
late 17th LANCERS

ELEVENTH EDITION
Revised
32nd Thousand

LONDON :
HUGH REES LTD., 47, PALL MALL, S.W.
1940

Title page of eleventh edition (1940) of *Marching or Flying by Night ...*
W.A.T. began working on this booklet immediately after his return from
the Boer War.

Lord Methuen, Commanding Officer 1st Division. W.A.T. (then a major) was ADC to Lord Methuen at the Battle of Tweebosch (1901) when they were both captured by the Boers.

Two officers and Major W.A.T., mounted (c1903) in full dress uniform, with czapska (helmet), plastron (breast plate) and gauntlets. This horse has a shabrack (saddle cloth).

Ladysmith, January 1900. W.A.T. about to ascend in the basket of the
observation balloon during the siege.

From left to right: W.A.T., Hylda (riding side-saddle), unidentified friend, and Ned Tilney.

Colonel W.A.T., Regimental Commander of the 17th Lancers
at the outbreak of the First World War.

Signed photograph given to W.A.T. by Queen Mary.

ABOVE W.A.T.'s sons, Dolly (Adolphus), b. 1903, and Ned, b. 1906. BELOW The Hall, Sutton Bonington, Leicestershire, the home of Sir Ernest Paget and later of his daughter Hylda and her husband, W.A.T.

POLO COMPETITIONS AND INCIDENTS IN
THE HUNTING FIELD

The Rifle Brigade had their Indian Inter-Regimental winning team in the English Inter-Regimental this year and were excellently mounted. Pope had bought Sailor and another first-class pony for our Regimental team, but none of us could do them justice, both refused to 'ride off'. By far the best pony we had was the pony I had trained before the South African War, Lightning. Up to the tournament we went, Carden (1), self (2), Fletcher (3), Colonel Haig (back).

In the semi-final we met the Rifle Brigade (Green Jackets). When half-time came, the position looked quite hopeless, for they led by five goals. I asked the Colonel what he thought we could do to save the situation and he cryptically replied: 'Pray as hard as you can and we will win!' When there was only a chukker and a half to play, the Rifle Brigade still led by four goals, so they ordered a dinner at the Naval and Military to celebrate the apparently certain victory. In the last chukker we were two goals behind, but we then equalised the match and had to play extra time. I had told Gordon and Fletcher what the Colonel had said. For the extra chukker I brought out Lightning, who had already done three chukkers. She played like one possessed and, getting the ball at the chestnuts end of Hurlingham, we raced down to get the winning goal. This was the first English Inter-Regimental the Regiment had ever won, and there were great rejoicings.

From 1895 when I was first elected captain of the polo team I had endeavoured to instil into the team that perfect discipline in every branch of the game was vital and that the captain's orders were final. In 1898 and 1899 I had kicked out two prominent players from the team because they would not comply with my orders. At subsequent mess meetings the officers upheld my decision.

There was little real soldiering to be done in Glasgow, so Hylda and I hunted during the week with the Ayr, Linlithgow and Stirling and Duke of Buccleuch. Incredible as it may seem nowadays, we used to train from Glasgow to Loughborough for the Quorn meets on Saturday and Monday, returning in time for parade on Tuesday. Together we had six horses at Sutton and when we took our second leave for hunting we were lent thirty horses in Leicestershire, so from Sutton we had to hunt six days a week, to keep thirty-six horses in exercise.

Much amusement was caused one day with the Quorn. Frank Forrester, the Master, used to get highly excited when we had a really good run. One day when a big crowd was out, we had a great run from Ella's to Welby Fish Ponds, but we checked on the road near Six Hills and Frank Forrester came galloping down the road, shouting 'Has anyone seen the fox?' In his mad gallop he caught Hylda's horse broadside, knocking horse and rider into the ditch. Thereupon I set about him with my crop, mounted combat fashion and didn't cease belabouring him until he had helped to pick up Hylda. To show what a good fellow Frank Forrester is, he never showed me the slightest animosity or bitterness for the beating I had given him.

Arthur Lucas had one of the best studs at Melton and he asked Arthur Coventry and myself to hunt them. All except one were magnificent performers, but this chestnut neither Arthur nor myself could make jump away from the crowd; it would refuse even the smallest place, yet would follow other horses over the very biggest. When Arthur Lucas sold his horses at Tattersalls, this rotten animal fetched the, then, record price for a hunter.

That year we bought a beautiful six-year-old at the Oakley sale for £75 and thought there must be something radically wrong with it, owing to the price, for it was one of the best-looking Leicestershire hunters I have ever seen. Hylda rode it when the next season began and went right at the top of the hunt, she and this beautiful animal being the admiration of everyone. One day we ran at best pace from Six Hills, through Hoton, then straight over the Prestwold flats, between Stanford and Prestwold, and killed the fox on the river bank between Loughborough and Barrow. An American came up to me at the end of the hunt and offered me a blank cheque to any amount for the horse, which we had named Raffles.

I refused at first to sell him, but eventually said he might have a fortnight's trial and if he liked the horse I would take £350. In a week the cheque arrived, and within six weeks he offered me to take back the horse for £100, as nobody could get him over a fence. It was one of the most curious instances of hands and mouth I have ever come across. If you touched his mouth at all when going at a fence, nothing would induce him to jump, whereas if the reins were dangling on his neck he would face anything. We had him till we went to India and he never fell or refused.

Portal took command of the 17th after Haig left, and he played back in the succeeding Inter-Regimental polo, which we won fairly easily. I then went on Lord Methuen's staff in London as military secretary, he having been given the London District and Eastern Command.

Allenby and Byng had cavalry brigades, and we used to have long arguments as to the future value of aerial photography and reconnaissance: they thought balloons were useless and only Hunter Weston, who was DAAG on Lord Methuen's staff, was on my side. I always affirmed that the dirigible balloon that Templer was endeavouring to make at Farnborough would be of the utmost value – especially for aerial photography. When he suggested dropping explosive bombs from balloons, he was told that this could never happen, as it was against international law. Mellor, who was now with the Aeronautical Section RE at Aldershot, succeeded with the help of professional photographers in developing his aerial photos taken from balloons within an hour, so his project appeared to be of the utmost value in war. I arranged through the War Office to give a demonstration of its practicality at the Berkshire manoeuvres, telling the authorities of its utility at Ladysmith. Being on Lord Methuen's staff as AMS on these manoeuvres I took the heads of the War Office to see for themselves the aerial photographs. Most of the high officials appeared to be most favourably impressed and I stayed behind to congratulate Mellor. Several of us were poring over these very clear photos of a flank movement with magnifying glasses, when Mellor remarked these bloody fool brass-hatted imbeciles would not even believe this, then looking over his shoulder saw Generals Altham and Reed, who naturally had heard his remark. Mellor stupidly said, 'I am very sorry but I did not know you were there!' He was subsequently called upon to send in his papers and I met him in London in 1916, still Captain Mellor late RE. He was a real genius and the first man to develop aerial photography.

Most of the chief officers at the War office and London District had been through the South African War, so we were a very happy family.

Lord Methuen had now recovered and took up golf. To keep fit he and I used to catch the 8 a.m. train to Mitcham daily and get back to the Horse Guards by 10 a.m. for our daily work. It was a strenuous enough life for anyone. He had the Eastern Command and London District. We were fully occupied in the daytime, and had to attend many dinner parties and public functions in the evening, till late at night. I frequently marvelled at Lord Methuen's incredible energy. At the first manoeuvres we had in Berkshire, the pioneering equipment of one of the infantry brigades carried on pack mules went astray and when the brigade was attacked no entrenching tools were available. This gave me the idea of every man carrying a combined pick, spade, graffing axe, entrenching tool on his person. I had a tool made at Vickers which a man could easily carry and could be used as a spade, axe and delver. Being made of bulletproof steel, it could also be used as a small shield. After submission to the War Office, I took out a provisional patent and at the instigation of General Hart, who commanded at Chatham, it was tried there against the tools then issued and won the trial easily. I endeavoured to point out to the War Office authorities that in a European war it would be impracticable for a battalion to bring up picks and shovels on pack mules when they wanted to entrench, but I could not get a favourable hearing anywhere.

Feeling convinced that the idea was logical and right, I pressed it home with the authorities wherever I went. I took one to India, where the idea was much more favourably entertained, especially after it had been given an exhaustive trial at the manoeuvres. Many native regiments adopted it. When the Great War broke out an almost similar tool was issued to all troops and used through the war. On the termination of hostilities when I claimed a reward with the Royal Commission for Inventions, I was told that as I was a serving soldier no award could be entertained. On the same grounds they turned down my claims for (1) my system of finding one's general direction at night by the stars, (2) the invention of a bulletproof aeroplane for flying low and bombing the enemy's trenches, which I had invented during the Great War and (3) the combined entrenching tool for which I had been granted a patent.

When I arrived with the 17th, who were then at Meerut, Nicholls, who was then in command, asked me to take over the polo. At an officers' mess meeting, I was again elected captain. They promised to conform to the rules I had laid down in 1903 when we won the English Inter-Regimental.

On taking up command of the Regiment in 1911, I retired from first-class polo, as that year, when on leave in England, I heard a rumour that war with Germany was inevitable. It happened in this year that Hylda and I stayed with the Ormondes at Cowes, where Prince Henry of Prussia had been the previous week. Lady Ormonde told me that he had openly chaffed her as to what the Germans would do when they had overthrown the British Empire and conquered England, and he actually told her some of their secret preparations.

On my return to India, I endeavoured to impress upon the higher military authorities the total unpreparedness of the army for a European war, but was only laughed at. However, Sir James Willcocks, then commanding the Northern Army, allowed me to mobilise the Regiment for war, when many of the items from the mobilisation stores were found to be defective or non-existent.

I wrote an article in the *Cavalry Journal* that year, 1911, on aerial reconnaissance and was admonished by the higher authorities for being a cavalry heretic and writing nonsense, but everything I foreshadowed came to pass in the Great War.

In 1903 Lord Methuen had asked for a greatly increased allowance of ammunition, all round, and was told by the Secretary of State for War, Haldane, that the extra cost would be prohibitive and the War Office Ordnance considered the existing provision to be ample. At the big cavalry manoeuvres in India I proved to the satisfaction of Sir James Willcocks that the allowance per gun and man was ludicrously insufficient, but at the end of 1913 he informed me that the Government would not entertain the idea of an increase in the quota.

The stupidity and lack of common sense of the War Office authorities was really comic, if not, under the circumstances, downright cruel. At the end of 1912 some of my friends in high positions were certain that the Germans were determined to bring about a European war. I believed they were correct so I requested that, if mobilisation took place, the men should be issued with boots at least half a size too big for them. When once soaked, the leather would shrink and the men would suffer agony at night, and never be able to get the boots on again in the morning. After two years' continuous war service in Africa, there was little I did not know about practical soldiering, for during that period I had filled almost every position on the staff.

In India, to keep all ranks fit in the hot weather, I instituted squadron and regimental tactical rides each weekend, choosing places where the officers and men could get good sport, shooting and pig-sticking. The latter was very popular and I have never seen better reconnaissance done than on these occasions. We would march to our bivouacs generally on Saturdays; that night they did night reconnaissances and from dawn to 9 a.m. on the Sunday various schemes. After church parade, which we always held, selected batches were allowed to go out pig-sticking and a more amusing sight could not be imagined.

On these outings the men were instructed in the rudiments of cooking and they lived as if on active service. All went well for the first summer, but the second year we had so many pig-sticking casualties among men and horses that it had to be stopped.

I was on General Kitson's staff for the Delhi Durbar and was ordered to lead the procession into Delhi. For this purpose, I selected to ride a very beautiful chestnut with four white legs – a real picture of a horse, but fiery. It went quietly enough for half the way, until a huge crowd of natives gave a hurrah of welcome to the King and Queen, at which my mount gave three bucks and the roughest ride imaginable. In full kit it was like being in a Turkish bath.

Apparently this magnificent capering horse pleased the native element, who thought it very fine. I received praise from all directions. The incident led to my meeting the Maharajah of Kashmir, who invited me to shoot in the special reserves of Kashmir. It was the best sport a man could ever wish for.

Hylda and I had a royal time at the Durbar, as we were bidden to dinner with the King and Queen and saw everything in the best manner possible. The scene at the Durbar itself passes description – many of the Indian chiefs had literally coats of pearls, diamonds and every sort of precious stone in such profusion that some of them resembled costermongers.

I asked the Prime Minister of Kashmir how they prevented jewels from being stolen, as some of the pearls on the Maharajah's coat were as big as hazel nuts. He told me that the hereditary chief jeweller counted them every night and that none had been missed since the Crown Jewels had been in charge of that family – some 600 years.

We had an exciting experience at the Investiture which was held in a huge marquee tent. When it was half way through, there were cries of 'fire'. The King and Queen and those on the platform were absolutely unperturbed, but the people around, where Hylda and I sat, got up and moved hurriedly towards the entrance and there was almost a stampede at the back. The comic side was well represented, for two peers seated on the dais shifted uneasily in their chairs at the cry of 'fire' and, as they were seated near the edge they both toppled over on to the audience. The fire was soon under control and those who had fled had some explaining to do!

THE GORGES OF KASHMIR

Soon after our return to Sialkot, I took up the Maharajah of Kashmir's invitation. I found out that the best shooting was to be had some 300 miles north east of Jammu. The Prime Minister of Kashmir informed me that only mule transport could get along the single track, 100 miles from Riasi.

I approached Sir James Willcocks, then commanding Northern Army, a very keen sportsman, and he expressed a wish to accompany me, giving me a job of reconnoitring that part of the Himalaya which had never been mapped by a white man. Our starting point, where I was to meet Sir James with our outfit of government mules, was Naoshera on the Chenab river. On my arrival I received a message that the C-in-C was unable to come, but that I had to carry on and return to Sialkot within six weeks. After a week's trek over the mountains, we came on to a track, not two yards wide, with a precipice on the left of 1,000 feet, above the river. We had fifteen mules in the convoy and lost three down this *khud* [precipice], but the guide was not in the least perturbed and we eventually came to a lovely valley with one of the Maharajah's palaces standing on the river. Being the Maharajah's guest, I was met by all the surrounding *theselders*.

The first day's shooting produced twenty-five peacock and every species of pheasant (except Argus), and thirteen brace of partridges, all to my own gun. The next week, I reached a spot in the Pir Penjal, from where we had a beautiful view of Everest. Here, as I was the Maharajah's guest, the whole countryside turned out to beat, and as they had never seen a white man before, I held an *indaba* with the headmen before I commenced shooting. We drove over very beautiful valleys, and as most of the headmen carried jingals, many loaded with old pieces of metal, stones and prehistoric powder, it was like a battle, for game of all sorts was very plentiful.

I was placed at the head of the valley and was shooting high rocketing pheasants and peacock when to my dismay I saw a leopard not twenty yards to my front. Luckily I was motionless, standing on a huge rock, and I allowed it to pass me not five yards below the rock. Had I been on the ground, it would have certainly mauled me. I dared not shoot with a 12 bore gun, as it was two weeks' hard marching from Jammu and the slightest maul would probably have been fatal.

The next day I did some *mahseer* fishing, much to the delight of the natives, for immediately I hooked a fish they dived in and brought it out in no time, running off with it to their village. Any that I happened to land myself, they would not touch, and this applied to my shikaris and mule boys, so at the end of the day, I had a pile of *mahseer* rotting on the bank.

It was amazing how these natives could swim. A large fish – it turned out to be 35 lb – took me down some falls and lay in the backwash under the fall. My own shikaris tried in turn to free my line and move the fish, but the water was too strong. A young native then dived in, and swimming under water brought back the fish with bait and line, a most wonderful feat. I engaged him forthwith as my personal fishing shikari. My own shikaris could not speak the dialect in these parts and this young native, whom I named Jummu, could also make himself understood in Hindustani. He subsequently proved himself quite invaluable and however bad the conditions were, he never lost a bait or failed to free my line, even in the most rapid water.

Every day I met game of all sorts in profusion, but as none of the coolies could touch meat I soon got tired of shooting. Even the bears and leopards were comparatively tame, never having seen a white man. The inhabitants of this district had no marriage laws at all, and worshipped stones in the shape of a man's 'parts', the consequence being that men and women suffered horribly from venereal diseases.

After a week's sojourn in the north of the Pir Punjab, I retraced my steps and heard of a white sahib a week's march down the river. He turned out to be a French medical missionary, who had been there three years, treating and studying native diseases, and one day I was present in his surgery during the hours of treatment. The ravages of syphilis would give anyone a horrible nightmare, ineffaceable for all one's life; even girls of ten or eleven were suffering from it.

All the way down the Tawi and Chenab rivers I met with the greatest honour and respect, for on my way up I had treated four natives for snakebites and they had all recovered. I just 'starred' the bite with a lancet and rubbed in permanganate of potash. Every evening patients were brought to me and to the best of my belief only one died, a woman bitten in the 'tender parts' by a krite snake.

On my arrival at Sialkot, the sportsmen of the garrison were much interested in my experiences, so Leader, our brigadier, begged me to take him up whenever we had an opportunity. We got a month's leave before the monsoon broke in 1912, and as this was far too short a time to get further than where I had lost the mules over the precipice, we decided to employ camel transport and ride ponies as far as Riasi, so as to allow us as much time as possible for shooting and fishing in the preserves.

We had excellent sport, but were caught in the mountains by the worst upheaval of the elements it is possible to imagine. About 2 p.m. very black clouds rolled up, with incessant thunder and lightning. Then there was minor earthquake with a waterspout breaking on a mountain nearby. The tributary of the Chenab which we were fishing suddenly became a huge river, which brought down goats, sheep and other animals as well as natives. Since we had crossed to the north side, our return was cut off till the floods subsided. This delayed us three days and there was no prospect of reaching Sialkot at the expiration of our leave. I discovered that some natives from the upper waters of the Chenab reached the plains on rafts of felled timber. After much persuasion the local *theselder* promised to have two rafts made for Leader and myself, but would do nothing until he had obtained the Prime Minister's sanction as he considered the project most dangerous.

While waiting for the rafts to be built Leader and I tried to solve the problem of saving one's life when swept away while wearing fishing waders. For this purpose we chose a deep pool (running into shallow water at its end) and for three days tried every conceivable dodge. When one was swimming, air collected at the foot end, submerging one's head. When we got into difficulties Jummu and the shikaris would jump in and rescue us. Just before we left, I was sitting in my waders on a sloping shore and in this position, with my knees up, paddled with my hands into the stream and found it was perfectly easy to float in a sitting position downstream, as the air rose to the knees. We had great fun paddling downstream in this way, but you had to face down the river, otherwise a bump on the back against a rock would disable you. (After the Great War I sent a full description of this method to *The Times*.)

The moment leave was given for us to attempt our return journey by the river, we embarked on our two rafts, each manned by four expert *khisti* wallahs with long bamboo poles. We had sent a runner to Sialkot for horses to meet us at the foot of the Jummu hills, so as to save time. The first day all went superbly, and we covered over thirty miles. The second day of our raft journey we had to leave our rafts with the *khisti* wallahs, whilst they were traversing some very dangerous rapids. These they managed successfully, and they met us at a village on the north side of the Jummu Hills. We were due in Sialkot the next evening, so made an early start, but when we approached a precipitous gorge nothing would induce the *khisti* wallahs to proceed until the heavy flood had partially subsided. We were desperate to reach Sialkot on time but the mountain through which the gorge ran was a very high one with only a foot track over it.

So, with the promise of liberal baksheesh if they got us to the plains, they consented to make the attempt. When we entered the gorge, Leader's raft led the way and it was amazing how the *khisti* wallahs avoided the huge rocks, whirlpools and falls, but eventually Leader's raft was caught in a whirlpool and I saw it gradually disappear, only to reappear some distance down with Leader hanging on and the *khisti* wallahs swimming.

The thunder of the waters in the gorge would baffle any description, for there were no banks to the river, only precipitous rocks towering some 2,000 feet up to the top of the mountain. Before we could land we traversed two or three miles in the dark, for the distance was so great to the top that the light failed to penetrate the narrow gorge as far as the river, the top of the mountain being overgrown with high trees and brushwood.

After this, we landed at the first available spot, and taking all our guns, rifles and anything of value, we told the *khisti* wallahs with the rafts to meet us where we expected our horses to be. Never shall I forget the tramp and climbs we had that day in the blistering sun; in the evening we lay down dead beat, still some forty miles from our destination.

We reached our horses next day, but not a sign of the rafts. Just as we were starting to ride homewards, a *khisti* wallah appeared in the river riding straddlelegs on two logs, and then five more eventually turned up. They told us, without any concern or excitement, that the rafts had been dashed to pieces soon after we had left them and two of the crew had been swallowed up in a whirlpool. Jummu thought this was an excellent joke, and told them they must learn to swim as he could. When we gave them ten rupees apiece they were in the best of spirits.

In 1913 the 17th won all the sporting events in India – polo, cricket, football – except the Khadir, when Carden was in the final. In 1911 I had bought Fireplant, a beautiful chestnut pony, the previous and only pony winner of the Khadir, from Captain Vernon of the Rifle Brigade. When going full tilt in the final stages of the Khadir, I was about to spear the hog when the pony somersaulted and completely laid me out. I was taken to Ludovic Porters Camp half senseless, but not unconscious of the terrible pain; for I had broken three ribs and my right collarbone, and my chest was not only bruised through, but flattened out. The next day I was conveyed two days' journey in a palanquin to the railway line, Hylda walking by my side. On arrival she met John Vaughan, with tears streaming down his face, for although he had won the Khadir Cup, he had killed his horse.

The only vehicle to contain the palanquin on the train was an all-metal luggage van, into which I was put, now half dead and suffering extreme agony. After a somewhat long sojourn in Meerut Hospital I was judged to be fit for duty, but being still in great pain, I took leave home and when x-rayed, which the military doctors in India had never done, it was discovered that both my shoulder blades were broken in half.

Hylda had spent two hot weathers with me in the plains, so in the autumn of 1913 she and I decided we would take our leave up the Chenab, instead of going home to England on short leave. With camels and ponies we got as far as Assisi, the junction of three rivers, Chenab, Ans and Rad, and were having a thoroughly happy time.

When fishing down the Chenab on our return, I noticed a fakir on the opposite side of the river gesticulating wildly. My fishing shikari Jummu begged me not to fish the pool, over which I had made two or three casts, as it contained holy fish. In deference to the fakir's entreaties, I stopped and returned to our camp. The fakir arrived in the evening and told us that only two sahibs had ever fished the pool and they had both died within a year.

That evening malignant malaria overcame me and the next day I was completely unconscious. How my most beloved wife ever got me back to Sialkot, God only knows, but I was afterwards told that it took her five days. Jummu and she had to walk for two and a half days over the hills which Leader and I had climbed over after we got through the gorge on rafts. For nine weeks I was completely unconscious, with malignant malaria and sunstroke, my life being despaired of. On 1 November 1913 I was dying, and Hylda sent for the chaplain to administer Holy Communion. He came on 3 November and in a lucid interval I partook of the Holy Communion, when I was told subconsciously, as clearly as any man can be, that I was not going to die, but that I should get perfectly well.

On 4 November, the following day, complete consciousness returned. When Boles, the adjutant, called to see Hylda, he was amazed to see me sitting up in bed. I weighed only nine stone, a mere skeleton, but by 4 December 1913, a month later, I had recovered sufficient strength to take a full dress mounted parade, when Sir James Willcocks commanding the Northern Army, inspected the regiment. Captain Purser, RAMC, had attended me throughout the terrible ordeal, but the Viceroy and Lady Hardinge had also sent down two specialists and two nurses to attend me. We can never be sufficiently grateful to them for their marvellous kindness.

Everyone, including the natives, loved Hylda and the Regiment surpassed itself in their kindly endeavours to help her. At the end of the training season, I was given six months' leave and returned home with Hylda.

When we reached Bombay, the Willingdons insisted on us staying with them for a week, so as to allow me time to pick up some strength, since I was still a semi-invalid and all the doctors thought I should never really recover sufficiently to be well enough to soldier in the East again. The voyage home did me a lot of good and on our arrival the Ormondes asked us to stay at Cowes, which we did.

We returned to the Ormondes after Cowes week, when the Fleet had been mobilised. We met many of the leading naval officers at the Yacht Squadron and at dinner with the Ormondes. Lord Ormonde, who was Commander of the Royal Yacht Squadron, told Harry Fowler and myself that the Fleet had received orders to sail at once, so Harry and I went down to the Royal Yacht Squadron and arranged with Willie Portal to go out in his yacht and see their departure. We heard that night that the situation was hopeless for the cause of peace.

The next day, before dawn, Harry Fowler, Charles Cust and myself saw the whole of the Fleet and most of the smaller craft pass before us going eastwards. It was a sight never to be forgotten. We little realised what a holocaust was to follow.

INDIAN MALARIA IN FESTUBERT'S TRENCHES

I was due to return to India but my orders were changed and I was to be sent to France if the medical board passed me fit. At this board they at first refused to pass me fit for active service, as they said I could not have had sufficient time to recover. I pointed out that all the doctors who had looked after me had certified that I had made a miraculous recovery. They insisted on interviewing my wife and although she knew I was still suffering from malignant malaria, she did as I asked and assured them that I was fit.

I received a great welcome from the Regiment in France which made me almost forget my state of health.

In 1915, at Festubert, the 17th Lancers relieved the Royal Welch Fusiliers who had sustained terrible losses. The Argyll and Sutherland Highlanders had also suffered very severely in the Battle of Festubert. It was piteous to hear the wails and cries of the wounded, who had become stuck in the mud, with no hope of rescue. At two points in our line the German trench was not five yards away. At some places in our trenches piles of dead formed the ramparts. The 17th were in these trenches at Festubert for four days during which we were continuously up to our armpits in water. As the ground rose slightly 100 yards to our rear, immediately we took over I begged the higher command to send a staff officer up to authorise our laying out a second line on this ridge, where the troops would be on comparatively dry ground. They agreed with my suggestion and said a staff officer would be sent up to lay out the new line. As no one came, I telephoned again and this procedure went on daily, until I was so exasperated that I telephoned to Sir Douglas Haig. When eventually the staff officer arrived, he only remarked that his journey to the trenches had been most unpleasant. He asked for some refreshments and retired till nightfall to a safe dug-out. He was a member of the Divisional Staff and appeared to think that it was the duty of the staff to avoid danger in any form.

After the fourth day of this hell, I remember nothing, for according to the medical report, I was suddenly 'knocked out'. For weeks I was only semiconscious and paralysed in both legs. Continuous attacks of trench fever brought me near the grave. I was sent to recuperate at Scarborough, in command of the cavalry depot. The doctor who had me in charge gave my case up as hopeless. I was about to be invalided from the Service when I went to see my old and dear friend the 13th Hussar polo back, Boy McLaren, who was desperately ill with fever and shell shock. A retired naval medical officer named Stuart was looking after McLaren and came in at our first meeting. He had been one of the members of the medical board which had recently passed me unfit for the Service. When I told him how heartbroken I was, he replied that if I could arrange to be under his care, he thought he could make me fit for home service in a few months. But that the cure was a very drastic one!

Lord Londesborough, who had been extraordinarily kind since our arrival at Scarborough, arranged with the authorities that I should be allowed six months' respite, during which period I was to be treated by Stuart. He told me the only chance I had of recovery was to take a dip in the sea every morning before breakfast and that he had arranged for me to start the next morning in the pool (an open swimming bath annexed to the sea). This was in the month of February and my first dip was during a snowstorm. As I had given my word of honour to carry out his instructions, I went down every morning until the boys (Dolly and Ned) returned for their Easter holidays. They most pluckily accompanied me daily to the pool and also had their dip, no matter what the weather was.

One morning it was so rough that the caretaker begged us not to go in and only by promising that we would not leave the side did he allow me to take my header, followed by Dolly and Ned. Almost simultaneously a huge wave burst over the outer sea wall into the dressing rooms and the backwash caught Ned, carrying him right across the pool. He mercifully gripped the top of the outer sea wall and was saved, by inches, from certain death.

Dr Stuart's drastic treatment proved a marvellous cure for trench fever, and before the prescribed time I was passed fit for home service and appointed Staff Officer I of the mounted troops, a division on the East Coast, under Lord Shaftesbury. I now had a wonderful opportunity to advocate the use of the aeroplane. I went to the War Office to show them plans for the construction of a bulletproof aeroplane that could fly low over the enemy's trenches bombing and machine-gunning the troops.

Our headquarters were at Colchester. During one of the Zeppelin raids, it was reported that signals had been passed from one of the largest country houses near the Colne river to the enemy Zeppelin. The report appeared to be entirely false, as the owner of the house was a well-known member of the London County Council. However, one day Shaftesbury and I motored over to call and ascertain for ourselves whether there was any foundation for these persistent rumours. We found a very nice elderly gentleman, his wife, daughter and a son (who was under military age). Whilst Shaftesbury made himself agreeable, I took a walk round the garden and then towards the river. An old man beckoned me from behind some shrubs. When I came up, he said, 'I am the gardener here and the place is full of German spies at nights!' When the next Zeppelin raid took place, the house was surrounded and three Germans, with the owner, were arrested and subsequently shot.

TABLING THE NIGHT SKY

Since the termination of the South African War, I had worked continuously with Reeves, the Curator of the Royal Geographical Society, to devise a simple method for men to find their way at night by the stars. We had been working on the problem since 1902, and had made out transit timetables of the first magnitude stars. These tables had already been of great value in India and the East. Whilst lecturing at Scarborough, I realised the usefulness of the first magnitude stars which rise in the East, are in our latitude south east when halfway to their zenith, due south when at their zenith, south west when half down, and west when setting. After a little observation, the men could recognise their respective altitudes or measure the altitude from the horizon using their closed hands. It was found that those men who could distinguish their general bearings from the heavens got the same uncanny pigeon instinct possessed by the Arabs, bushmen and others such as I had witnessed in long-distance night reconnaissance in South Africa.

My work was immediately recognised as being invaluable for troops when fighting at night. I was asked to expound it in detail before the Royal Society of Arts in London. I was then sent on a lecturing tour of troops in the United Kingdom, as well as most of the universities (including Oxford, Cambridge, and Edinburgh).

Lecturing before the professors and dons at Cambridge was a terrifying ordeal, but apparently they appreciated the worth of this system. At the end of the lecture the Master of Trinity congratulated me and emphasised the fact that it had not been suggested by any astronomer before – i.e. to make practical use of the heavens as a compass. I stayed with General Smith-Dorrien at Cambridge, lecturing to the troops under his command, for he at once comprehended that if every man knew his bearings, there could be no disasters such as Magersfontein.

In this connection, General Smith-Dorrien gave me a full account one evening of the early stages of the Great War and how helpless the men were during the night. He said that the confusion during darkness was indescribable and that through losing their way in the Mons retreat many units were cut off. One flank brigade actually fired into the brigade on its flank. Such things, he said, would never happen if every officer and man knew their direction and had the same night sense as the Australian bushmen. He was much impressed and afterwards asked me to make out star tables for Mesopotamia and Palestine. I received hundreds of letters saying how successful my system was.

When I was made Chief Staff Officer of the mounted forces on the East Coast, I was worked hard, for since my return from France and convalescence I had had to tour every camp in England and Scotland, travelling by day and lecturing in the evenings.

Part IV

IN THE IRISH MORASS

When Portal left Ireland, I was sent in his place to command the Reserve Regiment of Lancers at the Curragh, just after the Rebellion had taken place in 1916.[1]

At that time the condition of Irish society was fairly tranquil and if only Sir John Maxwell had remained as C-in-C, there would have been a different tale to tell and the Loyalists would not have been betrayed and murdered. Sir John ruled with a strong, just hand and would brook no interference from anyone in carrying out justice. This did not suit Lloyd George and the politicians, who deposed Maxwell and then began the persecution of all who showed any patriotism in Ireland. I

---

1 Ireland seemed to be drifting towards civil war when the First World War broke out. The IRB (Irish Republican Brotherhood), true to the traditional principle that England's difficulty was Ireland's opportunity, determined on armed insurrection. Help was sought from Germany. In 1916 about 150,000 Irishmen – all volunteers and mostly Catholics and nationalists – were in British uniform and recruiting was still going on. Independent of the British army, the Irish volunteers were tolerated by the authorities because it was thought they would defend Ireland's shores from foreign invasion. Those who in 1916 controlled the volunteers considered that Ireland was already in the hands of a foreign invader (Britain). On Easter Monday the volunteers took part in manoeuvres which became the Rising. They occupied a number of public buildings and proclaimed the Republic. British forces were taken by surprise. After a week's fighting, with 450 people killed and over 2,500 wounded as well as much damage to central Dublin, the rebels surrendered. General Sir John Maxwell had fifteen of the leading rebels executed. When the British Embassy in Washington reported on the extremely adverse reaction of Irish-American opinion to the news of the 1916 executions. General Maxwell, as Military Governor, was dismissed by Lloyd George.

The troubles continued until 1922, with the well-equipped British forces under General Macready – including the Black and Tans, recruited 1920 – considerably outnumbering the Irish Republican Army. The Government of Ireland Act, of December 1920, established the temporary partition of North and South. Although not particularly popular, the Act was generally acceptable as a compromise capable of leading to peace. The Anglo-Irish Treaty was signed 6 December 1921. The IRA did not accept the treaty and prepared to fight for a united Ireland. The Catholic hierarchy – which from 1918 had given support to Sinn Fein, the IRA political face – condemned the anti-treaty forces and placed them under excommunication. The struggle continued on guerrilla lines and became particularly bitter after the killing (in an internecine skirmish) of Michael Collins, a signatory of the treaty and Commander-in-Chief of the Irish Free State Army.

had been sent there as fit only for light duty (category C3), but could hardly have had a more harassing time.

I had hunted with most of the well-known packs while serving with the 17th at Ballincollig, and with the Meath, Kildares, Carlow and Queen's County when an ADC at the Curragh during Lord Cadogan's Viceroyalty, so I knew most of the hunting, shooting and fishing folk in Ireland. As all the Lancers and six regiments of Yeomanry were under my command, we had as many horses to hunt as we could keep in work. I encouraged hunting among the officers, as much as possible on troop horses.

There was the most extraordinary mixture of officers passing through the Reserve Regiment, some who had lived in a world of vice and skulduggery. We had three messes, one in Dublin and two at the Curragh, each of about 80–100 officers. It was hard to protect the young officers from the gambling sharks, and the mess at Dublin had to be closed down as it was found impossible to enforce the rule that bridge at 1/– per 100 was the only card game allowed in the mess.

A curious incident happened in this connection. An officer named Hickey was accused of swindling by his brother officers and ordered to be court martialled, one of his accusers being Davis, whom Haig had kicked out of the 17th Lancers, and subsequently from France, for gambling. Before his court martial Hickey asked to see me and explained that he knew what cards every player held immediately they had looked at their hands. He had repeatedly told his brother officers of his power and they would never believe him. The statement seemed incredible, but I arranged for him to give an exhibition in the officers' mess before a jury of his brother officers. There he proved his power to the satisfaction of the sixty or seventy who were looking on and his court martial was cancelled. Lord Enniskillen and Harry Greer asked Hickey to give an exhibition of his powers in Dublin for charity, and on this occasion he told what the players had in their hands before a card was played.

In 1917 a general call for officers and men to volunteer for the Infantry was made and splendidly responded to by all ranks of the Reserve Cavalry. I made a special application to be examined by a medical board in order to go overseas in any capacity, but they would not pass me fit and labelled me category C3.

Condemned to remain at the Curragh, I took a share in a very good grouse moor, Edenderry, with Percy La Touche. We also had Lord Castletown's shoot at Granston. We had splendid sport at both of these places, on Edenderry one day getting 200 brace of grouse and another time at Granston over 300 wildfowl in a day. Granston was an excellent duck shoot, untouched for two years, and the first year we had it it was extra good. The guns stood in tubs in the middle of the central stream and when all were in their places and the time signal gun was fired, the air was thick with birds. We lost a good number, however, as it was difficult to collect them after the shoot. The cars (we always motored out to the shoots) would be laden down with game for the officers' messes. We also gave the men game pies, which were much appreciated. If there was not enough to go round the three officers' messes under my command there were complaints that the Lancers were more favoured than the Yeomanry.

Jack Riddell, son of Puggy Riddell of Pytchley fame, said, 'Half these officers haven't tasted game in their lives and I'll prove it!' We had a two days' covert shoot at Edenderry, getting fine woodcock, pheasants and other game birds, and on our return shot gulls, kittiwakes, moorhen and crows. I then squared Sergeant-Major Baker, the caterer, to include all these a week hence in the dinner menu as 'woodcock'. He disguised them so well that everyone was taken in, including well-known sportsmen in the Lancer regiments. They all pronounced the woodcock to be quite excellent. Of course only the breasts and wings were served and all the cutting up was done behind the scenes.

The landlords were now receiving threatening letters from the Sinn Feiners, and some of the leading gentry had been shot at and some killed, so from the Curragh we could only hunt with the Kildares, Carlow and Queen's County. It was then a hazardous pursuit, with local sportsman being killed sometimes on their way home after hunting. Nothing however would or could deter the Irishman from hunting, which went on uninterruptedly through murders, wanton arson, burglaries and other crimes till the Provisional Government was established in January 1922.

THE FEISTY MISS TYNTE

The Irish really are different from any other type of human being. There was a chemist, for instance, a mad keen foxhunter, who was shot and killed on his way to a meet of the Carlow. The hunt heard the news about noon, when the hounds were drawing a good gorse. On it being drawn blank, the Master, George Grogan, assembled the field and announced the murder.

'I'm sure he wouldn't like to spoil a good day's hunting, so we will take off our hats for five minutes and then go on to the bog!'

'And we will have a great hunt from there,' added Miss Tynte, owner of the beautiful Tynte Abbey and some of the finest heavyweight hunters in Ireland.

'Begorrah, we will,' chorused most of the field – and a great hunt we had indeed, killing one fox when it was almost dark. I was riding that day what Irishmen considered one of the best hunters in Ireland, named Lunatic, a 16.1 dark chestnut gelding, almost thoroughbred by Equus out of a three-quarter-bred mare. I hunted him in Meath, Kildare, Carlow, Queen's County and Kilkenny regularly two days a week for three seasons and he never fell or gave me a fall. He finally died of tetanus after being trapped by some loose barbed wire the far side of a wall in the Carlow country. Anyway, when we had broken up the fox I rode with Grogan and the hounds back to the kennels accompanied by some of the field. Grogan begged me to stay the night at his house, as it was highly dangerous to ride the roads after dusk. No one mentioned the murder of the poor chemist that morning, but discussed every detail of the hunt.

Miss Tynte had turned a somersault into a broad open brook, from which she extricated herself and continued the hunt to the end, minus hat, coat and skirt. In appearance she was like the cinema star Fatty Arbuckle, but went very hard and straight out hunting. When deprived of her outer coverings she looked like a jellyfish mermaid, so we had much merriment at her expense on the way back to the kennels. Mrs Hall, the joint master of the Carlow, asked her to stay the night, so she rode along with us till we passed a house from which she borrowed a cloak, many sizes too small.

It was very dark and foggy by the time we reached Grogan's house at about 7 p.m. At this point one of the stable men announced that Mrs Hall had asked us both to dinner. Grogan was overjoyed at the invitation, announcing 'Mrs Hall has the best cellar in County Carlow. We will have a great evening.' 'Bring the lamp, Biddy,' he called and a girl appeared from the back premises carrying a stable lamp. 'This is the only light we have about the place,' Grogan explained, 'lamp oil's rationed; but if you come to my room, Tilney, I'll rig you out for the dinner party.' As all his clothes were far too small, I set off for the dinner party in his pyjama trousers and hunting coat.

'It's two miles along the road and a mile across the fields,' he remarked as we were starting. 'We mustn't be late, so we'll take the short cut.' Having reached the house with the utmost difficulty, owing to the fog and pitch darkness, we found Mrs Hall and her two daughters and Miss Tynte, the latter swathed in bath towels with an anti-macassar over her shoulders, looking like an eastern Begum.

Mrs Hall produced the best of her cellar and we had an extremely merry evening, talking hunting far into the night. When Grogan and I started our return home, I suggested we should go by the road. 'Most unsafe,' he replied. Then I began to realise what a lot of good wine had been consumed during dinner.

After Grogan had led the way with the lantern for at least an hour, I ventured to ask if he was certain he knew the way. 'Of course I do, don't I live here?' he replied testily, and immediately fell head over heels into a sunken ditch. Out went the lantern, which in the now heavy rain refused to relight. After taking a considerable time emerging from the ditch, Grogan told me thickly: 'Of course I know the way now, this is the bloody ditch near Mrs Hall's, so come on, old boy, it's quite all right.'

The wine was now well mixed in Grogan's body and he was also badly shaken. After we had stumbled on for what seemed hours, Grogan, who was leading the way, disappeared into another ditch just as he was saying for the hundredth time, 'Of course, I know the way, we're close to home.' This time he remained in the ditch, saying 'Itsh no good all these bloody ditches all over the place, we must shtay here till it is light!' And so we did, Grogan at first getting very cantankerous and annoyed with me for doubting whether he knew the way, then falling into a deep sleep.

At the break of dawn I woke him. His first remark was 'This is the bloody ditch we were in before, close to Mrs Hall's.' We got back to his house about 6 a.m. and I immediately got on my Harley-Davidson motor bike to return to the Curragh, for I knew how dreadfully alarmed Hylda would be at my not returning.

On my arrival, I found four cars had been sent to scour the country in search of me. One of the cars which had toured the Carlow District reported the murder of the chemist and the rumour spread that I had been done in as well.

PROTECTING THE TOMMIES

Soon after this I was sent for by the C-in-C, who informed me that I had been chosen by the troops as their representative on the Army

Representative Committee.[2] The whole committee sat in London every fortnight under the chairmanship of Sir Henry Mackinnon, who forwarded our views and recommendations to the Cabinet. After our first meeting in Dublin the ARC member for Southern Ireland was shot dead on his return to Cork. A Cork doctor, whose name I have forgotten, most bravely volunteered to take his place. He too was murdered soon afterwards and I was asked to take over Southern Ireland as well. This meant a great deal of travelling. In most districts the trains were constantly being held up, the roads were most unsafe and the Sinn Feiners took all motors seized on the roads.

Edward White was our chairman in Ireland. He was a solicitor and land agent in Dublin, a strong personality and a really good fellow. White and I discussed at length the best means of getting about the country. We decided that the only possible way for me was on a motor bike. I was provided with a new Harley-Davidson and given generous terms of insurance by the Car and General Insurance Co.

One afternoon, after attending a committee meeting in Dublin under the presidency of Lord French, I was returning to Kildare when I thought my bike began to backfire badly. I was in uniform and I did not want to meet any patrol of the Sinn Feiners after dark (at this time they hadn't the audacity to patrol main roads in daylight). As I was rushing down a hill at over 60 miles an hour near Kill, the tank burst into flames. Seeing a pond a little distance away alongside the road, I took a header into it, bike and all. When I had extricated myself from the wreckage, I walked to the nearest farmhouse. Luckily the farmer was an ardent loyalist. He told me that the rebels were in the immediate vicinity and gave me a safe hiding place in the roof of a barn. I was miserably cold and hungry, so this kind farmer, a tenant of the Mayos, said he would bring me some food and a change of clothing when it was dark.

Ages seemed to go by, then I heard voices in Gaelic below and the farmer saying in English: 'He only stopped an hour and then went on

2 On this committee, sometimes referred to by W.A.T by its sobriquet 'the Tommies' Parliament', sat three representatives from England, three from Scotland, three from Ireland and nine representing the Dominions and Colonies. W.A.T was the representative for mid-Ireland. He notes, 'Our job was to arrange for the resettlement in civil life of all ranks, when they were demobilised; to advise the British Cabinet as to the best way of finding employment for ex-servicemen; to co-ordinate the various army and navy help societies, and to organise in each country and county, committees to look after the interests of ex-servicemen of all descriptions.'

to Kildare in a car that he stopped on the road.' However, two men came and searched the loft and I thanked God when one of them said 'The b—'s not here!' I had to wait, however, till past midnight before the farmer arrived with some food. Coming down from the roof to the loft, I changed into the farmer's clothes and drove to the Curragh, arriving at dawn. When the motor bike was recovered from the pond by the Car and General, they found two tracer bullets in the tank and one in the side car. While repairs were being effected they provided me with a Sunbeam, which I found to be very slow after the Harley-Davidson.

Being unable to go far afield, I spent most of my spare time hunting and shooting, as well as fishing with friends in Southern Ireland who were on the county committee for the ex-servicemen. There in the South a positive reign of terror had been brought about in the Cork and Waterford districts, the rebels having murdered many of the leading loyalists and civilians who had espoused the ex-servicemen's cause. Threatening letters, some real bloodcurdlers, were regularly sent to me. I realised that only God could save me from being murdered, but that there was no cause for fear under His protection. I therefore went all over the country addressing meetings and organising ex-servicemen's affairs as if there was absolute peace in the land. It was only by God's miraculous protection that I came through safe.

That year (1917) the difficulties of the situation were increased a hundredfold through a manifesto issued by the trade unions in London and signed by Ramsay MacDonald and the TUC leaders, calling on all their members to copy the Russian Revolution and oppose all forms of patriotic effort in the Empire's cause. This was interpreted by Larkin, the Labourites and Sinn Feiners to mean that all loyalists in Ireland, especially those who had served or were serving in the Great War, were to be treated as pariahs, as well as their families.

The trade unions barred these poor fellows, heroes for always, from all forms of work. Most of them had gone through real hell in the war and had returned wrecked, disabled or invalided to their homes, only to suffer persecution in every form for their patriotism. Those who had volunteered for service were the victims of the worst enmity, and they had their families treated as outcasts. Many of the Roman Catholic priests were the men's bitterest enemies. They would not allow them to attend Mass, and refused them the Sacrament and extreme unction. This reign of terror gradually spread through Southern Ireland. Those who were foremost in helping the ex-servicemen did so at the risk of their lives and property. Lady Mayo, Lady Weldon and Lady Arnott, however, refused to relax their efforts – the former in conjunction with General Fry. Fry was the 'Scarlet Pimpernel' for members of the Royal Irish Constabulary who were doomed to die at the hands of the rebels (Sinn Feiners and Bolshies). In the most mysterious manner, Lady Mayo got some two to three hundred of these men from the clutches of their would-be murderers and, with the help of General Fry, sent them to the Isle of Man. Many succeeded in getting away with their families, but those families who had to be left behind were relentlessly persecuted, especially if they were Protestants. Lady Mayo carried on with this noble work until her house, Palmerstown, was burnt to the ground, with practically the whole of its contents.

I was told by an eyewitness that while the Mayos were at dinner, a gang of rebels (mostly Bolshies) burst into the dining room. The leader told Lady Mayo that they had been ordered to burn down the house and that the occupants could have an hour in which to remove personal effects. Lady Mayo treated them with scorn and remained seated in the dining room while they were drenching the house with petrol, refusing to move until they had set light to one of the rooms. When the fire was started they took her forcibly to the gardener's house. All the pictures, tapestries and Mayo miniatures of inestimable value were destroyed – not even jewellery and the wonderful Mayo pearls were saved. All this was done because, heroine that she was, she helped the ex-servicemen and RIC men.

She carried on this wonderful work until 1923 when the British garrison was withdrawn from Southern Ireland. She then took a small house in Chelsea. One day I commiserated with her on the loss of her home and everything she held dear, and she replied, with a seraphic smile, 'Yes, but they cannot take away the love and companionship of Jesus.'

Tony Weldon had been on the Viceroy's staff with me before the South African War. When he died in 1917 as the result of war service, the only asset he left his widow and three boys was the beautiful family place, Kilmorony Athy. Having been ADC to Lord Wolseley when he was C-in-C in Ireland, and being a prominent landlord, he exercised considerable influence over the Southern Irishmen, particularly over those who had any connections with the British services. On the outbreak of the Great War, Lady Mayo and Lady Weldon had been foremost in the recruiting campaigns and, as the men were all volunteers, the County Committees organised reception committees to welcome them home when they were disabled or wrecked in the war. These committees now found their work becoming impossible. In several counties, when a draft of men was due to arrive, they were met at the station not by their friends but by bands of rebels; and they and their families were most cruelly persecuted. Many serving Irish soldiers could not return at all – they would have been murdered at once by the Sinn Feiners.

Soon after I had been elected as the tommies' representative, a big batch of ex-servicemen was due to arrive at Athy and stations south. Information was received that these poor fellows were to be attacked on arrival by gangs of the Irish Republican Army. Lady Weldon met the contingent at Athy station and the RIC protected it, marching at the head of the troops, who all sang British patriotic songs through streets lined with armed rebels; and through Lady Weldon's heroism not a shot was fired, up to the contingents reaching the barracks. There they had to spend the night before proceeding to their homes. Two of these ex-servicemen were murdered the next day on their way to Monasterevin and their bodies thrown into a bog.

Reports from the Cork district being most harrowing, I decided to see what could be done there. Putting my whole trust in God, off I went. On my arrival at the Imperial Hotel, Cork, I endeavoured to organise a meeting of ex-servicemen but only a very few dared to put in an appearance. Meanwhile, reports of the ex-servicemen's terrible treatment fully confirmed everything we had heard in Dublin. Many had been taken prisoner on their arrival and either shot or 'gone west' in a bog, which meant that after a mock court martial, they were buried alive in a bog. Anyone who helped the ex-servicemen was in peril.

Lord Bandon had done everything possible to alleviate their lot and suggested that our chairman, White, should come to see for himself the state of affairs and endeavour to induce the British Government to stop this persecution.

On White's arrival in Cork we had another meeting at which many prominent landlords and citizens in the south of Ireland attended. White told the meeting that no 'military' action was to be taken by the Government and that the Army Representative Committee had been allocated considerable funds from the Field Force canteens to alleviate distress among ex-servicemen in Ireland. Lord Bandon suggested that White and I should meet the Sinn Fein leaders to see what could be done to stop this wholesale massacre of the men. Three days afterwards we met seven rebel leaders including Michael Collins – who was on the run and had a price on his head.

To my surprise a man named Fagan, whom I had known well while the Regiment was quartered at Ballincollig, greeted me most affectionately. He had been one of our mainstays when the Regiment had the Muskerry hounds, so we at once talked about fox-hunting. Only White, Lord Bandon and myself were at the meeting and White pleaded that the slaughtering of disabled and defenceless men was inhuman, and altogether made a most impressive speech. The line the Sinn Feiners took was that Ireland was at war with England, and they were within their rights in shooting our soldiers. They eventually consented to spare the permanently disabled and gave White and myself safe permits to visit Waterford and Yougal and the chief towns in Southern Ireland.

Terrible tales were told wherever we went. The edict had gone forth that no ex-serviceman was to be employed in any shape or form – if they expressed their views or attended pro-British meetings, their homes were raided, they were tried by mock courts martial and were shot or buried alive in bogs. We decided that the only chance to alleviate their lot was to approach the RC Church, so we met the Bishops and leading priests in Cork, but they were worse than the Sinn Feiner leaders. I never admired a man more than I did White when, at the meetings, he pleaded these poor fellows' cause most forcefully. Yet the churchmen refused to countenance stemming the tide of murder, boycott and every form of cruelty to the ex-servicemen's families. At such a meeting White instanced a case we had heard of near Waterford where a man of the Munster Fusiliers, sent home completely paralysed from his hip downwards, had within a week been tried by mock court martial, carried into his back yard and shot with his two sons, aged seventeen and fourteen. The boys had only begged for mercy for their father. White turned on the meeting with trembling voice and tears in his eyes and said, 'This is villainous slaughter of innocent and brave men. You are Ministers of Christ. For you to condone and support it can only lead to one end, general anarchy!'

Emissaries from Russia poured into Ireland to teach the people how to 'follow Russia'. All forms of employment and trade were closed to anyone who professed to be pro-British. Even the men who held no more than temporary commissions in the British Army found themselves barred from any form of work.

At the conclusion of our tour in Southern Ireland, I went to Lady

Weldon's at Kilmorony to report to the presidents of the county committees on what was happening in the south. Lady Mayo said that she would go at once to London to inform the Cabinet.[3]

The night after this meeting, the parlourmaid rushed into the dining room at Kilmorony while we were at dinner and said that a party of Sinn Feiners was at the front door demanding to see Lady Weldon. Lady Weldon showed no sign of agitation and went to the door. On her return she said that they wanted to see me. I found five armed men. They interrogated me and asked to see all my papers. These they took away, but since White and I had resolved at the first Army Committee meeting in Dublin that our efforts to help ex-servicemen should always be entirely free from political or denominational bias, all they got were various labour proclamations and reports of the different Army and Navy Help Societies. This was the first 'raid' we had experienced in Mid-Ireland.

The next day I was going to address a meeting at Castle Dermot and as usual rode my motor bike with a sidecar. When passing the Duke of Leinster's place, I saw two men standing on the far side of the bridge and as I approached they came into the road and held me up with revolvers. Having called me every name known in Billingsgate, they ordered me off the motor bike to go into the ditch, as they politely remarked, to have my 'bloody brains knocked out'. For some unaccountable reason I had kept the engine running. All the time I was asking God to save and preserve me from what appeared certain death. One of the men seized me by the shoulder, and at the same moment I accelerated the engine, let the clutch in and the bike bounded forward. Immediately they emptied their revolvers at me, and continued firing up the straight bit of road leading to Castle Dermot. I knew that it was only the hand of God that had saved me.

When I reported the matter on my arrival at the RIC barracks at Castle Dermot, the inspector said that they could do nothing, since if they tried to capture my would-be murderers, their motorcar would be ambushed and they themselves all murdered. I did not mention this incident to Lady Weldon, in fact I never discussed anything relating to matters connected with 'the Tommies' Parliament' except with White. At times, in critical situations, I longed to have some sound confidant with whom I could talk things over.

---

3 W.A.T notes: 'Subsequently I was told that the Cabinet, about this time, sent an influential mission to the Pope, begging him to stop these fiendish crimes, but that he refused to intervene.'

The trade unions at this period issued yet another edict debarring all ex-servicemen from every form of work or employment. At an Army Committee meeting it was decided to provide work for the able-bodied men and cater for all categories of the disabled. Before embarking on this policy, we tested the feelings of the trade unions in England by sending selected, fully qualified officers who had been disabled to some engineering and other works. The trade unions in question at once called their men out. At Kitson's works in Leeds a lightning strike was proclaimed and continued till all the ex-servicemen had been removed. The painters and decorators struck *en masse* when we started an ex-servicemen's building and decorating company in London. The manufacturers were forbidden by the trade unions to supply them with materials. So the only thing to be done was to form companies of demobilised men to enable them to get a livelihood.

We had the power to co-opt the best advice and experts for our many schemes. The first undertaking of any importance was a corporation of all ranks to obtain a direct supply of fish for the services. I was asked to be responsible for this scheme, and most interesting work it was. The sea work – trawling, delivering of fish – was undertaken by the Navy; the selling and transport by the Army Servicemen's Corporation. We estimated that some 10,000 disabled men would obtain perpetual employment by means of this organisation.[4]

This grand plan and scheme of work was a simple one: all labour was to be at the trade union rate or wage, and other trades and callings at the ordinary rate. Disabled men would receive their wage less a sum to be provided by the Government according to their category of disablement. Thus, supposing the wage of a mill-hand to be £2 a week, and the man was 50 per cent disabled, his employer paid him £1 and the Government £1. In this way we were assured of work for over 50 per cent of the disabled. The trade unions, however, would not cooperate or give a helping hand under any consideration. They obstructed and opposed our efforts whenever we endeavoured to find work for the men and although Northern Ireland was splendid, all ex-servicemen being helped and welcomed, elsewhere in Ireland it was a different story.

One of our efforts was to launch a scheme for harnessing the River

4 W.A.T notes: 'When the Army Representative Committee was wound up, Lord Leverhulme asked me to give him full particulars of our direct "fish supply to the forces" scheme. As the Cabinet offered no objection, I spent many a day with this wonderful old man, giving him full details of our organisation. From this sprang the present Macfisheries Co – providing for a direct supply of fish to the public.'

Liffey to supply Dublin and district with electric power. In this connection I was sent to ascertain the number of men available in the Waterford, Cork and Limerick districts. At the latter place a leader of the Sinn Fein party named Furness told me that our proposed scheme was useless, as when they (the rebels) came into power they were going to harness the Shannon, employing German labour, the contract being given to a German firm (Siemens). This was the latter end of 1918; and when I asked why they intended to give the contract to a German firm and employ Germans, he retorted that it was to give them a base of operations from which they would 'defeat your bloody country'. He claimed that from this base of operations they would:

1. Bring about a revolution and general strike in England by 1926 or 1927, by undermining the industrial world with agitators under assumed English names.

2. Be able to train with German NCOs a Sinn Fein army.

3. Endeavour to make the British Army, Navy and Air Force ripe for revolt, by means of agitators enlisted in the ranks.

4. Have the best aerial base for operations against English ports and shipping, for the Germans, without making an orthodox declaration of war, would be able to bomb our chief ports from the air and to refuel at their base in the Shannon peninsula.

5. Have an excellent submarine base from which to attack our shipping.

6. Have a base of operations impregnable from the land, sea and air.

I met more of the Sinn Fein leaders the following day. They confirmed what Furness had told me, and made it quite clear that none of the ex-servicemen would be allowed to work on the Liffey scheme; if they did so, it would be at the peril of their lives.

A CONFRONTATION WITH SINN FEIN

On my return journey to Dublin, via the Curragh, on the motor bike, I had an interesting and curious experience. It was a common rumour at this time that the rebels were importing foreigners – Chinese, Tartars and Russians – to carry out their nefarious assassinations, as on many occasions the Irishman had declined to perpetrate some of the worst crimes. About 9 a.m., as I was approaching Nenagh, I met a body forty to fifty strong of the worst-looking ruffians imaginable, consisting of

Mongolians and other foreigners, the only Irishman being the man in command. Of course they held me up and, being in uniform, I thought the end was come.

I was marched down a side road until we met a small party of Sinn Feiners, three of whom took me away to a small farm, where they interrogated me closely as to my doings. After my telling them that our work was non-political and solely for the welfare of Irish soldiers on demobilisation, they asked if I knew Vandaleur (an officer of the Irish Guards, Harry Greer's relative) and I told them I had never heard of him. They withdrew and had a long consultation. On their return they asked me why I should be treated differently from any other British officer caught in uniform – they had found me guilty of serving for and under the English Government and I was to be shot.

'Well!' I replied quite calmly, 'I shall see my God before you do, and what is the use of this safe conduct permit, signed by your leaders?'

The brandishing of the pass which White and I had received in Cork produced an instantaneous effect. Luckily I had no other incriminating papers on me. The other Sinn Feiners had gathered round and a man said: 'This is the b—— who used to bring down the women to hunt with the Limerick in Cadogan's time and he's a great sport!'

This quite turned the meeting, for when they heard I had hunted, fished and shot over most parts of the south of Ireland, the leader sent for my motor bike and sidecar and whilst waiting till it arrived, took me to a farm where bread, tea and eggs were served. I then heard of the fate of poor Vandaleur. As far as I could gather, he had been invalided from the front and had been given a temporary job in the south of Ireland. Three days previously he had been captured, somewhere down by the sea, tried by mock court martial and shot. It was low tide and they buried him in the sand, well below high water mark, so that his body would never be found. To everyone's amazement and horror the tide never came up to his grave and when they visited it, they found he was alive. They were much perturbed at this spookish incident, which they declared was God's miracle. They apparently dug him out and took him to the priest's house, but what eventually happened to him, I never heard. It had made a dramatic impression on these ruffians.

Just as I was hoping to be released, the band of foreign devils were marched up, now under the charge of a brutal-looking German, who gave his commands in good English. After talking with the OC of the Sinn Feiners, he came up and said: 'You know me well enough, I was one of the waiters at St Pancras Hotel and used to look after Sir Ernest and Lady Paget before the war. I was a Secret Service officer there from 1900 to the declaration of war, and then rejoined my regiment in Germany.' He was now the German propagandist for Southern Ireland and had given glowing accounts of the victories the Germans were gaining. The commanding officer of the Sinn Fein party remarked that the war would soon be over and the English kicked out of Ireland. I was about to tell them that the Germans had been heavily defeated all along the line and the end of the war was imminent, but refrained from doing so as I noticed there were some Germans among the foreign contingent who had joined the Sinn Feiners at the farm.

About noon I was marched before the leader, who told me that I would be released only on condition that I did not communicate my capture to a soul. After much formality in taking an oath, on my word of honour, I was ordered to mount the bike. When they heard I wanted to go to Athy to stay at Kilmorony, they mostly chorused what a grand fellow Tony Weldon had been, and became very voluble and even pleasant. Apparently he had had a command in Limerick, for they all eulogised his memory. As no man's life was safe with these foreign cutthroats in the district, I pretended that I did not know the way and asked if one of the Sinn Fein officers might accompany me as far as Roscrea. To my surprise the leader ordered two to accompany me as far as the Devil's Bit Mountain, and then one was to see me as far as the foot of the Slieve Bloom Mountains.

I had every reason to suspect treachery, but there was no alternative, so off we went, the officer in the sidecar and the Sinn Feiner on the back as pillion. The officer was related to Tom Donovan, the old Cork horse dealer, who was a great hunting pal of mine when the Regiment was at Ballincollig; and we talked sport all the way to Roscrea. It was very lucky I had him, as we met two parties of rebels on the way. The rebels' method of communication was uncanny in its rapidity. When we arrived at Roscrea, Donovan went into a grocery store to arrange for my safety as far as Athy. Although I passed two rebel patrols shortly afterwards they never questioned me.

A PUGILISTIC SOLUTION

The difficulty about my Tommies' Representative job was that I could not discuss the situation or my experience with anyone, for fear of losing the men's confidence. On arrival in Dublin I narrated the futility of our projected efforts to White. One of these projects, the Land Settlement Scheme, had already been launched and it looked hopeless to commence on the Liffey Electric Power Scheme. The whole situation was discussed at a conference consisting of the Viceroy, the C-in-C, White and myself and they ordered me to proceed to London at once to see Sir Henry Wilson. He was a personal friend of mine and we had ridden many a race together when he was in the Rifle Brigade. When I had disclosed the rebels' Shannon Scheme and the base of operations which they had arranged for the Germans, he was intensely interested and summoned the Chiefs of the Air, Army and Navy intelligence staffs. They were all agreed that the Germans could not have selected a better position. After consultation with the heads of the intelligence department, Henry Wilson summed up, as follows:

1. The Germans had the nearest air base towards America and within easy air range of Germany. Their bombers' flight would be in a direct line over many of our docks, great cities and harbours, with a safe landing base from which to refuel.
2. They had an excellent submarine base from which to attack our shipping.
3. Such a base would be impregnable by land, until the German-trained Irish army had been defeated.
4. The population would be mostly hostile, and without the concurrence of America a blockade would be impossible.
5. By poison gas bombs from air bombers, the UK population could be well-nigh exterminated.

He concluded with the remark: 'They are clever devils, these Huns. Immediately they are defeated in this war, they prepare for the next.'

I told him – as apparently he knew already – that the trade unions were filtering agitators into the ranks of regiments to bring about wholesale mutinies, and were also doing their utmost to keep the demobilised men out of all forms of employment so as to make them thoroughly discontented and ripe for the coming revolution. He said, 'Of course, no British Government would or could allow such a concession [i.e. the Shannon Scheme] to be made to the Germans, and we are dealing with the question of the trade union agitation in the ranks.' The authorities subsequently told me that the Cabinet had been fully informed of the suggested action of the pro-German rebels.

The Armistice was now under way and the men were being demo-bilised as quickly as possible. One day at the Curragh I received a message from Miss Sands of Sands' Home for Soldiers and Sailors asking me to go to see her at the Soldiers' Home. I had never met this fine old lady and on meeting her, in her private room, was much impressed by her appearance. She informed me that some of the men wished to speak to me, in private, and she thought her room would be the best place for the interview. Five men appeared, two from the Lancers. After Miss Sands's departure, they told me that a mutiny was to break out the following day, and they felt it their duty to tell me that it had been organised by the trade union delegates who had been enlisted into the various regiments.

This was a purely military matter, and it was no business of mine to advise the military authorities. I had always been scrupulously careful not to be biased for or against one side or the other, only to try to do everything possible for the ex-servicemen. I had been reluctant to have the interview with Sir Henry Wilson in case the men or Sinn Feiners might make it out that I was acting as a Secret Service agent. So on this occasion I did not mention my information to any of the military authorities. However, I felt I must have a confidant with whom to discuss this most serious and urgent matter, so I went down to Curragh Grange and told Harry Greer the whole situation. He knew Ireland from top to bottom and his opinion was the soundest procurable anywhere. We decided that no action could be taken until the mutineers had shown their hand.

The next morning I was up at reveille. At 8 a.m. a mob of over a thousand men surrounded the Lancers' quarters at Ponsonby and Steward barracks shouting, 'Come out the Lancers.' I walked on to the parade ground and was told that no parades or stables were to be held except by sanction of the men's leaders, and that the latter wished to see me.

After breakfast these men (all trade union agitators who had been expressly enlisted to stir up strife) slouched up to the orderly room. Millett, Kearns, Smith, Campbell, Jackson and Johnson were the most prominent and demanded the immediate release from service of all TU members. This deputation consisted of twelve men and there was not room for all of them in the orderly room at the same time. It was a bitterly cold October day with a strong east wind, so I asked two to come inside to discuss matters. I scribbled on a piece of paper to the adjutant: 'Detain the deputation outside the orderly room till I send for them', and then talked with the two selected men, Kearns and Campbell, for over two hours while their comrades were freezing outside. I then returned them to their comrades and changed to another two, and kept this pantomime going until nightfall, when they were all well nigh frozen and chilled to death. None of us had anything to eat or drink. Their attitude when they first made their demands was most arrogant and insubordinate; but when I released them about 7 p.m., they were lamblike. On their return to barracks, they were unmitigatedly chaffed by the men about the trick I had played on them. This happened on the Thursday, and although by then the mutiny was flourishing amongst the other troops at the Curragh, none of those under my command were contaminated.

On the following days I interviewed some of the prominent NCOs and men and learnt that a big meeting had been summoned for Saturday night to elect leaders and arrange a plan of campaign to combine with the Sinn Feiners, shoot the officers, and start an open rebellion. Having carefully checked this information among my tommy friends, I decided that Lord French must be advised of the situation forthwith, so I rode up to Dublin on my motor bike, arriving at the Viceregal Lodge about noon. Lord French at once sent for the Chief Secretary, McPherson, and a long discussion took place, ending in them both deploring the fact (after they had called in and consulted the C-in-C) that the commanders at the Curragh were a futile lot of incompetent old women and unable to deal with the situation. Unrest having been allowed to creep so successfully, it was impossible – without causing much bloodshed – to deal with it by force. The Lancer Reserve Regiment was the only one which had refused to be drawn into the movement.

When Lord French asked if I could make any suggestion, I put forward the following. If I were provided with a letter of indemnity signed by himself, I would return to the Curragh at once, collect a band of pugilists from the troops under my command belonging to the 9th, 12th, 16th and 17th Lancers, arrange for these men to attend the meeting the following night, and if possible 'lay out' the leaders of the forthcoming rebellion, but that all these pugilists must be covered by his letter of indemnity. I assured him and the Chief Secretary that I would in no way compromise them or the C-in-C. After a good deal of discussion and much laughter, Lord French wrote out the letter of indemnity, and I again promised that I would not give them away under any circumstances.

I arrived at the Curragh about dinner time Friday, in time to ask Jack Riddell, a major in the 16th Lancers, to have a bite of dinner with us. Jack (son of Puggy Riddell of Pytchley fame), who was nicknamed the 'King of East Africa', was one of the hardest nuts I have ever met. He had been one of the early pioneers in East Africa and owned vast tracts of that territory. He had been with Smuts most of the war and could speak many of the African dialects. After being wounded he had had a row with Smuts because some captured cattle had been branded J.R., rather than G.R.[5] Since his arrival at the Curragh he had taken the keenest interest in boxing and promoted some excellent encounters. When I had divulged to him my plan of campaign, he took it up with maximum enthusiasm, promising to have four first-class pugilists ready for me to see by 11 a.m. the next day – Saturday. These were to be the leaders, with four men under their command. The middleweight champion of England, a Kettering man, whose name I have forgotten, was a corporal in the 9th Lancers and he and three other bruisers turned up at my house at noon. After seeing Lord French's letter to them, they took on the job with great gusto. Jack Riddell was to be handy in case serious rioting occurred.

About 8 p.m. there was the devil of a noise proceeding from the Riding School. At some point before 9 p.m. Jack appeared and reported that fifteen leaders had been sent to hospital and that his men had suffered no casualties. All was quiet that night, everything passing off as if nothing had occurred. There was no more trouble with the mutineers.

Some weeks afterwards, I was asked by the GOC, Curragh, for my reasons in writing why I had been a party to creating a disturbance in the Riding School. I replied that troops other than those under my command had held an unlawful meeting on the particular Saturday night, and as they had no right to be there and the military police would take no action, my men had turned them out. I thought that this would settle the matter, but not at all, for when the Brigadier interviewed me and I declined to give any further explanation, I was hauled up before the GOC, who threatened me with a general court martial if I did not give a full account of the incident, as two of the trade union leaders were critically ill in hospital.

As I had been passed unfit for service (C3) at a recent medical board, and my army career was in any case finished, I rejoiced at the idea of a court martial, and was disappointed when a polite letter came from the

5 For Jack Riddell instead of George Rex.

War Office asking me to give an account of the insubordinate conduct of the troops at the Curragh. I briefly replied that as the Regiment which I had the honour to command had refused to take any part in 'the mutiny', they resented the action of the mutineers in trying to contaminate them and had therefore kicked the leaders out of the precinct of their barracks.

GALLOPING FOR DEAR LIFE

During the hunting season 1918–19 I was out with the Queen's County. When the field was proceeding to another covert after a good hunt in the morning, rifle fire was opened on us while we were going along the road between two hills. I was riding a four-year-old, Sane Boy (brother to my wonderful horse, Lunatic), and was talking to Sir Hutchison Poe, a Crimean veteran who had lost his leg in that war and who always came out accompanied by his old coachman with whose help he could mount and dismount.

We were luckily at the rear of the column when fire was opened. Old Poe, it was supposed, could not ride over fences with only one leg, but on this occasion he jumped a nasty bank out of the road, followed by the old coachman, and fairly flew over five or six fences until we came to a bog. He was not in the least discomposed or worried, and made his way home across country, a distance or four or five miles. I would have liked to accompany him, but as Sane Boy had only been out hunting once before I was doubtful whether he would negotiate seven miles across country to Athy. I had not gone more than a mile or so northwards before I saw two rebels, carrying rifles, trying to catch a loose horse with its saddle on, but without a bridle. These men at once turned their attention on me and opened fire. The field I was in was all wired, except the bank up the hill. I rammed Sane Boy at a real rasper stone-faced bank, a seemingly impossible obstacle. He got over with a scramble, and seemed to appreciate the danger we were in, for he jumped beautifully until we reached the Monasterevan-Athy road. There I found that he had lost two shoes.

It was now getting dark. Luckily, a blacksmith was handy and he soon got to work on Sane Boy. The blacksmith interrogated me closely, as to where I had left the hunt and if I had seen any of 'the boys'. On my replying in the negative, he said, 'You must have left before they stopped the hunt, for they were after Walsh and Poe, and will be back here soon to carry out a raid near Athy.' It was a nice situation to be placed in, for my young horse had already carried me over forty miles and I had at least ten more to get to Kilmorony. The blacksmith, when he had finished shoeing the horse, told me that he had recently been demobilised from the artillery, offered me tea and gave Sane Boy a feed of corn, after which we were ready for the road again.

Just as I was starting, the blacksmith seized my bridle, saying, 'The boys are coming down the road. Come back and I'll let you out the back way!' The back yard was enclosed with a wall and for a moment I suspected treachery, but he said, 'Lep over the wall and ye'll find a lane running north east, past Cushie's, and if the boys are not on it, ye'll get home.'

After negotiating three fences in the dark, I found the lane and reached Kilmorony after 10 p.m. The instinct of direction which I had acquired, like pigeon-instinct, stood me in good stead on this and several other occasions, for if I knew the bearings I never lost my way or had to ask the road to my destination. They were greatly relieved at Kilmorony when I turned up, for Walsh had sent a message to Lady Weldon that he had escaped from the rebels, after losing his horse, and that I had been seen galloping away with Sir Hutchinson Poe and his coachman. He had heard several rifle shots, so they imagined both of us had been killed or captured. The next day we heard that Walsh's horse had found its way home and that old Poe was also safe.

THE HOTEL MASSACRES

Every effort was being made by the revolutionaries of England, Scotland and Ireland to force the demobilised men into their ranks and also to capture control of the various soldiers' and sailors' associations. The Federation of Discharged Soldiers was being badly contaminated and a mass meeting was arranged to take place in Glasgow in November 1920, the advertised speakers being Jackson, Johnson, Campbell and Smith – all extremists of the Bolshevist type. The authorities asked me to attend this meeting for there were any number of Irish ex-servicemen in Glasgow. It was therefore arranged for me to say a few words on their behalf and to let them know of the various relief schemes which had been instituted to promote work for the disabled and unemployed.

It was a huge meeting of some thousands. As we were going on to the platform a man belonging to the North Lancashire Regiment drew me aside to tell me that Smith's real name was Schmidt and that he had served all through the war in the German Ordnance Corps. I asked the

chairman of the meeting if at some point I might say a few words. Each
speaker in turn advocated red revolution. Smith informed the audience
what glorious results had come from the Russian Revolution and
explained how it had been organised with the help of the demobilised
men. Being called upon by the chairman to speak, I said: 'As I have to
return to Ireland by tonight's boat, I have only time to say a few words.
I have met Messrs Jackson, Johnson and Campbell at the Curragh [they
were some of the men knocked out by Riddell's bruisers during the
mutiny], but Mr Smith I have not had the honour to meet previously.
From the information I have just received he has no right – it is indeed
the greatest insult that he should be allowed to address you, the greatest
heroes of all time, for his real name is Schmidt and he served till the end
of the war in the German Ordnance Corps.' Smith, trembling with rage,
endeavoured to speak, but with shouts of 'Well done, Colonel', the
tommies broke up the meeting.

That evening I sailed from Glasgow to Dublin. I had arranged to stay
the weekend with Harry Greer at Curragh Grange, but at Kingsbridge
station the following morning the station master informed me that a
general railway strike had been proclaimed and there was no chance of
my getting by train to Kildare. Deciding to stay in Dublin over the
weekend. I got into a sidecar to drive to the Shelburne Hotel. When we
were passing Guinness's brewery, the nearside wheel of the car came off
and I, with my golf clubs and hand bag, was precipitated onto the pavement just as a tramcar was heading by towards Kingsbridge station.
Having cursed the jarvey, I returned to Kingsbridge station in the tram
and was told by the station master that if I waited till the evening he
would smuggle me to Kildare in a luggage train. So down I went, most
uncomfortably, in the fish van, arriving at the Greers about 10 p.m.

The next morning we were horrified to hear of the massacre of all
British officers who happened to be staying at the Shelburne, Hibernian
and Ross Hotels. It was only by a direct intervention of Providence that
I had escaped. If the wheel of the sidecar had not come off, I would
have been either at the Shelburne or Ross's where every officer was
murdered that night, 21 November 1920.

Ross told me subsequently that the murderers broke into his hotel
after midnight. After holding him up, they demanded to know which
rooms the officers were occupying. There were five officers in all staying
at the hotel, three of them with their wives. The married couples were
all sleeping on the first floor. Ross took the murderers up to the top
floor and had the presence of mind to wake 'the boots' on his way up,

telling him to warn the officers on the first floor. No one expected that these devils would slaughter innocent men in cold blood, so when the married officers heard shots on the top floor, they thought that one of the subalterns above had fired on the intruders. Two rushed out in their pyjamas and were shot at their bedroom doors. When the assassins entered the third married officer's room it appeared only to be occupied by a woman, who told them that her husband was on the staff and had been called to headquarters for night duty. Ross told me that her calmness allayed all suspicion, and after they had searched the room and cross-questioned Ross, they were satisfied that she was speaking the truth and left. When Ross had seen them safely away, he returned to tell the wife. Her husband emerged from under the mattress. His wife had had the presence of mind, when 'the boots' arrived, to persuade her husband to lie face down between the springs and mattress and she then lay on the top and calmly awaited the arrival of the murderers.

Fifteen Sinn Feiners carried out this butchery; they were the slaughtermen. Every one was in turn murdered by his own side by the end of 1925, except Mulcany who received – and I believe still holds – a high post in the Free State Government.

The Bolshie elements in Ireland were gradually getting the upper hand. Arthur Vicars, who had been on Lord Cadogan's staff, was taken from his home and shot. Every day horrors of the worst kind were reported.

Hunting, however, went on as if nothing untoward was happening. Rigney, one of the horse dealers in Athy, remarked that it was better and more profitable to deal in 'cool meat' than live animals, so bought a hearse and changed his trade from horse dealer to undertaker.

After the massacre of the twenty-one officers in Dublin the British Government appealed to the Pope to denounce these wholesale assassinations. He refused. On that same night a private soldier who had been badly disabled in the war, and lived with his family near the pier at Kingstown, was murdered in his bed by some Sinn Feiners. His son, mad with rage, ran a bayonet into the stomach of one of the murderers and killed him. Of course they slaughtered the poor boy, so there were three corpses to be buried. An appeal for funds for the family was made to the Army Committee. I went down to Kingstown the day before the funeral to see what could be done to help the widow and her remaining three children. They were very respectable people with a nice home on the sea front. The husband had been one of the first to volunteer for service in the Great War, joining the Dublin Fusiliers, and was only hit

during the last month. On my way to the house I met a funeral procession conducted by seven RC priests, with censers, and a big crowd. This
was the murderer's funeral!

On my arrival at the soldier's home, I found the widow completely
collapsed with grief. The whole family were RCs and the Bishop had
ordered that no priest should conduct the burial service and had put a
ban on anyone helping the poor woman. There lay the Dublin Fusilier
and his son, just where they had been killed, both shot through the
head. I was a bit nonplussed what to do. Being a Protestant, I had no
chance of making the RC Bishop feel any pity, so I rode up on my
motor bike to Dublin in the hope of finding the valiant White. As he
was a very busy man, I thought I had little hope of catching him. Luckily I met him just as he was going out on business and he at once put
me into his car and drove to Kingstown. It was now getting dark.
Having called at various places in Kingstown, he drove to the house,
carrying a large parcel with him. We did not attract any unpleasant
attention from the group of people standing near the house when White
made it known that he was a solicitor belonging to one of the biggest
firms in Dublin.

We went in to find the poor woman in the same state and position as
when I had left her four hours previously. No angel's words could have
been more beautiful than White's. He opened his parcel, which contained buns, cakes, eggs and a host of other goodies, and gave them to
the widow and children. The youngest was about four. Never have I
seen human beings eat so much as that family did on this occasion, for
they had had practically nothing to eat since the Bishop had put a ban
on the house. They had been boycotted by the tradesmen and everyone.
After they had finished their meal, White explained the arrangements
he had made for the funeral the next day, for he understood that no
priest of their faith would be allowed by the Bishop to officiate. I had
never encountered such pathetic sorrow. She seemed to feel this boycott
more than the death of her husband and son.

White then took her by both shoulders. 'These priests of yours pose
as being the ministers of Christ on earth. They are nothing of the sort,
for they condone the murder of your husband and behave in exact
opposition to what Our Saviour teaches, namely love and goodwill
towards men. They are party to the wholesale murder of defenceless
and innocent men, whose only crime was serving their country in the
Great War.' He then told her of one of the finest types of what a Christian should be, a naval chaplain, and that any naval man in Kingstown

would confirm this. She seemed much reassured and asked us to go and see the minister and make all arrangements for the following day.

It was now about 7 p.m., and the minister (a Wesleyan) was having his supper when we arrived. When he heard White's story, he asked us to have some food at his table while he visited the poor woman. We had finished our food and were beginning to think he would never come back, for the house was quite close and he had been away over an hour. When he did return he said: 'I'm sorry to have been away such a long time, but I persuaded Mrs —— and her children to pray with me and we were lost in prayer. She rose from her knees a different woman and said that Christ had brought great comfort to her soul. It is all right now, and I will see to everything tomorrow.' He was a handsome, sailor-like man of about thirty-five and impressed both of us enormously. We subsequently heard that he had treated the widow and her children with the utmost kindness and Christian love.

On our way back to Dublin I asked White how he managed to conduct his very big business and lend a hand to the welfare of the ex-servicemen at the same time – when I had caught him that afternoon he was rushing off for some important meeting. He replied, 'To work for Jesus is the greatest pleasure and happiness I have, and I put His work before everything.' Near Ballsbridge about 11 p.m. we were held up by a Sinn Fein patrol. We were later informed that they had been on their way to raid and murder a magistrate.

SKIDMORE'S MAGIC

My younger son Ned and I had been to fish in the spring of 1920 with Bertie Hall Dare at Newtownbarry on the Slaney. I had often been there in previous years and had caught the record fish. The people around were most friendly and outwardly loyal to the British Government. Bertie, who had about six miles of the best pools, had not been molested or raided. In the spring of 1921 I was surprised to hear from him that the Bolshies had claimed equal fishing rights on his reach of the river and were ruining his fishing. He asked if I would come down 'to peg out his claim to fish' and that it would be doing him a real kindness if I could manage to come, as having shot, fished and hunted around there for so long, the people liked me very much.

As I have already told, Old Skidmore of the antique shop at Askrigg, Yorkshire had showed me his ancient volume on how to catch salmon. All poachers' tricks were included, and among them the following: 'Put some salmon roe on the top of some large worms. Feed the worms with the roe mashed with bread and milk for a few days and if a salmon is in a pool, it will take these worms more readily than anything else and come from afar to do so.' Before going to Bertie's, having a good collection of roe, I fed some worms and took them down. The smell was awful. The first day I went to fish I found the best pools occupied by the Bolshie element, who ordered me to quit in the most threatening and insulting terms. Smilingly I begged them to allow me to start on the top pool and fish the river down, after they had tried any bait they liked. After much abuse they agreed.

It being a Saturday there were a good twenty men fishing Bertie's beat, the top pool being occupied by the local tackle maker, Fitzgerald. Naturally, as I had bought fishing tackle from him off and on for twenty years, he was tolerably polite and invited me to fish the pool down, but I airily replied: 'Oh, no, Fitzgerald, you go first and I'll try with a worm.' He was fishing a prawn, since many other rods had already flogged the pool with fly and spinners. Waiting till he had gone to the pool below, which was round a bend of the river, I commenced worm fishing with my roe-worms and at once got into a salmon which when landed was 22lb. This fish I hid in some scrub.

When Fitzgerald had vacated the pool below about noon, I sauntered down and got another fish of 19lb, which I also hid. Now came a straight stretch of the river with two excellent pools, but they were being fished by four men. I thought it best to make myself as pleasant as possible, so confined myself to watching them fish. I'm afraid that I prevaricated and lied in a horrible manner that day. They were having no sport at all, and I remarked that no fish could be caught that day with the number of rods flogging the water. This tactic bore fruit, for they all went off to Newtownbarry to have a drink. No one was about, so in went my roe-worm and in the very pool above the bridge got a fine fish of 15lb, which I hid in a hole in the bank and then went up to lunch at the house. In these times one couldn't speak openly about anything, so when Bertie asked what sport I had had, I dissembled and told Mrs Bertie in front of the servants that, as far as I had heard, none of the numerous rods fishing his Newtownbarry water had caught a salmon.

Going out after lunch I fished the lower water with a salmon fly the wings and hackles of which I had thinned and trimmed so that I was able to slide a good big worm over the feathers. The river was now bank-full with fishermen, so I had to wait till they had all flogged the water and were out of sight before commencing to fish. Having waited till 5 p.m., I thought – stupidly as it turned out – that it would be safe to fish the pool above Bertie's private bridge, for I could see no one there. It was a very difficult place to throw a fly, yet a certain lie for a salmon. I soon got into a good fish and had to wade into mid-stream to avoid some trees and prevent him getting through the bridge. Being intent on playing the fish, I did not at first notice six armed men who were on the bank behind me. When eventually I succeeded in getting the fish mid-stream, I saw that Fitzgerald was one of the party.

On my reaching the bank, they asked if I had a permit to fish from the IRA. When I replied mildly that I was fishing Mr Hall Dare's water, they used their usual Billingsgate language and abuse, took my rod and tackle and confiscated the fish – one of about 27lb – threatening that if I was caught fishing again I would be shot. The fish was well hooked and when disgorging the fly I removed all traces of the roe-worm, so they thought I had caught the salmon with a fly. Other fishers had seen me playing the salmon and there was now quite a throng of people on the bridge. Seeing them, Bertie Hall Dare rode down on his cob to discover what all the excitement was about. I briefly told him. He at once rode after them and quite unperturbed by their demeanour ordered them to return my tackle and the fish immediately. I thought we were most certainly in for trouble when one man threatened to shoot Bertie, but Fitzgerald, who was a tenant of Bertie's, intervened. With hangdog looks they brought the fish back with my rod and tackle.

After dinner that night, when we were alone, I told Bertie of the great sport I had had and where I had hidden the three fish. Before dawn on the Sunday he and I went down to the river – he on his cob, with an old pair of waders over the pommel. We collected the salmon without anyone seeing us, and brought them up to the house in the legs of the waders.

On our way to morning service, Roark, the father of the polo players, met us. Up till the Troubles he was one of the most successful horse dealers in Ireland, but had since become a bankrupt; so Bertie allowed him to live in one of his lodges. Beckoning us aside he told us that the Sinn Feiners planned to murder me that night. On our way to the Protestant church we passed the RC church and convent, on the doors of each of which was a large placard saying that for every RC who suffered, two Protestants would be killed. The old RC canon, whom I had known and liked for many years, was standing outside his church. Bertie at once tackled him for allowing this unchristianlike placard to be put on his church. He was much distressed at Bertie's invective, and told us it was by order of the Bishop that the proclamation was posted and that he was powerless in the matter. He and Bertie were lifelong friends and they mutually respected one another, for Bertie was an ideal landlord and had done much for people of all denominations in New-townbarry.

The canon walked a few yards with us, and when we were out of anyone's earshot, said, in a very pointed manner: 'Look here, Colonel, you must be away this afternoon, the Sinn Feiners are going to murder you tonight.' I replied, 'Canon, I thank you most heartily for your advice, but I have been miraculously preserved from death by my beloved Saviour, and if God protects me, no Sinn Feiner can do me any harm.'

During our service the lesson from Chapter 11 of Hebrews was read: it seemed a direct message to me that if I continued to have faith in God, all would be well. My conscience told me to make no alterations in my plans, but to remain at Newtownbarry till the end of my visit the following Thursday. On our way back to the house, Bertie was much perturbed as to my safety and suggested that I should get away through the gardens immediately after lunch and that he would drive me to Thurlee or Carlow. I told him the feelings I had had in church and said that if he would keep me till Thursday, I would stay, to which plan he reluctantly agreed.

As I was going to bed that night I heard voices outside the front door, demanding that Bertie come down. Mrs Bertie, sister of John Gordon, insisted on going down in his place, and I heard her giving the callers a proper dressing down for raiding the place and ordered them to the back door. There Bertie appeared on the scene, cool and quite unperturbed. They demanded provisions for a contingent of the Republican Army quartered in the Wicklow Hills, and took most of the jam, hams (some of the best I have ever tasted), and my 27 lb. salmon.

A LIFE FOR A LIFE

On the Monday I got three fish on the roe-worms and continued to have good sport till Wednesday, including a 32 pounder which was the record fish of the year. On Wednesday afternoon the IRA men would not allow me to fish any of the pools. The river was lined with fisher-men using all forms of bait, so I asked if there was any objection to my fishing a deep run under a tree with a worm, as I liked watching them fish.

It was an impossible place to throw a line, so I cut a bit of stick to a boomerang shape, attached this onto the line, and floated out the bait, otter fashion. To my great surprise a fish bit at once. I couldn't give him a yard of line, for fear of getting hitched up in the tree and also attracting the attention of the rebels who were occupying the pools above and below me. My tackle was strong enough to hold almost any salmon and just as I had the fish floundering and was about to gaff, three armed rebels came up behind me and asked what the hell I meant by fishing without a permit from the IRA. I replied, 'Can one of you use a gaff?' for the bank was so steep and high, with branches overhanging the deep hole where the fish was floundering, that it was impossible for me to gaff him. When they saw the size of this real monster they put down their rifles, linked hands and made a chain down the bank. The fellow who said he could gaff missed a very easy chance twice. On his making a third snatch at the fish, the bank gave way and the three slid into the water. My line was meanwhile hopelessly hung up in a branch well out into the stream. By this time a crowd of over a dozen rebels had come up and the cry went up, 'The commandant is drowning!' Not a soul on the bank attempted to help the two men who were clinging to a branch and unable to swim, while the young fellow who had tried to gaff climbed to safety on the bank. So, thrusting my rod into the hands of the nearest bystander, I rescued the commandant and then his mate, the latter half-drowned and in need of artificial respiration. I gave a sovereign to a fellow to get some whiskey, which revived the casualty in an incredibly short time.

The fish was still on, with the line entangled in the branch midstream, so I swam out, hoping to release the line and land the salmon; but when I got into the main current I had to snatch at the line from downstream and off the fish went with twenty yards of my line, which broke at the branch. The commandant, named Kelly, had recovered by the time I regained the bank and walked with me towards the house. He thanked me most touchingly for having saved his life, and said, 'You saved my life and I must save yours. The Republican Army council has issued orders – you're known as the man we cannot kill – for you to be captured and shot tomorrow. If you don't believe it, here are the orders.' Whereupon he produced a piece of paper with orders written in Irish in which he had been deputed with five others to carry out the job. I told him of the miraculous manner in which God had preserved

me hitherto and here had been another wonderful example of His intervention, for if I had not hooked the big fish and the Commandant Kelly
had not fallen in – to give me the chance of saving his life – I should
have been murdered within twenty-four hours. He was much impressed
when I told him of my previous escapes and said that it was wonderful
that God obviously protected those who put their trust in Him. He then
discussed various ways and means by which I could get out of the place
without compromising him. He had been ordered by the IRA authorities not to lose sight of me until I left Newtownbarry the next day,
Thursday, and I was to be waylaid at a cutting where the road touched
the river.

In parting, he instructed me to go that night via Shillelagh and
Tullow, and avoid the Carlow road which was patrolled at night. I
would not meet any patrols on the Shillelagh-Tullow road after midnight. It was now about 5 p.m., and for fear of being overheard I said
nothing to Bertie, but filled the bike up with petrol, giving it out that I
was starting after breakfast the next day, Thursday.

We had a cheery dinner and laughed over the immersion of the three
rebels. Then the ladies left. Bertie, his son Charlie and I were talking
over the general situation when I noticed the door was ajar, so telling
Charlie, in French, to go on talking, I crept to the door to find two maids
eavesdropping – they were Sinn Fein spies! This decided me to trust no
one and not to make any preparations for my departure till everyone
was in bed and asleep. My bedroom was over the front door, and on
entering I threw open the window, calling to Bertie: 'May I have breakfast about 9 a.m., and start at 10, for I must be at the Curragh before
lunch and have to call at Carlow on my way to see the vet Walsh.'

Instead of going to bed, I dressed for the journey in the dark. At
about midnight, on peeping out of the window, I saw two men; there
might have been more, for it was pitch dark and I could hear only low
whispers and see the end of two lighted cigarettes. About 3 a.m. nothing could be seen or heard, so I crept down to the back door and out to
the stables. My motor bike started at the first kick, a most unusual
occurrence. In the stillness of the night, I thought its noise would
awaken everyone.

As I left the front gates, the star Altair (the brightest star in the con-
stellation Aquila) was visible for a few seconds between the clouds. I
knew my direction. Had I not been able to find my way by the stars I
could never have succeeded in getting away, for I had never been along
the Shillelagh road and only knew that my general direction was north

east. The North Star was not visible, owing to the blackness of the night.

I shall never forget that terrible ride. At every moment I expected to be stopped by a Sinn Fein patrol, miss the direction or have a mishap with the bike. It was my first experience of bolting for my life and most harassing to the nerves. I had hitherto never carried a revolver, but would have given anything to have had one that night.

When approaching Shillelagh I was challenged by a Sinn Fein patrol who barred my path. Pulling my hat well over my face, I charged the two men who stood with rifles advanced on either side of the road. Luckily at this point the road was dead straight, and the day just dawning so that one could see 100 yards ahead. I made straight for the man on the right, a much smaller individual than the one to my left; he was holding his rifle at the advance in a half right direction. Having done so much fighting on horseback, I directed my line of attack towards his right shoulder. The impact was terrific and I thought for a moment I was over, but the sidecar on my left saved an upset and the man seemed to fly yards: the big man on the left was so surprised that he forgot to fire. I reached Tullow without further adventures. My bike, however, could only wobble along, as the steering gear was badly bent. When I dismounted outside Tullow, I found the sidecar was quite out of true. I therefore had to change my plans and make for Athy. Had I gone direct to the Curragh all the facts of the night's adventures would be known, whereas in Athy I had an ex-service mechanic friend to repair the motor bike without making any enquiry as to the cause of accident.

In Athy there was an old town councillor named Pleuman, a great loyalist and most religious man, belonging to the Church of Ireland. He was suffering from cancer in the stomach, which was pronounced by the doctors to be inoperable, because of his weak heart. He told me that he had asked God to allow him to undergo the operation without anaesthetic and subsequently to make him perfectly well. The Dean of Kildare, Waller, had promised to pray with him during the operation which was to be performed by Sir Courcy Wheeler of Dublin. I told him of the miraculous happenings which had occurred in my life and how God had saved me on many occasions in the past from what seemed certain death. Dean Waller told me subsequently that the operation had been successfully performed without anaesthetic: old Pleuman's stomach was opened up and the cancer successfully removed before his very eyes. When I next visited Athy, he was in seemingly perfect health. I met him and Dean Waller on many occasions afterwards when the Dean corroborated the above account.

SYLVESTER'S PLOY

On my return to the Curragh, Sylvester the bookie, reputed to be the cleverest dry fly fisherman in Ireland, suggested that I should come to fish some water he had leased in King's County. I was to provide the lunch and he the motor to take us there. He asked if two jockeys, Beary and Fraser, might also come as his guests, to which proposal I naturally assented. Starting very early we motored a good fifty miles, reaching a beautiful trout stream about 10 a.m. Sylvester told us how lucky he had been to get this fishing on lease for two years at the ridiculously low rent of £20 for the season, as it was one of the best trout streams in Southern Ireland. Sylvester was a loyalist at the Curragh and an ardent Sinn Feiner among his countrymen, so he gave most amusing descriptions of military doings at the Curragh and Dublin to those rebels whom we met on the way. Being renowned for his wit, he stopped frequently at the pubs to see his friends and I was amazed at the amount of whiskey they all consumed without becoming dead drunk. On our arrival at the river, he asked me to fish above the bridge in the morning while he took the two jockeys below and we would all meet at the bridge for lunch. I had an excellent morning's sport, but the sun came out very strongly and, suffering from sunstroke, I had to take shelter under the shade of the bridge. While waiting for Sylvester's return for lunch I had a snooze.

I was awakened by voices overhead and could not help hearing the conversation, which alluded to the favourite in the Irish Derby which was to be run in about three weeks' time. Sylvester, who was representing a syndicate of bookies, was arranging the race with the two jockeys – a rank outsider was to be allowed to win. Immediately I realised the purport of the conversation I shouted, 'Is that you, Sylvester? Let's have our lunch', and appeared from under the bridge. They were surprised and crestfallen. Towards the end of lunch Sylvester remarked, 'Did ye hear us having a conversation about the Derby?' When I told them I could not help hearing every word, they asked me on my honour not to mention to a soul what I had heard. I laughingly replied that I had given up all interest in racing many years ago, since I could not afford to keep bookmakers, and made out that in fact I was asleep when they arrived at the bridge.

In the afternoon I fished the lower water and they the upper. Before starting Sylvester explained that his water extended to a part of the river some two miles below. I was busy disgorging a fish on the bank when someone behind said, 'What the hell do you mean by fishing my water without leave? What is your name?' Looking up I recognised an Irish gentleman called Denny, whom I had known years before. I explained that Sylvester had invited me to fish his water and that he and two friends were fishing above the bridge.

'Well, I'm damned,' was all Denny said, and asked me to come with him to find Sylvester, whom we soon came across with his basket full of beautiful trout.

Sylvester's first words were: 'Ah, Mr Denny, I was just after coming down to tell you we are having great sport. When you asked me at the races to have a day on your water, you said I might bring a friend, so I brought the Colonel and we have had a splendid day. Will you have some of the fish?' Denny was speechless, but drew me aside to ask who Sylvester was and how I had made his acquaintance. He had never seen or heard of the man before in his life! I told him Sylvester was a well-known bookie at the Curragh and one of the best dry fly fishermen in Ireland. When we rejoined the party, Denny asked him how he managed to catch such a splendid basket of fish. He showed us something I had never heard of before – how every fly, especially may flies, sedges and spinners, changed their hue every hour of the day. His knowledge of insect life seemed quite uncanny, for he showed us how a fish would not look at a female March brown, but speedily swallow a male. Denny told me that he had never seen anything like as good a basket of fish as Sylvester caught, and was so pleased that he asked us all down to tea.

This meant whiskey, which was at this time very hard to get in the country and sixteen to eighteen shillings per bottle. As Denny was a keen racing man and had a horse in the Irish Derby, the conversation soon turned to that race and my companion assured him that Golden (the horse that they had arranged should not win) was an absolute certainty. They were brimful of whiskey when we started on our homeward journey. Sylvester the driver was very garrulous, and the others sleepy. We had not gone more than ten or so miles when there was a tremendous bump and the car flew into the air, up a bank on the driver's side, and overturned in a ditch. We had run into a donkey lying in the road.

It was now almost dark. We were at least twenty miles from our destination, the Curragh, with the car hopelessly smashed up. Sylvester instructed the two jockeys to commandeer another car. When they had started on their errand, I remarked that I would pay for the hire of a car to take us home. He replied: 'Devil a bit of it, we officers of the Sinn Fein army have authority to commandeer any car, and we only brought you so that we shouldn't have any trouble with you bloody English.'

In a short time a nice saloon, driven by a chauffeur, pulled up – evidently a squire's property, yet whose car it was I could not ascertain since my companions addressed one another in Gaelic and did not speak a word of English until we had reached the first guardroom of the Curragh, where I was requested to get the car passed through the lines.

Prior to the running of the Irish Derby I did everything in my power to dissuade my friends and brother officers from backing Golden, but the 12th Lancers were obdurate, one officer plonking his all on the horse. A week before the race I had insisted on Sylvester advising Denny that his 'certain winner' tip would not materialise. As I explained, it was too bad first of all to poach his water and then cause him to lose a packet of money.

When the horse arrived at the tape, the jockey reined it back a yard so that when the tape went up the horse's spring was disunited. Unless we had heard that the horse was not going to be allowed to win, few people would understand how Golden had got such a bad start, for it lost two lengths then and finished fourth. I went to the start when the race took place and have never seen an example of more consummate horsemanship than Golden's jockey displayed. I had the satisfaction of seeing Denny at the Curragh races and he had not backed Golden.

PEPPERED BY THE FRENCH

In 1919 I was invited to shoot at Lord Cowdray's place in Scotland – Dunecht. He had a good moor, Birse Castle, and sport should have been excellent, but the guns were mostly celebrities who had been asked there to discuss the formation of the League of Nations, which Lord Cowdray was in no small measure financing. On my arrival, there was a huge house party, including Colonel House, Lord Grey, Asquith, General Diaz (son of the Mexican President), and representatives from France, Belgium, Italy and elsewhere, none of whom I knew.

After dinner a young-looking fellow asked me to play billiards, and when we were towards the end of our game a housemaid rushed into the room, crying: 'Oh, Mr Sheppard, Mr Sheppard, do come quick.' She then fell down at the door, seemingly in a dead faint. Naturally we rushed to her help, undid her dress, and went to tell the party in the drawing room. On our arrival everyone roared with laughter, for the fainting maid was Lady Cowdray who had borrowed one of the maids' dresses and bet the ladies that she would take in Dick Sheppard, the famous preacher with whom I was playing. After this improbable introduction Dick Sheppard and I became great friends.

The next day Lord Cowdray asked me to run the shoot, the guns being a French marquis, who had given out that he was one of the best shots in France, two Mexican generals, a Belgian, Lord Huntly, Dick Sheppard and myself. Dick came out in ordinary shooting kit, with an I.Z. tie, and I placed him in the drives between Lord Huntly and the Belgian, who, from his kit, looked like a sportsman, whereas the marquis and the Mexican generals admitted they had never been out grouse-driving before. The Frenchman's guns were inches longer than the ordinary English gun, and on our way to the butts he boasted that he had killed wildfowl at a hundred yards' range.

Before starting the first drive, I gave them a lecture on what *not* to do when grouse driving:

1. Not to follow the birds round with the gun.
2. Never shoot towards the beaters when they come within range.
3. Never shoot at birds when passing between the butts.

I did not add never get excited or make a possibly dangerous shot.

It was a perfect day for grouse driving with plenty of birds. In the first drive the head keeper, who was loading for me, remarked that the Frenchman was making some most dangerous shots, and at almost the same moment shouted, 'Duck, sir.' I luckily looked upwards expecting to see a flight of duck, but at the same moment was knocked sideways, the Frenchman having shot both the keeper and myself. The keeper got about five pellets into the side of his face; my wounds were mostly in the neck, through my suddenly looking skywards. Not wishing to upset the day's outing, particularly as it was such a momentous occasion, I begged Burrell, the keeper, not to say a word to anyone. At lunch, which was attended by the whole house party, Lord Huntly remarked that Dick Sheppard was the best shot he had seen for years, and would not believe that he was a parson until Lady Cowdray described the great work that Dick was doing.

After three days Burrell had to go to the Aberdeen Hospital and that night Lady Cowdray suggested that I should see a doctor owing to the swellings on my neck. The Frenchman having taken his departure, I then made a clean breast of what had happened. It appeared from what

the doctors told us that he must have been shooting with highly poisonous powder, as many of the birds killed that day were found to be unfit
for human consumption.

USING THE STARS

After this incident Lord Cowdray persuaded me to manage the shooting at Dunecht for him, as he had not the time to attend to it. Consequently in the following two years I met some very interesting people,
among them Bishop Browne of Bristol. Lord Cowdray had deputed
him to write a book on the Druid circles of the United Kingdom and the
world in general, in collaboration with the Royal Society. In 1920
members of the Society inspected many of the circles in Scotland,
making Dunecht their headquarters. They were evidently intent on dis-
covering the secret of these mysterious circles, which had many details
in common with Stonehenge.

Some years previously I had joined forces with Reeves, the director
of the Royal Geographical Society, to devise a method whereby people could know their way at night by the help of the first magnitude
stars. We discovered that primitive people in uncivilised parts used
similar devices to tell the time, seasons of the year and direction. In
fact they made use of the heavens as their calendar, compass and
clock, with the help of the first magnitude stars at night and the sun
by day. On these lines, Reeves and I invented the 'Anaspace
Compass', which gave the true time, bearings and day and month of
the year. The Royal Society and the Royal Astronomical Society were
extremely interested when I told them of our work and experience.
After visiting a large number of circles, the professors were fully convinced that we had hit upon the real clue to the purpose of the Druid
circles of the world.

The facts are embodied in Bishop Browne's book *Druid Circles*. For
instance, when the Druids saw Regulus appearing from the horizon in
England they knew the month was January, and the time about 9 p.m.
They marked the times of the clock stars with stones. When a star was
over a particular stone they knew it was due east; and if Altair was not
visible, since it rose from the east till then, they knew it was midnight
on the 1 May. By calculating the procession of the most commonly used
twelve first magnitude stars in relation to the stones the professors of
the Royal Society and Royal Astronomical Society were able to esti-
mate roughly the age of the Druid circles by the position of the stones.

In my book *Marching or Flying by Night without a Compass with Time Table of Directional Stars*, this is made quite clear.[6]

CONCEALING ARMS

In 1921 I was still engaged in Ireland on the Army Representative Committee, and was staying with Lady (Winnie) Weldon at Kilmorony Athy when her son Anthony returned for the school holidays. Mabel Kirkpatrick, Winnie Weldon's sister-in-law, was also staying. We had early supper to allow Anthony to hunt rats, which were swarming about the place, and I was busy perusing legal documents, having become one of Winnie's trustees. Suddenly the door was burst open, and looking up I saw Winnie being held up by two men, who were pointing revolvers at her head. Three more men held me up in the armchair in which I was seated. They demanded to know where the arms were that she had hidden, and threatened us all with instant death if they were not voluntarily given up. She replied: 'You cannot be Irishmen, for they are not such miserable cowards as to hold up women with revolvers. Put them down. There are no arms here; they were sent to Dublin in 1916. I'll take you round the house; but I won't answer any questions till I know where my son is.'

Some minutes later Anthony was marched in by two ruffians, both foreigners. He had narrowly escaped death. Chasing a rat, he was suddenly knocked on the head by one of the raiders in the stable yard. They were about to dispatch him when the yardman explained that he was only rat hunting. The leader, as horrible a looking ruffian as you could meet anywhere, accompanied by two other men, then took away Winnie to search the house. The only domestics in the place were the cook and a maid-of-all-work named Josephine who were compelled to accompany the raiders round the house with Winnie. Winnie was marched all over the house and through the cellars: it seemed an age before the raiders returned with her. Anthony, Mabel and I were meanwhile held up in the library by five men who covered us with revolvers.

It was now getting on for midnight. At that point I was seized and marched outside. I certainly thought my last hour had come when the leader accused me of being a British spy, and said that Lady Weldon had told them that I knew where the arms had been hidden – which in fact I

6 First published in 1914, by Rees, Ltd, 47 Pall Mall, London SW1. Studied by officers at Staff College, it ran to at least eleven editions.

did, for I had put all the old weapons that had adorned the walls into the disused ice-house. It meant certain death if they found them. The IRA had proclaimed some months before that all weapons were to be handed over to their county representative, and that anyone disobeying the order would be shot.

I thought the search would never end. They took me all over the house, cellars and stables. It was a little too exciting when they visited the disused ice-house, entered by a short ladder from the outside of the house. Three days previous to this raid there had been torrential rain, which had left a foot of water in the ice-house. My relief can be imagined when the man who had descended shouted, 'This bloody place is full of water', and up he came. They then seized all my private correspondence from my room, which included the private letters Lord Haig had written to me from France, all most friendly and many of great interest.

When they took me back to the library, Winnie remarked to the leader, 'After all your hard work I expect you will like something to eat, so you had better come into the dining room.' This they did – seven of them – and they finished all the victuals and whiskey we had in the house, and took their departure at dawn.

For some months both IRA and Bolshies had made the wood adjoining the River Barrow, near the Kilmorony private bridge, into a night rendezvous and camping ground. I had often set night lines under the bridge, and you could get there unobserved through a deep spruit that ran parallel to the private road. Soon after the raid described above, I stalked a large contingent that had assembled on the north side of the bridge before starting on a raid in Queen's County. With a rod and night lines I arrived close to their rendezvous unseen. From my position I could see everyone arriving, the maid Josephine and yardman Johnnie from Kilmorony, with the blacksmith Kelly, all of whom we had considered loyalists.

These were among the first arrivals. When the meeting had assembled, Kelly was selected chairman, and it was soon apparent that he held a prominent position in the IRA in addition to being 'staff officer' for murders. I could hear every word they said, and their plans to raid the vet, Holland's house in Athy, and the Barringtons who lived in the south. Kelly reported the several ex-servicemen who had refused to join the IRA, and by a show of hands they were condemned to death. The meeting lasted well into the night, and I was chilled to the marrow when they had all left and it was safe for me to leave my hiding place.

The next day I saw young Holland, who had won a VC in the war, and told him about the recent raid at Kilmorony. I advised him to send any guns or arms they had about the place to Dublin. However, he said he would give anyone who dared raid his father's house a hot reception, adding that they were friendly with all the people around, and he felt sure that they would never molest his father, who was eighty years old and much respected. This made no difference to the Bolshie element, for soon after ten men broke into Holland's house and got the reception they deserved, for young Holland shot three dead and wounded two. All had come from Tipperary. The Hollands were ardent RCs, and it was so typically Irish that after the scrap was finished old Holland sent for Canon Mackay, who was the RC priest at Athy, to administer the last rites over the dead and dying. No action was taken against Holland or his assailants, three of whom were taken to Athy hospital.

The raid on the Barringtons took place in 1921, and I learnt the details, some months after the tragedy, from a tommy who lived nearby. The Barringtons were highly respected, large landowners. Their house had ancient associations and there was an accepted legend among the country folk that anyone who robbed or raided this house would meet with instant death. On this occasion the IRA were accompanied by three of their foreign assassins. Presumably the party was out to kill.

Barrington received information of the raid that was about to take place, and welcomed the party on the front doorstep with the greatest politeness and *sang froid*. He invited them to have some supper before they commenced to raid the house. Seven of them accepted his invitation, and when they were seated, having left three to guard the front door, Barrington reminded them of the old legend. 'To hell with such priest's fables,' they replied. 'Well,' said Barrington, 'before we commence supper, we will drink to the health of the IRA with no heeltaps,' at the same time giving the seven men a glass of port. My informant told me that Barrington's carefree acting was extraordinary, for he made them a speech in Irish, gave the toast, and every man finished his glass, at a gulp. In a few minutes all seven men were dead as they sat at the table. When Barrington fetched the three sentries, who had been posted at the front door, he said, 'I warned you all what would happen if anyone raided this place; come and see!' One look was sufficient, and dropping their rifles they fled as if the devil were behind them. I was subsequently told the story by Canon Mackay of Athy, who said as the Barringtons were RCs they were immune from harm and would not be murdered, but he had not taken into his calculations that the raid had been made by the Bolshies and that the port had been 'doctored' some time previously with poison. After this Miss Barrington was shot dead, and the family had to flee to London.

THE BLACK AND TANS

I had many opportunities of seeing the work of the Black and Tans, and the impossible task they had been set by Lloyd George's Government.[7] Their chivalrous behaviour, under the most trying circumstances, was the admiration of all decent citizens in southern Ireland. They were employed as a mobile constabulary force to break up unlawful organisations and arrest leaders who were guilty of murders, raids and other atrocities. Their base of operations was constantly changing so the men who were temporarily sick were cared for, under cover of the Red Cross, in 'mobile' hospitals. While I was doing some work on the borders of Tipperary, a large body of Sinn Feiners and Bolshies raided one of these hospitals near Cashel, murdered seven invalids in their beds, assaulted the two female attendants, and burnt down the house of the doctor who was in temporary charge of the hospital. This inhuman cruelty was planned and organised by a well-known Sinn Feiner who lived near Cahir. The Black and Tans therefore raided his house the next night and shot him dead. The main party of the Black and Tans in that sector were billeted at an inn near Bansha. At the time of their reprisals at Cahir, the Bolshies, dressed as women, slaughtered five Black and Tans at the inn in cold blood while their comrades were away.

There was a tremendous howl in Parliament over the death of the Sinn Fein leader, the Labour Party clamouring that the commander of the Black and Tans should be tried for murder. The Labourites carefully concealed the facts, and the leader – an ex-officer who had won the DCM, MC and DSO – was arrested. Hearing I was in the district, he appealed to me for help, which I was very loath to provide as I wished to avoid anything savouring of politics at all costs. But as this occurred a few months before the advent of the Provisional Government I felt it my duty to accede to his request. I therefore visited him in Limerick gaol.

---

7 Reinforcements for the Royal Irish Constabulary were now being recruited in England. With the expansion of the force there were not enough traditional bottle-green uniforms to go round and some of the new recruits were equipped with khaki additions to their uniforms. They were first seen in County Tipperary in their mixed uniforms where they were given a nickname after a famous pack of hounds there called the Black and Tans. They were not a special force, but there to swell the ranks of the RIC.

The Black and Tans were furious at the treatment meted out to their leader, and that night a party of them brought me some photographs, which had been taken from the Sinn Feiner's house prior to his execution. They depicted, in the most cold-blooded manner, how the slaughter of the seven men in hospital had been carried out. I took these proofs that evening to the C-in-C in Dublin, and the arrested Black and Tans were released. This was the only occasion when I took an active part in any of the political disturbances in southern Ireland.

Shortly before the Black and Tans were demobilised I was walking down Grafton Street, Dublin, at about 4 p.m. when a terrific explosion occurred at the corner of Dame Street. The streets were crowded at the time. When I approached the scene Grafton Street was littered with dead, dying and wounded of both sexes. A lorry load of Black and Tans had been passing when a bomb was thrown from the top of the corner house of Grafton Street on to the wire netting covering of the vehicle, and luckily for the men inside it bounced off into the crowd below, where it exploded with terrific violence. The Black and Tans did not hesitate for a moment, jumped out of their lorry and when I arrived were all engaged in tending the wounded. Every moment I expected to see one of them shot, but without a thought of the danger they ran they worked incessantly until all the injured were removed to hospital. The Irish newspapers, commenting on this occurrence the next day, remarked the English had conquered a quarter of the globe by force of arms, but it had taken the Irish no time to force them into wire cages.

Some of the Black and Tans who had relatives and friends in Ireland were foolish enough to believe in the word of the Provisional Government that they could settle as peaceful citizens, without fear of victimisation, and that they would be welcomed as citizens of the New Free State. Many of these fine fellows, therefore, commuted their pensions to purchase farms or a business, and by the time I left Ireland in 1924 many had been murdered or forced to flee to England, quite penniless.

THE MURDER OF A HERO

Towards the end of 1921 a man named Dan Broon and a party of ten rebels tried to kill Lord French as he was driving back to the Viceregal Lodge, accompanied by Mrs Seymour, the wife of one of his ADCs.

A week after this had occurred, Hylda and I were bidden to spend the weekend at the Viceregal Lodge. The only others were Seymour and his wife and Eddie Saunderson (Lord French's *fidus Achates*). On the

Sunday, Hylda and I were about to walk to church and had gone a few yards outside the front porch when Lord French rushed after us saying: 'It's not safe for you to walk to church; you must come in the motor.' A more extraordinary service I have never attended, for the Viceroy's car was escorted by his armoured cars, and a body of mounted RICs, guarded the precincts of the church during the service. These precautions had to be taken because the Sinn Feiners meditated an attack in force. On our way back we saw plenty of them but not a shot was fired. Lord French's bravery and determination were extraordinary, for he refused to be intimidated, and when iron shutters were fixed in all the lower windows that night, he ordered them to be removed.

On the day the armistice between the British Government and the Sinn Feiners was signed, I met an ex-sergeant of the Irish Guards near a village called Suncroft. He had been ordered by the rebels to rendezvous that night at a bridge some distance away, and he asked my advice whether he should obey them. Up till then he had ignored their threats and orders. I told him that the Armistice had been signed,[8] and he replied: 'Well, then, I certainly shan't go.' He had been wounded four times in the Great War, and then invalided as unfit for further service: an extraordinarily fine type of guardsman, with a wife and five children. From the rebel's point of view his only crime was his eagerness to help his fellow ex-servicemen in their misery.

That night fifteen rebels came to his house, which adjoined the RC church, tried him by mock court martial, and compelled his wife and children to watch him being burnt alive in the back yard. As he was not dead at dawn, they mutilated his body in the most horrible manner. The next day, when I heard of this awful tragedy, I motor-biked over to see what help could be given to his wife and family.

The priest was standing outside the door of their little house, chaffing and laughing with two other men.

I said, 'Isn't it too terrible about poor O'Gorman? I hear he has been burnt alive. I have come to see what can be done for his wife and children.'

He replied, 'Ach shure, didn't he open his mouth too much. He deserved everything he has got.' Words, which I really believe were inspired, rushed out of my mouth and I rated him for ten minutes, beginning: 'You, a minister of Jesus Christ, condone and encourage murders and every work of the Devil. You knew the Armistice was

---

8 On 11 July 1921 a truce was signed between all the Crown forces and the IRA.

signed yesterday, and you came and watched this poor man being burnt alive, before his wife and children.'

When I paused for breath in my tirade, he held up his hand as if to bless me, saying, 'You, Colonel, will be next for it.'

I then broke past him into the house. The wife and children were literally stunned with fright and grief. They sat in the back parlour, moaning and groaning, within sight of poor O'Gorman's body smouldering in the back garden. At the foot of the pyre lay a dead Irish cocker spaniel, with two puppies whimpering round her body. I asked Mrs. O'Gorman if I might take away the puppies, and she replied: 'Yes; the mother bit one of the raiders when they burnt my husband, so they killed her.'

I wired to the Guards Association, and within three days the family were removed to Bournemouth. The puppies were put into the sidecar, and one lived with us at Sutton to be fourteen years old. We called him Sinnie and he was a most amusing character, but useless for sporting purposes.

White, Lady Mayo and myself had many occasions to deal with the Guards Association in the relief of ex-servicemen. We never discovered the secret of its really amazing efficiency and promptitude in action. It was far and away the best organisation of all the naval and military help societies. The Army Representative Committee had been endeavouring since the conclusion of the Great War to amalgamate the various naval and military and air force societies into one organisation, so as to minimise expense and overlapping, and this we succeeded in doing, under the heading, first of all, of the United Services League, which was affiliated subsequently to the British Legion. To begin with, this amalgamation appeared simple enough to carry through; but when we tackled the problem, many vested interests had to be overcome and the salaried staff opposed the project most strenuously. The Army Committee controlled the Field Force Canteen Funds, amounting to over two million pounds, and much of this large sum was allocated to the United Service League for the relief of suffering among ex-servicemen.

LORD FRENCH'S MEMOIRS

On one occasion Hylda and I were staying with Lord French at the Viceregal Lodge. One night after dinner he said: 'I want you in my study.' I thought I was in for a good wigging, and every sort of deed of omission and commission flashed through my brain, but Eddie Saunderson, who was the only other person staying at the Lodge, said: 'It is all right, Tilney; he wants to ask your opinion about his book.' When we reached the room, he said: 'I want your views about my book relating to the events in the Great War.' He then proceeded to tell me all the incidents from the commencement of hostilities to the time he returned to England. It was early dawn before he had finished, when he snapped out, 'Well, what is your opinion as to whether I should publish it now or not? Eddie thinks not.' I replied that I had known General Smith-Dorrien well for many years, and I felt sure he would never deign to answer his (Lord French's) criticisms, and that I should omit all bitter aspersions on several commanders and officials, however justified they may have been.

I said: 'I am sure people don't realise the impossible task you were given to perform, although the authorities knew that there was a lack of all the necessities for a war on such a scale.' Lord French then pointed out that this had been pressed upon the Government by the military authorities since 1902, but they refused to listen. I know this is a fact, for Lord Methuen was on the committee dealing with the munitions that would be required in a European war. Whilst I was his military secretary at the Horse Guards, I saw all the correspondence. The Government under Asquith would not consider any increase in the munitions quota, although the absolute necessity for such an increase was constantly pressed upon them by Lord Roberts, Kitchener, French and all the leading Army commanders.

Lord French told me that before the battle of Le Cateau the Signal Corps had completely broken down, and intercommunication between units and divisions was well nigh impossible. The artillery after the first day's fighting had to be limited to a few rounds per gun per day. On his urgent appeal to the Government to send an adequate supply of ammunition for all arms, Asquith replied that it was impossible, as the ammunition was not in the country.

Lord French concluded this most interesting evening by saying, 'You agree, then, with Eddie that I should not publish my book at present?'

THE HARVEST IN JEOPARDY

Ireland was now in the most terrible state. The rebels, both Bolshie and Sinn Fein, issued a proclamation that no agricultural work was to be done without the sanction of the local Sinn Fein authority. Winnie

Weldon was farming some 300 acres at Kilmorony, and was dependent on any profit that could be got out of this land for her income. The local (rebel) authority there was the blacksmith Kelly, who held the appointment of chief staff officer for murders over a considerable area. He and his family had done the horseshoeing for the Weldon family for generations, and as he had received much kindness and consideration in the past, Winnie had no hesitation in going to see him to ascertain the full facts of the situation. As he had done my shoeing since we had been staying at Kilmorony, I accompanied her to the blacksmith's shop.

It was about 10 a.m. As we arrived he came up in a mud-covered car, apparently after a night raid. He and his companions had two days' growth of beard and were armed with revolvers. He was most insolent and comically offensive when Winnie questioned him as to the purport of the edict. Fearing that I should lose my temper with the little swine – for he was most abusive – I asked Winnie to come away. In the afternoon a deputation, headed by Kelly, came to interview Winnie. They told her that no one would be allowed to work in the fields without the sanction of the Sinn Fein Committee, and that anyone who did so would be shot.

Three days after this incident, I heard a motor sounding its horn outside the front door, about 3 a.m. and thought we were in for another raid. Cautiously looking out of the window, I saw a Ford tractor, with a man and a boy on the seat. On going down, I found the man was a farmer from the district of Monasterevin. Having heard of Winnie's treatment by the Sinn Feiners, he had driven his tractor through the night, some twenty miles, to do her ploughing, and had brought this son, aged twelve, to assist him. After a good feed, they got to work on the big field and had finished half of it by 10 a.m. We all then went to breakfast. As none of the farm hands had turned up I thought the rebels would certainly destroy the tractor during our absence.

On our return we found the old gardener, Farley, standing guard over the machine, with his son, who had served throughout the war in the Air Force. Old Farley had been with the Weldons all his life, he and his wife being the very best type of Irish folk. Their three sons had joined the Air Force, Navy, and Army and had done exceptionally well in the war. I told him what Kelly and Co. had threatened to do, but he merely laughed, saying we would finish the field before the local Sinn Feiners returned from a raid some fifty miles away. By dinner we had finished the field and we all went to the house to get some food. The boy went back to get his coat when we reached the house. As he did not return we walked down the drive to find him. To our horror we found him almost thrashed to death, but not a rebel was to be seen. Lady Weldon and her sister-in-law Mabel took the lad back to the house and nursed him back to consciousness, while we went to bring the tractor to the house. We never discovered who had done this cowardly deed, and the wonderful thing was that the rebels did not waylay the farmer on his return that night. He was an extraordinarily brave man.

About this time the whole countryside attended the funeral of Colonel Cosbie, who had been shot. He was a much-respected Protestant landowner in Queen's County, and was not only a loyalist but an ardent supporter of the ex-servicemen. Colonel Megan, of Levitstown, and I attended. I will not forget the ceremony, for when the coffin was being lowered into the grave with the words 'earth to earth' and so on, a certain Lord L, a confirmed drunkard, stepped forward saying: 'Poor old Dick, what a good schap you were', tripped and fell headlong into the grave. Almost simultaneously shouts were raised from 'the bhoys' 'Throw in the earth quickly and bury the — with the Colonel.' There was pandemonium and Lord L narrowly escaped with his life, having been half-buried and badly mauled by the congregation.

THE BIRTH OF THE BRITISH LEGION

Before the establishment of the Provisional Government in Ireland in January 1922, all members of the Army Representative Committee were summoned to London for a meeting under the chairmanship of Sir Henry McKinnon. We had had no warning of the purport of this meeting. All the schemes for the welfare and employment of the ex-servicemen had had the full approval of the Cabinet and were being pressed forward with the utmost speed, in spite of the strenuous opposition by the trade unions. Everyone therefore was much surprised when Winston Churchill turned up at the meeting. He told us that most of our schemes had been favourably received by the Cabinet, but that they could not be carried out owing to the opposition of the Labour Party and Trades Union Congress. Sir Henry pointed out in reply that if our schemes were backed and carried through by the Government, all ex-servicemen would obtain decent employment in civil life. Every category of the disabled would be well cared for and have a good chance of recovering their normal health, which they had lost in the service of their country.

General Tim Harrington, representing the Imperial General Staff, then strafed Winston and the Government. He said that the ex-service-men of the Empire had done their duty in the face of the enemy and never imagined that the British Government would run away at the first threat of trouble from socialists, many of whom had been conscientious objectors during the war. With heartfelt vehemence he described how the trade unions were endeavouring to debar ex-servicemen from every opening, and gave instances of fully qualified men who had been bitterly persecuted at the hands of the trade unions simply because they had served their country in the Great War. Tim Harrington paid dearly for his straight speaking for he was shortly afterwards removed from his appointment at the War Office.

The next speaker was the representative of Northern England. He was an extraordinarily fine-looking man, a resident of Northumberland. He had enlisted in the Northumberland Fusiliers at the commencement of the war and wore three wound stripes on his private's uniform. Without taking his eyes off Winston for a moment, he began: 'So Mr Lloyd George and the British Cabinet propose selling us, who have saved the country, to the trade unions. You can go and tell your colleagues that we refuse to be slaves.' He then trounced Winston with such effect that the latter slunk out of the room. This was the end of the Army Committee – we were shortly afterwards thanked for what we had done and told that our services would no longer be required.

The great betrayal, as this Northumbrian tommy had described it, had a far-reaching effect on the future welfare of those who had served in the war. Up till now the demobilised were 'under the wing' of the Army Committee, officially backed by the British Government and the profits from the Field Force Canteens, amounting to over a million. We had started big undertakings for those who could get no work, and all the disabled had been catered for. The men were now thrown on the common labour market, where they had to compete with the stay-at-home, and conscientious objectors. Having already amalgamated the various service help societies into the United Services League, we now formed the British Legion, under Lord Haig's help and guidance. Since the formation of the Army Committee, I had kept him fully informed of our proceedings and he was most solicitous as to the lot of the demobilised when they returned to civil life. It is my lasting regret that the many private letters I received from him on this subject were all taken by the Irish Bolshies when they raided Kilmorony in 1922 and 1924.

Considerable sums were now allocated to the United Services League and the new-born British Legion by the Government. White and I were asked to administer the monies allotted to Ireland, and establish the British Legion there in various centres. Lord Haig had repeatedly stressed the point that the Legion must be non-political, non-denominational and run solely for the benefit of those who had taken part in the Great War. As was inevitable in Ireland, we encountered opposition from almost every quarter. For instance, at Cork, where the Legion secured excellent premises and promised to flourish, the club was attacked one night. Several men were murdered and the building burnt to the ground. Law and order, as understood in civilised countries, ceased to exist, for the Royal Irish Constabulary were replaced by Civic Guards, many of whom were the scum of the towns and villages.

HOW BRIDEY GOT TO HEAVEN

In the spring of 1922, after the formation of the Provisional Government, I was trout fishing at Kilmorony on the River Barrow when I heard a woman's screams coming from the direction of the private bridge about half a mile upstream. I walked as fast as I could in my waders, and when I came within sight of the bridge saw a crowd. On my approach, a woman told me that Lady Weldon's maid, Bridget Fitzgerald, had been drowned. When I arrived the local doctor informed me that during a Sinn Fein meeting Bridey had fallen into the river and drowned. 'There is the carpse,' he added, 'with Father O'Sullivan praying over the puir girl's body.' He then held forth on the girl's extraordinary beauty, and what a pity it was that she had met such an untimely end. I was the only occupant of Kilmorony except Martha (the cook), for Josephine, the Sinn Fein spy, had been dismissed and Lady Weldon and the others had gone away for a few days. I therefore suggested to the doctor, it being now about 6 p.m., that poor Bridey's body might be taken up to the house. 'Ach,' said he, 'we must not disturb the Father's prayers.' So we waited for another half-hour before the priest arrived.

By this time a big crowd had assembled on the bridge, it being a Thursday and half-holiday in Athy. I suggested to the sergeant of the Civic Guard that the body be removed before dark. He timidly replied that he could not approach the holy father, but that he saw the necessity of getting a move on. Perhaps I, being a heretic, might suggest that the body be removed to the house, where the father could continue his prayers for the dead?

The body was lying on a steep bank, the Queen's County side of the bridge, the priest kneeling with his back to the river. On my approach his head was bowed, apparently lost in prayer. Having reverently stood beside him for a full quarter of an hour, while he was muttering incoherent Latin sentences, I ventured to touch and then tap him on the back. He looked up, exclaiming 'Wash ish that?' and rolled back into the river – he was blind drunk. Some of the onlookers rushed to his assistance, but not a man got into the water – which at no place was over four feet deep – where the priest was floundering. As no one made an effort to haul him out, I stepped in and held his head above water till the Civic Guards had fetched a rope. He was inordinately fat for a middle-aged man, and being so drunk, incapable of helping himself. It was no easy task to get the cart rope fixed round his fat stomach. Since no one would get into the water to hold his head up, I held his head between my legs while I was making a bowline, adjusting the rope as best I could. I shouted to the Civic Guard to heave him up. The bank at this spot was very steep, it took ten to fifteen men to haul him up. Had I tied my ordinary slip knot he would have been seriously injured by the pressure of the rope on his body. When within almost handshake of the sergeant, he threw his arms over his head, released the bowline, and this time came a real thumper back into the river.

The crowd now became menacing, for they thought I had done this on purpose, and in the bedlam that followed they shouted, 'The Colonel is drowning the holy father.' At last I persuaded the sergeant to come in and give me a hand, and the priest was soon hauled safely on to the bank. Whilst the doctor was rendering first aid and pumping him out, I went to fetch the only bottle of whiskey we had in the house. In those days this was not only very expensive (18/– a bottle) but very hard to procure, so I acceded to the doctor's request with much reluctance. To my dismay, on my return, the doctor said, 'Are you sure this is good stuff?' and putting his mouth to the bottle consumed a good quarter before the priest had 'a pull', which left only enough for the sergeant of the Civic Guard to finish. The crowd's demeanour was still ugly, and I heard remarks such as, 'Ach, it is all the work of this dirty blackguard of an Englishman.' At last the doctor said 'Glory to God, the father is recovering; he was so overcome at Bridey's death, that he must have fainted.' I was truly thankful, for had he succumbed I think the crowd would have given me a bad time.

When the priest had been deposited in the doctor's car, I asked him how Bridey could have been drowned in only three or four feet of water. Wasn't there a man among that big crowd gallant enough to wade in and rescue the poor girl? He only replied, 'Ach, the divil had her, Colonel! She had the evil eye on her.' As it was getting dusk, and it was highly dangerous for any decent person to be out of doors after dark in these times, I gave the order for Bridey's body to be taken to the house. The sergeant said that this could not be permitted under any circumstances as by the law a body found drowned must be taken to a public house. Here he was right, but as the nearest public house was about four miles away and there was no conveyance at Kilmorony, the sergeant consented to the removal of the body to Kilmorony. The sergeant and I were laying Bridey on the bed in her room when Martha rushed in screaming, 'I won't sleep in the house with a carpse.' I did everything possible to quieten her down, but to no effect, so we had to remove the body to the stables.

The coroner at the inquest was a very decent-looking old fellow from County Kildare, and made a long speech to the jury. Then they all proceeded to inspect the body. 'Aye, she was a mighty beautiful girl,' they all chorused, while one asked, 'Is there no mark of violence on the body?' 'We could see that,' replied the coroner, 'so the body must be stripped.' There wasn't a woman on the place who would touch the corpse, which they credited with having 'the evil eye'.

It was after noon before I sent my groom to fetch my horse-coping friend Rigney. He who had turned his horse-dealer's establishment into that of an undertaker. About 3 p.m. Rigney arrived with the most horrible-looking old hag, whom he introduced as his 'stripper'. His get-up as an undertaker would have made anyone laugh even under the very saddest circumstances. I had known him for years as a good roughrider and dealer, and on this occasion could hardly recognise him. He appeared in a long frock coat, green with age, shiny black evening trousers pulled over his hunting boots and a top hat that must have belonged to Beau Brummel. His first remark was: 'Ye don't know me in this rigout, Colonel; why, I almost live in it these days.' After the old hag had done her work, the coroner and jurymen inspected the body, and on their return to the dining room, to my horror, the coroner said, 'I can have nothing to do with this case as Bridey Fitzgerald was drowned in Queen's County and I am the coroner for County Kildare. So the court is adjourned.' Before he dismissed the jury, I asked him to see me for a few moments in private.

Hastening to the cellar, I opened two bottles of very excellent old port and told my groom to gallop to Athy for two bottles of whiskey, which was all he could safely carry. I then invited the jurymen to have some tea before their departure. As soon as the port was finished, the whiskey arrived, but there was no sign of tea as Martha had bolted from the house. They were now thoroughly enjoying themselves, so I produced a sheet of paper headed 'Kilmorony, Kildare' and said I would just get a drop more port and then we would get the business quickly finished. Three more bottles produced the required result. The coroner was now incapable of writing himself, so at his dictation I drew out a lengthy document for him to sign. He then made a long oration, extolling Bridey the beauty and concluding by saying, 'The carpse may be removed.'

Rigney was the only semi-sober man present, so I gave him a telegram to Bridey's father announcing the sad news and asking him to remove the body. I retired to bed early. Before dawn the next day I heard mournful noises outside the front door, and peeping out of the window saw an old man in a sidecar driven by a jarvey. On going down I found the old man to be Bridey's father, quite overwhelmed with grief. All he could say was: 'Ach, the divil has taken her, and she has gone to hell.' He insisted on viewing the body, which was stark naked, and his emotion was such that I feared he would collapse, so I obliged him to return with me to the house, where the jarvey, old man and myself partook of the best breakfast I could provide (Martha still absent) of boiled eggs, bacon, tea and some very stale bread. At the end of the meal he said, 'If I could only give her a habit she would be sure to go to heaven.'

This was quite unintelligible to me, so I asked him in the kindest manner possible how I could help him. He told me that there was a 'habit' in Athy that had been blessed by the Pope. If this covered her body till burial, she would be sure of going to heaven. To send anyone to heaven was an opportunity not to be missed, so I rode to see Canon Mackay in Athy and asked him to give me this magic article. After an hour's wait, he produced with great reverence a black pall covered with gilt stars, half moons and zodiac signs. I told him of Fitzgerald's profound grief and his belief that this 'habit' would send Bridey's soul direct to heaven. Knowing the canon very well I expected a quizzical smile to come over his face. Not a bit of it. He affirmed in the most serious manner possible that it was a sure remedy against the power of Satan, and for a fee of two guineas it would be sent up to Kilmorony. As my horse was outside I suggested that I should ride back with the precious article, but he scornfully replied that no one but a holy priest was allowed to touch it.

At Kilmorony, Bridey's father was in an ecstasy of joy when the priest arrived with this wonderful relic, done up in a brown paper parcel. After a good whack of neat whiskey in the dining room, the priest asked for his suitcase from the motor and donned his vestments. It was now about 11 a.m. After another tumbler of whiskey he repaired to the front hall, where he unpacked the relic, muttering incoherent Latin prayers. The jarvey, Fitzgerald and the yardman Johnnie now joined us and we made a procession to the stables, the priest leading. Old Fitzgerald made me promise before he mounted the car that I would attend the funeral. When we reached the stables he covered the naked body with the habit and told the jarvey to bring the car down. When the ramshackle car arrived, the body was hauled on board while the priest muttered more Latin prayers. As the holy relic only half covered the poor girl's body, I suggested that a horse rug might be used to hide her nudity through the streets of Athy, on her journey towards Monasterevin. On my groom, Ball, producing a good rug, the priest shouted to the jarvey: 'Now, jump up, Mick, and be off wid ye. Whew! I'm very thirsty, that was mighty hot work.' The last I saw of Bridey, in the flesh, was being driven down the drive towards the bridge at Kilmorony, with the father holding her on the right, the jarvey on left, and her bare legs dangling out behind, the old father crying, 'I thank you, Colonel, for sending me daughter to heaven.'

I was aroused from my sad reverie by a tug at my sleeve from the priest: 'Now, Colonel, how about a drink? That is mighty good whiskey you gave me.' So up we went to the house, where he quickly finished the bottle. 'Ah that is grand stuff. Now let me take me togs off, and I will make out the bill.' After he had disrobed, we repaired to the library, where he wrote with much difficulty, for he was more than half-tight:

BRIDEY FITZGERALD

Masses for the dead	£2.2.0.
Attendance of Father O'Hagen	£1.0.0.
Hire of Motor Car	£2.0.0.

'And what did the canon charge ye for the holy relic?' To which I replied, 'Two guineas.' 'Ah, that is chape, for a send-off to heaven. You will give me a cheque to take back to the canon? ' So I made out a cheque for the total, inwardly congratulating myself that £7.4.0. was a fairly cheap rate to ensure a soul's journey to paradise. Then, not without difficulty, I packed him into the car, telling the driver to take him direct to the canon's house, where I hoped he would get a good ticking off for being drunk.

On the Monday I drove fifteen miles to old Fitzgerald's house for

Bridey's funeral. The wake was still going on, with Bridey laid on a table surrounded with candles in the sitting room and the small cottage full of maudlin drunken men. Versed though I was in stenches, this was too much for me, and I rushed outside for fresh air. Old Fitzgerald followed me out with tears in his eyes, imploring me to drink the wake, so I returned to the corpse chamber and golloped down a tumbler of potheen (raw whiskey). At this the old man was much relieved and ordered the corpse to be taken to the graveyard, about a mile away. She was wrapped in my new horse rug instead of a coffin, which old Fitzgerald explained 'would save expince'. The bier was an old door, laid on a pair of old carriage wheels, which I expected to collapse at any moment. A red-faced, bloated priest stood at the graveside, and after he had said a few words of Latin, Bridey was dropped into the grave, her only covering being my new horse rug, which was quickly covered with earth. While the shovelling was going on the priest said to Fitzgerald, 'And who will be paying for all this?' After a little conversation between the two, the old father came to me saying, 'Will ye pay £3 for her masses and some holy water?' He was overjoyed when I made this final settlement, which brought my outlay up to £10.4.0. and a new horse rug; but as he was fully convinced – on the assurance of the priest – that his expenditure on 'the habit' had sent his daughter to heaven, it was worth it. It was a time when one had to be extremely careful not to give offence.

'UP-TO-DATE WEAPONS'

After the establishment of the Provisional Government in January, 1922, the various Irish factions began to fight amongst themselves. The British garrison was gradually removed, but I was specially requested with White to continue our work for the ex-servicemen. Lady Weldon most kindly invited Hylda and me to stay at Kilmorony, for our house at the Curragh was being handed over to the rebels.

I happened to be in Dublin while the fight for the Four Courts was raging between the official Sinn Feiners and the Bolshies. The Bolshies had burnt down the Post Office and many of the finest buildings in the city, but the Four Courts was successfully held by a Sinn Fein garrison. White was quite unperturbed at the fighting which was taking place around his office, and asked me to come up for some important committee work in connection with the United Services League. By making a long detour on my Harley-Davidson around the southern fringe of

Dublin, I reached the city when the fight for the Four Courts was at its height.

The next day, when we had finished our work, White considered it would be unwise to return the same way and advised my taking the train from Kingsbridge to Athy, leaving my bike with him in Dublin. The only chance of getting to Kingsbridge was on foot, through the slums at the back of Liffey Street and Guinness's Brewery. I had not gone half a mile when I met a mob of Bolshies halted in the vicinity of the Brewery, as theatening a lot of men as could be seen anywhere. To have turned back after they had seen me would have meant instant arrest and possibly death, besides my missing the only available train: so I walked straight towards them. The commander advanced, revolver in hand, and quite politely asked where I was going and about what business.

With equal politeness I told him what White and I were trying to do for the ex-servicemen of Ireland, adding that as we had finished our work for the day, I was endeavouring to catch the only train that was going to Athy that day at 4 p.m. It was now about 3 p.m. Some of the men apparently knew me, for they remarked to the commander, 'This is the colonel we can't shoot', an unpleasant remark at any time, but on this occasion I firmly believed they were going to give that the lie without further waste of time. When I was taken down a small slum street by the commander and five men I felt my end had come. I was considerably surprised therefore when having arrived at a small store, the commander remarked: 'Now, Colonel, you must help us. Come in here and tell us how you load these bloody guns.' He then produced an American ten-shooter. On examination of the cartridges I found they were of slightly smaller calibre than the bore, consequently the repeating action would not work. The floor of the store was covered with arms of every description. After we had tried a variety of ammunition the Bolshie commandant arrived and asked the commander why he had not brought his party to the rendezvous for the attack on the Four Courts. The language was terrific when they had realised they had been hoaxed by the firm who had provided these 'up-to-date weapons'. After the hubbub had subsided, I asked if I might be escorted to Kingsbridge Station, as one experience of these ruffians, many of whom were foreigners, was quite sufficient. Three men took me along, and I caught my train.

THE INVISIBLE WIRE

In 1922 I was offered a good appointment by the War Office subject to my being passed fit by a special medical board in London. The week before this was to take place, I was riding my motor bike to Kilkenny, where with the help of Lord Ormonde we had successfully established a Legion Club. About five miles from the town I was suddenly somersaulted backwards. On regaining consciousness – I had been completely knocked out – I found myself surrounded by a mob of Bolshies. It was a common trick to trap anyone they wanted by means of an invisible wire stretched across the road, with a man behind a wall at each end. By tightening the wire they caught the motorist or cyclist across the face, neck or body. On this occasion the wire got me across the neck, cutting my gullet badly, and I have the marks to this day. After I had gone through a long cross-examination, the leader noticed that my suitcase was labelled for the Castle, so called me aside to explain that he had a great regard for Lord Ormonde and that I was to tell him that orders had been issued for a Sinn Fein-cum-Bolshie attack to be made upon the Castle in the near future. Shortly after, I was released.

On my arrival Lady Ormonde was horrified at my appearance. She summoned a doctor. After bandaging me, he insisted that I should take to my bed. Lord Ormonde came to see me in the evening and refused to believe that the Castle would be attacked. The next morning I received a wire ordering me to appear before a medical board the following day in London, so there was nothing to be done but catch the night mail to London, in spite of the doctor's protests.

I arrived with my neck swathed in bandages and feeling very ill, but realising that if I did not succeed in passing this special medical board I should have to leave the Army permanently disabled. I prayed the Board to pass me fit for home service, but they would not entertain the idea for a moment. I was heartbroken. A day or so afterwards, Philip Chetwode, who was Military Secretary, sent for me, and I shall never forget his kind words of consolation.

Well, that was the end of my Army career. As I was still working with White for the Irish ex-servicemen, I returned to Kilmorony to try to get over my sorrow in hunting, fishing and shooting.

Southern Ireland was now in a state of turmoil. Lord Ormonde was all that could be desired as a landlord and was seemingly loved by his compatriots, but it was not long before the attack took place on Kilkenny Castle. The IRA attacking force was largely composed of foreigners. The castle was saved through the heroism of an old Life Guardsman, whose lodge was at the front gate. He got wind of the coming attack a few minutes before it was launched, and sent his son to warn everyone in the castle. When summoned to open the gate, he refused and the attackers endeavoured to scale the walls, which were stoutly defended by Lord Ormonde's retainers till help came. The gallant old Life Guardsman and his son were shortly afterwards murdered in cold blood, when shopping in the town.

TRUSTING IN THE LORD

On a Wednesday evening in September 1923 I was walking down to the stables at Kilmorony when five armed men held me up at the point of their revolvers. After a torrent of abuse the leader demanded the sum of £1,500 for the IRA, and ordered me to appear before a court martial at a place in the hills south of Carlow on the following Tuesday. I endeavoured to explain that such a demand was, for a man of moderate means, impossible to meet at a moment's notice. I was so absorbed in asking God to help me that the full danger of the situation never crossed my mind until two of the ruffians began to manhandle me. I said to the leader: 'Come up into my room, and I will give you a cheque and a letter to the bank manager.' I had remembered that I had an old cheque book of Cox's for the 17th Lancers Funds. After much theatrical formality and bluff, I produced a cheque for £1,500 together with a letter to the manager instructing him to sell various securities to meet the demand. The leader and another ruffian stood over me with revolvers, threatening me with death if the money was not paid by the following Tuesday. I replied that they had better post the letter themselves and that I would give them a letter to the bank manager of the National Bank at Athy, instructing him to make payment on the due date. This appeared to satisfy them, and after searching my room they withdrew. Luckily Lady Weldon was away and I was the sole occupant of the house, with the exception of two servants.

On the Friday I was walking over the Kilmorony private bridge about midday when I met three men who stopped me in a polite manner and said they had been instructed by the Sinn Fein Government to demand a sum of £1,200. It was a nasty cold day, so I equally politely asked them to come up to the house to explain the grounds for this demand as I was an Englishman and had no property or lands in Ireland. They based the claim on the fact that I had been for four years a resident in Ireland, and that I had not contributed anything towards the upkeep of the Government. I thought it best not to point out that the Sinn Fein Government had been in power less than two years.

Having given them all as much whiskey as they could drink, I told them that my solicitor in Dublin, Edward White, would settle the matter on my behalf. I was now indeed between the devil and the deep sea, for I had arranged to hunt from Kilmorony that season and had all my kit there as well as three exceptionally good hunters, one of which I had sold at the beginning of the week to Reid, the horse dealer, for £500. The value of the horses together was well over £1,000, and there appeared to be no way of escape from the payments – or death – on the Tuesday. If I bolted forthwith they would seize all my belongings including the horses, ill treat my great friend and benefactress, Winnie, and possibly burn down her house with all her belongings, as they had frequently done elsewhere. She was expected home on the following day, Saturday, which was too late to allow me to escape from the clutches of the Bolshies.

An almost immediate answer came to my prayers in the form of a wire saying she was returning that night. I drove the dogcart to meet her and on our way back to the house from Athy told her everything that had happened. She was one of the bravest individuals it is possible to imagine, very wise and sound in counsel where the Irishman was concerned. After deep thought she insisted on my leaving Ireland the following night, Saturday.

Knowing the place was full of spies, she asked me to meet her in the dogcart in Athy on Saturday evening to pick up her purchases for the weekend and rode there in the afternoon on her bicycle. On my arrival at the station, O'Neill, the station master, told me in a loud voice – for there were a lot of people on the platform – 'Her ladyship wants you to go by this train to fetch the horse from Kildare, and she will drive the cart back to Kilmorony. You had better ride in this horsebox, and ask the station master to return it with her ladyship's horse.' His acting was excellent, for he insisted on my paying the return journey for the horsebox. As I was stepping in, he seized my hand and said in a whisper: 'Goodbye, Colonel, the next carriage goes straight through to Kingstown, and don't get out till you arrive alongside the boat.'

It was dark on arrival at Kildare, so there was no difficulty in slipping into the first-class carriage which went through to Kingstown. I thanked God when I stepped aboard the boat. I had no luggage, not even a toothbrush, and no overcoat, but luckily I knew the captain well, so when the ship had got well out I went to his cabin and told him the reason for my ignominious flight from 'a civilised country'. He most kindly lent me a warm overcoat, and I arrived at our little house in Chelsea about breakfast time on Sunday.

Hylda's surprise at my sudden appearance can be imagined for we had arranged to start hunting from Kilmorony the following week, when she was coming over. The next day, Monday, I went to see the manager at Cox's bank. The man laughed heartily at the trick I had played on the Bolshies. He, too, played up well, for instead of marking the cheque 'R.D., no account', after consultation with his colleagues he decided to take no action whatever in the matter.

Soon, however, threatening letters began to arrive, some real blood-curdlers, and I was advised to lay the whole case before the Government. McPherson, late Secretary for Ireland, was most kind and helpful, but they could do nothing to help poor Winnie in Ireland and I trembled to think what form of revenge the Bolshies would take when they found I had escaped.

To give her a reason for our non-arrival for the hunting season, Hylda wrote to say that I was very seedy, which was quite true, and we sent a verbal message by her son Anthony to ask her to send our horses and kit over at the first available opportunity, as Hylda wanted to hunt in Leicestershire. As Winnie's every movement was being watched by the rebels and all letters being opened by the Sinn Feiners, were not very helpful. But she succeeded in sending all our kit and horses by the end of the year to Sutton Bonington.

Winnie repeatedly refused police protection, and in spite of terrible threatenings remained at Kilmorony. But O'Neill, the station master who helped me to escape, was murdered a few months afterwards.

We came to live at Sutton Bonington after my father-in-law's death in 1924. Threatening letters continued to arrive with great regularity until 1932, when they ceased.

At the beginning of 1935 I had incessant 'trench fever' but carried on to the best of my power until by 8 April I had become very weak. Jeffares recommended our going to Brighton. On 14 April, while still staying at the Metropole, Hylda took my temperature in the morning. It was 103 and she sent for the doctor. He said I was very ill and must remain in bed a fortnight. I told him that I had asked God what I should do, and a vivid message came back – that I must return home to Sutton Bonington. So I did, in spite of the remonstrances of the doctor who said it was madness to attempt the journey. Although travelling third class, we had a comfortable journey, and on arrival home I collapsed.

On 28 April I felt that I was passing away, and about midday I was roused from a coma when the nurse announced Lord Dawson of Penn.[9] He told me that I was critically ill, but I told him that I believed God would answer my prayer. So strong was my conviction that I told him I would be well enough to hunt and shoot in the autumn, which I did.

When I had felt I was dying I asked God to allow me to see Queen Mary again for she had been my friend and guiding star throughout my married life. On 15 July I was invited to stay at Kensington Palace, to meet Queen Mary at dinner that night. Only the Athlones were there and H.M. was most friendly and kind and she consented to be Dolly's son's godmother. What struck me most was her amazing memory, for she remembered events at White Lodge as vividly as if they had happened this year.

Now in the autumn of my life I realise that my innumerable escapes from death have been solely due to God's miraculous kindness.

9 George V's physician-in-ordinary.

Envoi

W. A. Tilney lived at Sutton Bonington after his retirement from the Army in 1923. With the aid of various diaries, notes and letters he wrote his memoirs. The diaries have not survived.

He and Hylda regularly rode to hounds until the mid-1930s when both were in their late sixties. W.A.T. played tennis enthusiastically and followed the Paget family in being churchwarden for St Michael's.

His father-in-law, Sir Ernest Paget, Bt, a generous patron of the church, had been a wealthy man with around 3,000 acres. He was chairman of the London Midland and Scottish Railway from 1891 to 1918. However, the racecourse was his downfall and the patrimony was reduced to a little over 300 acres. Sir Ernest was succeeded as churchwarden by his only son, Sir Cecil (Hylda's brother). Cecil was a character who made some significant inventions for the LMS. Stories are told of him dressing up as a chef and concocting some amusing, if not delicious, dishes. He married, but died childless, so Sutton Bonington came to Hylda and W.A.T.'s son Dolly. While Dolly was a young man making his way in the world, his father took on the responsibilities at Sutton.

Jocelyn Tilney, widow of W.A.T.'s first cousin, the Rev. H. A. R. Tilney, recalls how my grandfather's religious ardour could verge on the embarrassing. She also remembers him as a wonderful raconteur. No matter who were his listeners – Queen Mary, the stable lad or local parson – he could keep any company spellbound for hours. She has told me that if ever she had been tempted to think he might embellish a point or two, the following incident taught her to be sparing with her reservations. She and her husband (known as Freckles) were in Norway fishing. Their gillie asked them if they might be related to Colonel Tilney. When Freckles said they were first cousins, the gillie said he was an extraordinarily clever fisherman and that he had caught the largest fish caught in Norwegian rivers. It had been stuffed and put on the wall in the local pub and might he be allowed to take them to see it? From that time on when W.A.T. talked of weighty fish, they dared not doubt he was telling the truth. Another recollection of Jocelyn's from that period of the 1930s is of Hylda wheeling a frail dog around in a little cart, and of giving Christmas parties for her friends' dogs with cutlets dangling from the tree.

When Dolly and his brother Ned were at Eton their parents would come down to visit them at the school, as likely as not on W.A.T.'s trusty Harley-Davidson motor cycle; and, as likely as not, then they would all go to lunch or tea at Windsor with Queen Mary. Dolly had been christened Robert Adolphus George after Prince Adolphus of Teck, brother of his father's protectress Queen Mary; both were known to family and friends as Dolly. When W.A.T. and Hylda were in India, Dolly spent many holidays at Tusmore because Lord Bicester's son Steven Smith was a school friend of his. Lord Bicester was a director of the Hudson Bay Company, which led to Dolly's placing in Sale & Co., an offshoot of Hudson Bay. Dolly threw himself into life with energy, determination and charm: a natural leader, he was successfully climbing the business ladder when the outbreak of war in 1939 precipitated him into the Leicestershire Yeomanry. He rose rapidly to the rank of brigadier and was captured by the Germans on the island of Leros in 1943.

Meanwhile, my grandparents lived on at Sutton Bonington. As staff melted away to fight or work in armament factories, they were left with one couple. Mr Berridge, an elderly resident of Sutton Bonington, recalls an example of W.A.T.'s characteristic energy. In the interest of saving petrol, only workers were supposed to use the buses at peak periods of the day – a rule which my grandfather took to mean he did not have the right to use the bus at all. So he walked to Quorn for lunch – a distance of a good eight miles – and walked home afterwards.

At the outbreak of war my brother, two sisters and I had been packed off to my mother's relations and friends in the USA. My brother Robert and I returned to England in 1946 at the ages of nine and eleven to renew our infantile acquaintance with Grandpa. He had only one more year to live and most likely was already weakened by the cancer which was to carry him away at the age of 79 in 1947. We children had little notion of the daring adventures and physical toughness of his earlier life.

Hylda lived on until 1959 and so we knew her much better. She would have loved to have danced professionally, but her position in life forbade it. A special treat was to be taken by her to Covent Garden and to go backstage after the performance to be kissed by Margot Fonteyn. She had stayed at Sutton as a young dancer when the ballet company performed in Nottingham.

As for my father, very much his parents' favourite, he built Sale &

Co. into the flourishing mini-conglomerate of Sale Tilney. He was a hero in the eyes of his children and the soldiers of his regiment. Chosen by the local Conservatives to fight the Loughborough seat, as the election drew near he felt obliged to resign because of the demands of Sale Tilney. When at last he was no longer under financial pressure he realised a life-long ambition to be Master of the Quorn with which W.A.T. had so often ridden out. In 1959 he lost his only son, my beloved brother Robert, in a motor accident at the age of twenty-one. Then years later came my father's all but fatal fall while leading the field out hunting, and the consequent inheritance by my elder sister, Anne, Lady Elton, of the family home at Sutton Bonington.

Index

ILLUSTRATED HISTORICAL PUBLICATIONS BY
"REPRINT" ، DAVID DOVER.   Tel. 01509 267450
Beacon Views, Abberton Way, Loughborough, Leics, LE11 4NX

e-mail. reprintuk@yahoo.co.uk   www.reprintuk.com

LOUGHBOROUGH:

- ☆ Loughborough War Years by Ted Sharpe. Includes photographs and posters. £3.50.
- ☆ Loughborough's Past in Old Postcards. £4.50.
- ☆ Loughborough in Black & White. A Collection of Old Postcards. £4.50.
- ☆ Loughborough in Black & White. Vol. 1. £6.00.
- ☆ Loughborough in Black & White. Vol. 2. Thorpe Acre. £4.50.
- ☆ Loughborough in Black & White. Vol. 3. The University & The Old College. £4.50.
- ☆ Loughborough Grammar School. The Early Years. £4.50.
- ☆ Loughborough Street Directories, 1901 & 1951-2 & 1962. Alphabetically listed streets with names and advertisements. £6.00 each.
- ☆ 1927 Street Directory - includes "Humorous and Literary Companion". £6.00.
- ☆ 1881 Handbook to Loughborough. Includes Burleigh, Knightthorpe, Woodthorpe, Loughborough old parks, churches and charities. £4.50.
- ☆ A Brief History of BRUSH, with past and present photographs. £4.50.
- ☆ A History of the Salvation Army in Loughborough. £4.50.
- ☆ A Century of Progress. Morris in Loughborough. £4.50.
- ☆ The Bell Hangers (John Taylor Bell Foundry). An unusual book. £4.50.
- ☆ Bells of Memory by the late Maurice Bray. A History of Loughborough Carillon. £6.00.
- ☆ A History of Clemerson's, Loughborough 1848-1948. £3.50.
- ☆ A Brief History of the Royal Mail in Loughborough. £4.50.
- ☆ Rosebery School, Loughborough - 1897-1977. £4.50.
- ☆ Historical Gazetteer and Directory of Loughborough, Shepshed, East Leake and the Surrounding Villages. Volumes 1 and 2. £4.50 each.
- ☆ The Blackbrook Dam Disaster in Charnwood, Leics, 1799. £6.00.
- ☆ The Windmill Inn - the oldest public house in Loughborough. £4.50.
- ☆ Glimpses of the Brush. £4.50.
- ☆ History of Baxter Gate Hospital. £4.50.
- ☆ Charnwood Chamber of Trade 1922-1982. 60 years of shopping in Loughborough. £4.50.
- ☆ Loughborough - A Pictorial and Descriptive Guide, 1907. £4.50.
- ☆ Loughborough Wharf. £6.00.
- ☆ Bygone Loughborough - Chapters of Local History from Earliest Days to the Incorporation of the Borough by Herbert W Cook. £6.00.
- ☆ Local Legends. £3.50.
- ☆ Rambles Around Loughborough 1868. £6.00.
- ☆ The Loughborough Job - The Luddites. M. Hornsby, Old Bookshop, Church Gate. £4.50.
- ☆ Loughborough in the XIX Century, Old Loughborough, Walks Around Loughborough, St. Bernard's Monastery and War Memorial. £6.00.
- ☆ Loughborough's Own Fox Cover. A nature story through the seasons of the year. £4.50.
- ☆ Loughborough Almanac, Street Directory 1941 + ARP Information. £6.00.
- ☆ Loughborough during the Great Civil War. Historical Account. £3.50.
- ☆ A Brief History of the Windlass. £4.50.
- ☆ Loughborough - 1966 Municipal Tenants Handbook. £3.50.
- ☆ A Chronology of Loughborough – Historical Dates Remembered. £3.50.
- ☆ Loughborough Today and Yesterday – An Interactive History. £6.00.
- ☆ History of Framework Knitters in Loughborough and Shepshed. £4.50.

- ☆ Old Footpath Walks Around Loughborough, a 1950's book containing much historical information, 26 local views and map. £4.50.
- ☆ The Parish Church of All Saints, Loughborough. A 1954 reprint by Rector W J Lyon. £1.00.
- ☆ A Brief History of the Great Central Railway and Victorian Season Tickets. P Courtenay. An easy to read account of this important railway. £2.00.
- ☆ In the Service of the Cross. Loughborough Congregational Church, 1828-1928. An in-depth history of the Church. £3.50.
- ☆ Loughborough's Art Deco Heritage. £3.50.
- ☆ Colouring Book of Loughborough and Surrounding Area. £4.50.
- ☆ Loughborough and its Carillon Tower -1923. An account of Loughborough's history and its new carillon tower in that year. £3.50.
- ☆ A Tiger's Tale, R Blood. An in-depth account of one Loughburian and his comrades in the First World War in the Leicestershire Tigers. £6.00.
- ☆ Shepshed Lace Manufacturing Co Ltd – 50 Years of Lace 1906 to 1956. A history of the early years of this company. £3.50.
- ☆ Loughborough Lock to Bishops Meadow Lock by Malcolm Dark. This presentation is a sequel to Loughborough Wharf and Charlie Lewis, a BWB employee 1956-1994." £4.50.
- ☆ A History of Charnwood Forest Railway. M Helsey. An in-depth history of this lost railway. £6.00.
- ☆ Great Paul by Trevor S Jennings, John Taylor's Bell Foundry. The history and casting of this renowned bell and its journey to London. £3.50.
- ☆ History of Loughborough Family in the Community, 1841-2002 by Rezia Begum. A detailed account of immigration into the Loughborough area. £6.00.
- ☆ Railway Lines: 1920s Working the Bluebell Line by Louie Carr. An amazing story related from written information by the author's father. £3.50.
- ☆ A History of Loughborough Markets and Fairs. M W Green and G H Green. An in-depth account of these renowned events in Loughborough's history. £4.50.
- ☆ Yesterday's Child in Loughborough – World War Two by Maisie Walker. An evacuee's true story. £6.00.
- ☆ Loughborough 1892. A most interesting and descriptive guide to Loughborough; also with industry and local traders in detailed write-up and many, many photographs of interest. A very rare reprint. £6.00.
- ☆ Messengers – Information on this lost but well remembered firm. £4.50.
- ☆ Loughborough Public Library Centenary 1905-2005. Many photographs and articles on the Library. £6.00.
- ☆ Night of the Zeppelin by D Long. A most detailed account of the air raid on Loughborough, with many photographs. £6.00.

SHEPSHED:
- ☆ History of Framework Knitters in Loughborough and Shepshed. £4.50.
- ☆ A Brief History of Shepshed. £4.50.
- ☆ Shepshed in Black and White Postcards. £4.50.
- ☆ Shepshed Vol. II – in old postcards. £4.50.
- ☆ A History and Survey of Shepshed Mill. £4.50.
- ☆ A Shepshed Street Directory - 1960's. £4.50.
- ☆ Shepshed Wakes Parade, 1950, with an array of old advertisements plus a history of the War Memorial and information on the Wakes of Shepshed; also included is a variety of old Wakes photographs. £3.50.
- ☆ The Freeman's Shepshed Almanac for 1923. An account of village events. £3.50.
- ☆ The Freeman's Shepshed Almanac for 1927. An account of village events. £3.50.
- ☆ The War Memorials of Belton, Hathern and Shepshed. R Blood. £4.50.
- ☆ Belton – Historical Points of Interest with old photographs. £4.50.
- ☆ Belton in old Pictures. Reprint. Many old photographs of this village. £6.00.
- ☆ 160 Years of Belton School by Liz Threadgill and Stuart Hicks. £4.00.
- ☆ History of Shepshed 1086-1969. An in-depth account of Shepshed with photographs and many interesting facts. £6.00.

LEICESTERSHIRE:
- ☆ Victorian Day on the River Soar by M Dark. £6.00.
- ☆ "Theme". An illustrated poem in vibrant water colours, Leicestershire Waterways. £4.50.
- ☆ Leicestershire Legends and Stories. £3.50.
- ☆ Inns of Leicestershire by Eric Swift. £3.50.
- ☆ Changing Times in Quorn, Mountsorrel, Barrow and Sileby. £4.50.
- ☆ Mountsorrel. £3.50. ☆ Old Mountsorrel. £3.50.
- ☆ Old Quorn Tales, Volumes 1, 2 & 3. £3.50 each.
- ☆ The Quorn Hunt by William Dixon. 1920s History of the Hunt, tips when riding and the calls of the Hunt and what they mean. Many photographs of the time. £4.50.
- ☆ The Quorn Hunt by William Fawcett. An in-depth history of the Quorn Hunt in the 1930s; includes many photographs. £4.50.
- ☆ Sileby in Old Postcards. £4.50. ☆Woodhouse Eaves. £4.50.
- ☆ Sileby Historical Information 1800s to 1900s – Documents of the business run by the Cooke Family of Cossington Road. £4.50.
- ☆ Recollections of Thorpe Acre. £4.50.
- ☆ The Civil War at Cotes Mill. £4.50.
- ☆ A Short History of Barrow on Soar (a reprint). £3.50.
- ☆ Barrow upon Soar in Old Postcards, including some original correspondence. £3.50.
- ☆ The History of Humphrey Perkins School by Bernard Elliott. £6.00.
- ☆ The Navigation Pub and the Canal to Barrow Deep Lock, Barrow upon Soar. A History from 1794. £6.00.
- ☆ Prestwold and its Church. £4.50.
- ☆ A History of Wymeswold. £6.00.
- ☆ Wymeswold – Old Postcards of this Village. £4.50.
- ☆ A History and Description of St Mary's Church, Wymeswold, 1846. £6.00.
- ☆ A History of East Leake. £6.00.
- ☆ A History of Walton on the Wolds by Ann Jones. Includes maps, past and present photographs, census returns, wills, family trees, monumental inscriptions, etc, with colour plates. £15.00.
- ☆ A Compilation of "A History of Walton on the Wolds". £5.00.
- ☆ John Bird, 1826-1894 and his son, Montague Bertie Bird, 1869-1942, Rectors of St Mary's Church, Walton on the Wolds, by Ann Jones. Illustrated with photographs and drawings. £12.00.
- ☆ St Bartholomew's Church and St Mary's Church, Walton on the Wolds. Ann Jones. £6.00.
- ☆ For the Millennium 2000, Walton on the Wolds in past and present photographs and post cards.

- ☆ St Bartholomew's Church and St Mary's Church, Walton on the Wolds. Ann Jones. £6.00.
- ☆ For the Millennium 2000, Walton on the Wolds in past and present photographs and post cards. Ann Jones. £6.00.
- ☆ The Normanton Ferry. £4.50.
- ☆ Melton Mowbray in Olden Times, 1879. £6.00.
- ☆ Melton Mowbray Town Estate - Its Origin and History - 1882. £4.50.
- ☆ Melton Mowbray - Recollections and the past, by the late Oliver Roe. £3.50.
- ☆ Leicestershire Parish Registers of Marriage (16th century to 1837) – villages around Melton Mowbray. £6.00.
- ☆ Ladies of Melton Mowbray's History. Philip E Hunt. £3.50.
- ☆ The Story of Melton Mowbray. Philip E Hunt. £6.00.
- ☆ St Mary's Parish Church, Melton Mowbray by the late Gilbert M King. An in-depth history with photographs of the church. £4.50.
- ☆ Woodhouse Eaves Millennium Village Trail. £4.50.
- ☆ Recollections of Woodhouse Eaves. £3.50.
- ☆ The Beaumanor Estate Sale Catalogue, 1946, Woodhouse Eaves and Old Woodhouse. £10.00.
- ☆ The History of St Mary in the Elms Church, Woodhouse 1338-2003 by Mr M J Kirk. A detailed account of this church in the hamlet of Woodhouse. £4.50.
- ☆ The Unicorn in Bradgate Park by John Harrison. £4.50.
- ☆ Hathern Historical Information, 1863, 1868, 1951 Street Directory with old postcards. £3.50.
- ☆ A History of Hathern by the late Rev. A J Ison. A detailed account of this village's history. £3.50.
- ☆ A Kegworth Walk Guide. 12 walks with historical information from the villages around Kegworth. £5.00.
- ☆ Within an Open Book by Sheila Sharpe. Accounts of the author's life , looking back at her ancestors, and a history of Kegworth past and present. £8.00.
- ☆ Tom Moore and Kegworth. An account of Thomas Moore's stay in Kegworth and two stories full of historical tales of Kegworth. £4.50.
- ☆ Barrow in the 20th Century. Millennium publication. £5.00.
- ☆ History of Kibworth by G W Barratt, 1911. A book of great detail of early history. £4.50.
- ☆ History of Kibworth and Personal Reminiscences. F P Woodford. A most in-depth account of Kibworth and the people who lived there in the 1860's. £6.00.
- ☆ History of Kibworth Beauchamp Grammar School, B. Elliott – a history from its origins to the 1950's. £6.00.
- ☆ Historical Walks with Old Postcards, Kibworth Beauchamp to Kibworth Harcourt. £3.00.
- ☆ Kibworth in Old Postcards, with original correspondence. £3.00.
- ☆ Historical Survey of Shoemaking from its origins to the 1930's. £3.50.
- ☆ The Folville Cross by Raymond Taylor. The ruined and reduced shaft of this medieval cross stands in the south-western of the four fields formed by the crossroads at Ashby Pastures. £3.50.
- ☆ History of Whitwick Methodists. E Jarvis. John Wesley's movements in the North West of Leicestershire. £4.50.
- ☆ City to City. E Jarvis. A journey through Whitwick from the City of Dan to the City of Three Waters. Many black and white prints. £6.00.
- ☆ The Story of Whitwick Park or King George's Field. E Jarvis. £3.50.
- ☆ Banded Together (Part I). An in-depth account of Leicestershire's worst mining disaster at Whitwick Pit No. 5 in 1898. Many photographs. £6.00.
- ☆ Banded Together (Part II). Details of the families of victims and survivors and information about many of the rescuers. £6.00.
- ☆ A Railway Excursion from Ashby, Swannington, Coalville, Bardon Hill and Bagworth to London St Pancras -1950. Detailed account in this souvenir programme, with many interesting points en route and around London. £2.00.
- ☆ The King's Head. Charles I and relics of the King's head. Where lies Charles I? Mysterious and strange coincidences throughout the search. £6.00.
- ☆ Porter to Signalman by Eric Jarvis. An in-depth account of the railways in the coalmining and quarrying industry in Leicestershire 1937-1965, includes many photographs. £6.00.

- ☆ Leicestershire Watermills, N. D. Ashton. Many old photographs of lost water mills of Leicestershire. £6.00.
- ☆ Good and Bard Days out in Leicestershire and Rutland. John Harrison. A quest to discover our history and heritage. So you thought you knew Leicestershire and Rutland? £4.50.
- ☆ Donisthorpe at War by Jenny Wright. This small village under attack during World War II. Many stories and photographs from the time. £7.00.
- ☆ Bradgate, Groby and Lady Jane Grey by P Dare. 1920s lost publication. Many interesting points and photographs. £3.50.
- ☆ Ashby-de-la-Zouch, History and Description. Also includes surrounding villages in the year 1852. £6.00.
- ☆ Ashby-de-la-Zouch - History and descriptive account of the castle, with maps. £6.00.
- ☆ Charnwood Forest by T R Potter. A most in-depth account of this area. Includes village information in 1842 and many pen drawings of the time. £10.00.
- ☆ Railway Connections – Leicester to Burton Railway. This publication is an in-depth account in photographs of the lost railway system in steam. £6.00.
- ☆ Anecdotes of Bygone Leicestershire and other stories. Colonel Pen Lloyd. A most interesting book containing many amusing stories and covering many topics. £4.50.
- ☆ Foxton Locks. A history of the locks and the inclined plane. Reprinted by demand. £4.50. [A new publication is in process and will be available in the near future.]
- ☆ Crime and Murder in Victorian Leicestershire. A most absorbing book – a credit to its author, Michael Turner. £4.50.
- ☆ A Miner's Child. Nora Chambers. A remarkable life story from the coalfields of Leicestershire – it all starts in the year 1921. £6.00.
- ☆ Leicestershire Men at the French Wars of 1346-1347. W. E. D. Fletcher, 1911. Detailed account of how the army was formed – includes names and other information. £3.50.
- ☆ The Leicestershire Mystery of the Green Bicycle Murder of 1919 by H R Wakefield. Printed a decade after the event Contains many photographs and transcripts of the trial. £6.00.

LEICESTER:

- ☆ Leicester Symphony Orchestra. A History and Celebration by Neil Crutchley. An interesting account of the orchestra over the years. Many photographs, over 100 pages in all. £8.00.
- ☆ City of Gods. Adam Richards. Historical poetic ramble through Leicester. £4.50.
- ☆ Leicester Blitz Souvenir - 1940's War damage in photographs. £4.50.
- ☆ 1936 Leicester - Detailed account of that year. £3.50.
- ☆ Leicester 1881 by Robert Read Jnr. Volume I - Corporation Undertakings. £6.00. Volume II Leicester Military Centre. £6.00. Volume III - Amusements Old and New. £6.00. Volume IV - Manufacturing and Commercial Progress. £6.00.
- ☆ Leicester - Our War by Jean, Eileen and Olive. Recollections of their lives during the war years. £3.50.
- ☆ The Story of Leicester's Industrial History, 1933. Historical facts on Leicester's Industry in the Heart of England city. £6.00.
- ☆ A Chronology of Leicester - 844BC to 1926 AD. £6.00.
- ☆ The Mystery of the Humber Stone by John Harrison. £4.50.
- ☆ Who Killed King Charles I ? by John Harrison. £4.50.
- ☆ City of Leicester Coronation Souvenir. Reprint. 1953 - Events of the Coronation and many photographs of Leicester at that time – many colour photographs. £6.00.
- ☆ Leicester As It Was by Alan Broadfield. A collection of old 1900s photographs of Leicester combined with in-depth information. £4.50.
- ☆ Leicester Old and New by William Kidd, 1975. Old photographs with a 1975 view, now an old view itself – a most amazing book. £6.00.

NOTTINGHAM and NOTTINGHAMSHIRE:

- ☆ A Popular History of Nottingham - 1893 by the late W Howie Wylie. £6.00.
- ☆ A History of Tollerton by Sidney Pell Potter. £6.00.
- ☆ Allen's Illustrated Hand Book and Guide to all the Places of Interest in Nottingham and its Environs - Part 1. £6.00.
- ☆ Allen's Illustrated Hand Book and Guide to all the Places of Interest in Nottingham and its Environs - Part 2. £6.00.
- ☆ Drake's Street Directory 1860, Nottingham. Nottingham and adjoining townships, parishes, and villages. £6.00.
- ☆ As The Years Have Passed by in Nottingham by William Leaning. An in-depth account of Nottingham's history including the Kings and Queens that have frequented Nottingham. £6.00.

RUTLAND:

- ☆ Much in Little – 100 years of Ruddles Brewery. £3.50.
- ☆ Ruddles and Rutland – sketches of all public houses and historical information. £3.50.
- ☆ Rutland - The Great War. Volume I - A Comprehensive List of the Distinguished Fallen, with Awards of Merit, Photographs and List of Action. ☆ Volume II - A Comprehensive List of the Fallen, Village by Village, with old church photographs. £6.00 each.
- ☆ An Arthurian Mystery in Victorian Rutland by John Harrison. £4.50.
- ☆ Uppingham by the Sea, 1876. An event in Uppingham School's history. £6.00.

LICHFIELD:

- ☆ Truths, Myths and Legends in and Around the City of Lichfield. R A Gilbert. £5.00.
- ☆ Lichfield in Old Picture Postcards. R A Gilbert. Some lost scenes in and around Lichfield. £5.00.
- ☆ The Road to Rocquigny by R A Gilbert, son of Lichfield, who paid the ultimate price in the 1914-18 War. £4.50.

FURTHER PUBLICATIONS OF INTEREST.

- ☆ Blimey, It's A Girl! Norma Flowers. World War II accounts from an Auxiliary Territorial Service driver. £4.50.
- ☆ Marriage and Muslim Women. Rezia Begum. £3.50.
- ☆ Recollections of a Postman. 37 years on the post. Some unbelievable stories. £4.50.
- ☆ The Awesome Voyage. The Atlantic can be a cruel sea, especially when things are not shipshape. £4.50.
- ☆ A Collection of Short Stories for Everyone. Seven stories by a nonagenarian. £3.50.
- ☆ A 'Tail' To be Told. A guide dog's story of faith, love and companionship. £4.50.
- ☆ Coventry - My War. Living in Coventry and 8 years old in war-torn Britain. £4.50.
- ☆ Boyhood to Boathood by M Dark. Water related stories. £8.99.
- ☆ Little Content by Molly Blackwell. Featured in the Millennium Book - now the full story. £4.50.
- ☆ A Little Red Van by P Wood. Nostalgic story of one Royal Mail Morris Minor van. £4.50.
- ☆ The Book of Luck 1900 Talismans, Birth Stones and Old Customs. £3.50.
- ☆ Telephone and address book with views of Loughborough and surrounding villages. £4.50.
- ☆ From Silence, To Speech and Beyond by Hazel Rennick. £4.50.
- ☆ Reflection of My Life by Maisie Walker. Looking back over 70 years of life, with down to earth poems. £3.50. Animal Crackers by Maisie Walker. £3.50. A Journey Down Memory Lane by Maisie Walker. £3.50.

☆ My Wife - Her fight. Cancer takes Paul's wife, leaving him to bring up their two small children. This book contains the story in pictures. £3.50.

☆ You Are My Grandchildren by Olive McBride – My Early Life in Barrow-on-Soar. £3.50.

☆ A Brother Loaned by Mandy Crane. A Child's Memorial. £3.50.**

☆ Poems of Love from the Heart of A Mother and Child. Poems of Compassion for Parents of Very Ill Children. £4.50.**

☆ Donisthorpe at War by Jenny Wright. Many wartime stories and photographs from this coalmining village. £7.00.

☆ Billy's Battle. The life of one soldier leading up to and after the Battle of the Somme, 1st July 1916. £4.50.

**[A donation from the sales of these two books will be made to Rainbows Hospice].

e-mail. reprintuk@yahoo.co.uk   www.reprintuk.com

☆☆ = Available Shortly.

All publications are available from "*Reprint*" post-free. Please enclose remittance.
Certain publications are available in large print. Please ring for details.